The Politics of Language Education

NEW PERSPECTIVES ON LANGUAGE AND EDUCATION
Series Editor: Professor Viv Edwards, *University of Reading, Reading, Great Britain*
Series Advisor: Professor Allan Luke, *Queensland University of Technology, Brisbane, Australia*

Two decades of research and development in language and literacy education have yielded a broad, multidisciplinary focus. Yet education systems face constant economic and technological change, with attendant issues of identity and power, community and culture. This series will feature critical and interpretive, disciplinary and multidisciplinary perspectives on teaching and learning, language and literacy in new times.

Full details of all the books in this series and of all our other publications can be found on http://www.multilingual-matters.com, or by writing to Multilingual Matters, St Nicholas House, 31–34 High Street, Bristol BS1 2AW, UK.

NEW PERSPECTIVES ON LANGUAGE AND EDUCATION
Series Editor: Professor Viv Edwards

The Politics of Language Education
Individuals and Institutions

Edited by
J. Charles Alderson

MULTILINGUAL MATTERS
Bristol • Buffalo • Toronto

Library of Congress Cataloging in Publication Data
A catalog record for this book is available from the Library of Congress.
The Politics of Language Education: Individuals and Institutions/
Edited by J. Charles Alderson
New Perspectives on Language and Education
Includes bibliographical references.
1. Language and languages--Study and teaching. 2. Language policy.
3. Language and languages--Political aspects.
I. Alderson, J. Charles.
P53.6128.P65 2009
418.0071–dc22 2009001470

British Library Cataloguing in Publication Data
A catalogue entry for this book is available from the British Library.

ISBN-13: 978-1-84769-143-9 (hbk)
ISBN-13: 978-1-84769-142-2 (pbk)

Multilingual Matters
UK: St Nicholas House, 31–34 High Street, Bristol BS1 2AW, UK.
USA: UTP, 2250 Military Road, Tonawanda, NY 14150, USA.
Canada: UTP, 5201 Dufferin Street, North York, Ontario M3H 5T8, Canada.

Copyright © 2009 J. Charles Alderson and the authors of individual chapters.

All rights reserved. No part of this work may be reproduced in any form or by any means without permission in writing from the publisher.

The policy of Multilingual Matters/Channel View Publications is to use papers that are natural, renewable and recyclable products, made from wood grown in sustainable forests. In the manufacturing process of our books, and to further support our policy, preference is given to printers that have FSC and PEFC Chain of Custody certification. The FSC and/or PEFC logos will appear on those books where full certification has been granted to the printer concerned.

Typeset by Techset Composition Ltd., Salisbury, UK.
Printed and bound in Great Britain by Short Run Press Ltd

Contents

Acknowledgement vii
Contributors ix

    An Overview
    J. Charles Alderson 1

1. Setting the Scene
   J. Charles Alderson 8

2. Professional Advice vs Political Imperatives
   Alan Davies 45

3. Micropolitical Issues in ELT Project Implementation
   Tom Hunter 64

4. The Politics of ELT Projects in China
   Ron Kerr 85

5. Teaching Immigrants the Language of the Host Community: Two Object Lessons in the Need for Continuous Policy Development
   David Little and Barbara Lazenby Simpson 104

6. The Commercialisation of Language Provision at University
   Glenn Fulcher 125

7. The Role of Micropolitics in Multinational, High-Stakes Language Assessment Systems
   Mark Crossey 147

8. Challenges and Constraints in Language Test Development
   Gary Buck 166

9. The Politics of Examination Reform in Central Europe
   Karmen Pižorn and Edit Nagy 185

10 Language Educational Policies Within a European
    Framework
    Neus Figueras 203
11 The Micropolitics of Research and Publication
    J. Charles Alderson 222

Acknowledgement

Several extracts in Chapters 1 and 11 of this volume have been reproduced by permission of SAGE Publications, London, Los Angeles, New Delhi and Singapore, from David Buchanan and Richard Badham, *Power, Politics and Organizational Change: Winning the Turf Game.* © D. Buchanan and R. Badham, 1999.

Contributors

J. Charles Alderson is Professor of Linguistics and English Language Education at Lancaster University. He was Director of the Revision Project that produced the IELTS test; Scientific Coordinator of DIALANG (www.dialang.org); Academic Adviser to the British Council's Hungarian English Examination Reform Project; and is former co-editor of the international journal *Language Testing* and the *Cambridge Language Assessment Series* (Cambridge University Press). He has taught and lectured in over 50 countries worldwide, been consultant to numerous language education projects, and is internationally well-known for his teaching, research and publications in language testing and assessment, programme and course evaluation, reading in a foreign language and teacher training.

Alan Davies is Emeritus Professor of Applied Linguistics in the University of Edinburgh where he has been attached since the mid-1960s. Over the years he has spent long periods working in Kenya, Nepal, Australia and Hong Kong. He has served as Editor of the journals *Applied Linguistics* and *Language Testing* and includes among his recent publications: *The Native Speaker: Myth and Reality* (2003), *A Glossary of Applied Linguistics* (2005), *An Introduction to Applied Linguistics* (2nd edn, 2007), and the edited volume *The Handbook of Applied Linguistics* (2004). His book *Academic English Testing: 1950–1989* was published in 2008.

Tom Hunter has had over 35 years experience in ELT. In most recent years this has largely been in international aid development contexts where, as a trainer-trainer, curriculum expert, project manager and policy specialist, he has honed his skills. He has worked on both long and short term consultancies in a number of countries, including Bangladesh, Kenya, Ethiopia, Mexico, Iran, Sri Lanka, Afghanistan and Uzbekistan. His research interests are in teacher-training and curriculum. He currently works at the University of Ulster where he is course director for a foundation diploma course. Tom is married with two grown-up children.

Ron Kerr worked as a teacher developer and project manager in China, Ukraine and Russia. He has a PhD in Linguistics from Lancaster University and has published on critical development management, leadership and knowledge transfer. He has been teaching at Lancaster University Management School, the Open University and the University of Birmingham.

David Little established the Centre for Language and Communication Studies at Trinity College Dublin in 1978, was first head of TCD's School of Linguistic, Speech and Communication Sciences from 2005 to 2008, and recently retired as Associate Professor of Applied Linguistics. He is the author and co-author of several books and numerous articles on the theory and practice of language learner autonomy. From 2001 to 2008 he was director of Integrate Ireland Language and Training, a government-funded unit that provided English language support for newcomers to Ireland.

Barbara Lazenby Simpson has been involved in English language teaching since the early 1970s. She is currently a research fellow at the Centre for Language and Communication Studies, Trinity College Dublin, and was deputy director of Integrate Ireland Language and Training from 2001 to 2008. Her work focuses on migrant second language learning from primary pupils to older adult learners and involves course design, materials development, and research across the domain.

Glenn Fulcher is Senior Lecturer in Education (Applied Linguistics) at the University of Leicester. He studied Theology and Philosophy at the University of London and Education at Christ's College Cambridge, before gaining an MA in Applied Linguistics at Birmingham University. He received his PhD in Applied Linguistics from the University of Lancaster in 1993. He is author of *Testing Second Language Speaking* (Longman/Pearson, 2003), and *Language Testing and Assessment* (Routledge, 2007) with Fred Davidson of the University of Illinois.

Mark Crossey was British Council Peacekeeping English Project ('PEP') manager for Poland from 1996 to 2003, and then the global programme's Poland-based testing coordinator from 2003 to 2005. He then moved to British Council London to become the Global PEP Director. Mark left PEP in 2007 and is currently Deputy Director, British Council Romania.

Gary Buck is an applied linguist with a strong assessment background. His first degree, from Oxford University, is in Oriental Studies, he has an MEd from Temple University with a specialisation in TESOL, and his PhD is from Lancaster University in second-language assessment. He wrote his dissertation on The Testing of Second Language Listening Comprehension. He has published in leading journals on assessment-related issues, including his book, *Assessing Listening Comprehension* (CUP, 2001), and has made numerous presentations at international refereed conferences, and given a large number of invited talks and workshops on a variety of assessment-related issues. He is co-founder, President, and Technical Director of Lidget Green, and in that capacity has designed and developed a number of internet-based testing systems. He joined the University of Michigan in September 2006, as Director of Testing, where he directs a large international language testing programme.

Karmen Pižorn is Assistant Professor of English Language Methodology at the University of Ljubljana, Faculty of Education, Slovenia. She coordinates The Early English Language Teacher Training Programme and teaches English Language Methodology for Teachers of English to Young Learners, Assessing Young Language Learners, Grammar for Teachers of English to Young Learners, and General English courses for undergraduates. She has been Testing Team Leader of The National Testing Committee for English in Primary School for seven years and has published articles and books on language testing and assessment.

Edit Nagy was English Programmes Manager for the British Council in Hungary 1995–2007, and in that capacity she managed several English language teaching projects. She set up a national network of English teachers, a set of resource centres/points and established a network of ESP teachers. Under her management, the Examinations Reform Project developed the model of the new English school-leaving examination in Hungary, delivered a suite of six accredited exams-related teacher training courses and published the INTO EUROPE series of exams preparation materials as well as a website for English teachers. She has worked with professional associations, experts in ELT and hundreds of English teachers in Hungary and in the region.

Neus Figueras Casanovas holds a degree in English Philology and a Phd on Oral Testing, both from the University of Barcelona. Since 1996 she coordinates the development and administration of standardised certificate exams for adult students of foreign languages at the local Ministry of Education in Catalonia, Spain. She has participated in testing-related European projects (Speakeasy, DIALANG, Ceftrain, ENLTA, Dutch CEF Construct, EBAFLS) and collaborates with the Council of Europe in relation to the uses of the CEF in testing contexts; she co-authored the pilot version of the Manual for Relating Examinations to the CEF (2003) and coordinated the CD with Reading and Listening pilot samples. She has worked as a teacher trainer in regional, national and international contexts and published articles on language testing and assessment. She was the first president of EALTA, the European Association for Language Testing and Assessment (2004–2007).

An Overview

Language learning has always been an important part of a well-rounded education, and language policy, as an academic discipline as well as a practical political activity, has an important role to play in modern societies. Policies determine which languages are to be regarded as official, and which are to be the medium of education. Policy-makers decide which second and foreign languages should be taught in schools and universities, and those responsible for policy implementation determine how the languages are to be taught, learned and assessed. In the last two decades, language education has become increasingly concerned with innovation and change. This is partly as a result of the increased interest in English language teaching as global demands for English grew and as new approaches to English language teaching developed in the 1970s, 1980s and 1990s. Governmental agencies and textbook publishers were all instrumental in encouraging teachers and institutions to become more effective in their endeavours and as part of that to innovate in teaching methods, teaching materials, tests, in-service and preservice education for teachers, and more. Numerous Government- and NGO-funded projects were set up to encourage such innovation and to foster change. Initially, such projects concentrated on the content of their innovation: the nature of the textbook, the design of the test, the methodologies of teaching and teacher training. However, project members came to realise that the process of innovation was at least as important to the success of the project as the content of the innovation. Increasingly, project participants and managers turned to the evaluation and innovation literature in general education for guidance on the factors that might influence whether an innovation might be successful or not. Authors like Fullan (2001), Henrichsen (1989) and Rogers (1995) have been increasingly cited in the ELT literature, and their insights and precepts have been taken into account when evaluating and planning change projects. As a result a literature has developed within ELT focusing on change management (e.g. Kennedy, 1988; Markee, 1997). Such books also have recourse to the management literature for insights, and management authors are increasingly seen as relevant to ELT.

However, the image of rationality and logical processes that characterise both the educational and the management literature do not tell the whole story. Experience suggests that systematic logical analysis, careful planning and project monitoring can have an effect on the course of a programme or project, but at least as important are individual factors: the personality of the players themselves, their emotions, their ambitions, their agendas and their influence. This has been recognised for a number of years, both in the management literature (Ackroyd & Thompson, 1999; Buchanan & Badham, 1999) and in language education even as early as 1984 Jack Richards was writing about 'The secret life of methods'. However, it was very rare for anybody to publish either accounts of such factors, or theories that might address related issues and help professionals understand better the politics of language education.

Nevertheless, a literature is developing within language education that addresses issues of what we may call the macropolitics of education: authors like Phillipson (1996) and Pennycook (1994) have argued that English language education in particular is a neo-colonialist enterprise serving the needs of capitalism and the national interests of the UK, the United States and Australia. In language testing, too, authors like Shohamy (2000) and McNamara (2001) have asserted that language testing, serving the function of gate-keeping in many contexts, is a tool to enforce or maintain the power and influence of the ruling elites.

Thus, one can argue that, as the field of language education has become more self-critical, the ethos of the times is receptive to a volume that examines in some detail aspects of the politics of language education. What makes the present volume different, however, from other volumes such as those cited above is that it looks, not at the macropolitics and the ideological agendas of nations and multinational or global organisations but rather focuses on micropolitics, the agendas and motivations of individuals within organisations, and on the agendas of those organisations.

Politics can be defined as action, or activities, to achieve power or to use power, and as beliefs about government, attitudes to power and to the use of power. But this need not only be at the macropolitical level of national or local government. National educational policy often involves innovations in language education, be that to revise the curriculum, to introduce new teaching methods, textbooks or tests, in order to improve the foreign language proficiency of citizens, to open up or restrict access to education and employment and even immigration opportunities. But politics can also operate at lower levels, and can be a very important influence on educational developments and their deployment. Politics can be seen as methods, tactics, intrigue, manoeuvring, within institutions which are themselves not political, but commercial, financial and educational. Indeed, Alderson (1999) argues that politics with a small p includes not only institutional politics, but also personal politics: the motivation of the actors themselves and their agendas. And personal politics can influence language education both in day-to-day affairs, and in projects for innovation and change.

Experience shows that, in most institutions, development is a complex matter where individual and institutional motives interact and are interwoven. Yet the language education literature has virtually never addressed such matters, until very recently. The literature, when it deals with development matters at all, gives the impression that language education is basically a technical matter, concerned with the development of appropriate materials, the creation and revision of appropriate tasks, textbooks and tests, and the analysis of results from piloting of innovations. But behind that facade is a complex interplay of personalities, of institutional agendas and of intrigue. Although the macropolitical level of language education is certainly important in a globalised world (as Pennycook, 1994; Phillipson, 1996; Shohamy, 2000; and others discuss), one also needs to understand individual agendas, prejudices and motivations. However, this is an aspect of language education which rarely sees the light of day, and which is simply part of the folklore and gossip of language education.

Exploring such issues is difficult because of the sensitivities involved, and it is difficult to publish any account of individual motivations for proposing or resisting innovations or status quo situations. However, that does not make it any the less important. Alderson (1999), for example, argues that language testers need to take account of the different perspectives of various stakeholders: not only classroom teachers, who are all too often left out of consideration in test development, but also educational policy-makers and politicians more generally. Although there are virtually no studies in this area at present, the aim of this book is to begin an open debate about such matters, to contribute to a better understanding of language education and particularly educational change and resistance to change, but also the processes of language education more generally.

After the first chapter of this volume, which attempts to set the scene by reviewing relevant theories in related disciplines like psychology, management and intercultural communication, as well as some of the references above, each chapter first addresses and discusses a key theme in politics and language education, followed by one or two case studies that illustrate important issues relating to the roles of individuals and institutions within that specific theme or context. The final chapter discusses practical, theoretical, methodological and ethical issues in researching and publishing accounts of the politics of language education.

In the first chapter, Alderson sets the scene by describing a range of different circumstances where micropolitics can be said to have influenced language education. In order to understand micropolitical behaviour better, he then explores various literatures and theories for insights, first from the perspective of the individual, where personality types, individual needs and the role of individuals within groups and organisations are implicated. The contribution of management theory is then explored as well as the relevance of a broader understanding of society and culture. The latter is seen as of particular interest to a profession which operates at the interface between different cultures. Finally the nature of misbehaviour in organisations is examined in some depth as background to the case studies that follow in subsequent chapters.

The second chapter by Davies addresses the conflict between the professional and the political (a theme also taken up by other authors). He shows the importance of key players in language policy decisions. In his first case study, in Nepal, he shows how the role of the professional consultants involved was essentially to recognise the need for the personal opinions of the key educational and political players to prevail, and the status quo with respect to the starting age for the learning of English was maintained. In the second case study, in West Africa, on the other hand, the strongly held opinions of the external consultant prevailed, but only briefly, and, in time, policy reverted to the status quo. Davies points out that the passage of time allows him to see more clearly the important role in the formulation of language education policy of the attitudes and beliefs of individuals, and indeed to write about this more openly than would undoubtedly have been possible closer to the events described.

Hunter discusses the projectisation of English language education in the context of development aid. He describes the role of consultants to such projects, and the part that vested interests among the different stakeholders can play in a project. His account of the role of a country's elite in determining language education policy is reminiscent of Davies' interesting distinction between the 'sentimental' and the 'instrumental'. The interaction between politics and personalities is at the heart of Hunter's chapter, with a case study showing how affective factors can influence decision-making and resistance to change. Political psychology is invoked as helping us better understand the behaviour of the various stakeholders involved.

Kerr's chapter follows on from Hunter in addressing the politics of ELT projects in China at a time of change in the management of projects, and the consequences of macropolitical decisions on the actors involved. The chapter describes how UK Government policy is translated into institutional policy, filtered through the agendas and ambitions of institutions and individuals. The resulting micropolitics of the interaction between project members, their managers and their host institution is described in detail in a case study which describes how ELT 'experts' had to learn how to play the political game.

Little and Simpson locate their case study in an Ireland which is coming to terms with a greatly increased influx of refugees and migrants. They show how language education policy is influenced by immigration policy, the impact of both these areas on the micropolitics of setting up a professional Refugeee Language Support Unit and the resulting necessity to reconcile professional principles with political expediency. An initial emergency policy decision to cope with newcomers' language needs is shown to be increasingly problematic as the authorities assume that the same policy and its implementation can be extended to cover different target groups. Inertia within bureaucracies, as well as possible turf wars between government departments, and a hope that problems will eventually disappear of their own accord, appear to result in the authorities preferring the status quo and minimal investment to meeting the needs of learners as identified by the language education professionals.

Fulcher describes how the internal politics of UK universities results in the teaching of English for academic purposes (EAP) to international students being treated as a cash cow in order to cross-subsidise departments of modern foreign languages which are unable to cover their costs because of declining student enrolment. Ironically, these latter departments look down on 'mere' language teaching as being academically inferior. In a self-fulfilling prophecy, the insistence of university management that EAP activities maximise income results, firstly, in their being unable to do research as well as teach, and then, secondly, being outsourced to commercial operations which claim they can provide EAP services more cheaply while at the same time allegedly enhancing universities' recruitment of lucrative international students. Language education is clearly the victim of academic politics and snobbery, as well as of the increasing commercialisation of UK universities.

The next chapter by Crossey describes in some detail the interaction between macro- and micropolitical issues in the context of the North Atlantic Treaty Organisation (NATO) and its language policies. He addresses the difficulty of developing coherent language education policies in an international setting, namely the circumstances leading up to the collapse of the Soviet bloc, the extension of NATO eastwards and the increasing importance of the use of English for military purposes. He presents a case study of attempts to develop standardised language proficiency tests across the member states of NATO and how personal and political motives intertwined to influence such attempts, against a background of macropolitical developments.

Buck discusses the tensions between the professional standards of language test developers and theorists, and the constraints of the real world. The concerns of the former often appear to be compromised and frustrated by the demands of organisations and the different departments and individuals within those organisations. Whilst recognising this classical micropolitical situation, Buck points out that it is often hard to distinguish between individual agendas, ambitions and resistances, and the legitimate concerns of those responsible for financial probity and commercial considerations. His view is that language education (in this case in the shape of test development) is perhaps inevitably a matter of principled compromise, which 'ivory tower' theorists need to recognise.

Pižorn and Nagy's chapter is set in a rapidly changing Central Europe, where the need emerged for educational reform as part of government policy to engage much more closely with Western Europe, to join NATO and the European Union, and where macropolicies of reform, accompanied by the professionalisation of language assessment in both Slovenia and Hungary met considerable institutional and individual resistance. The micropolitical role of both individuals and institutions is examined in some detail and it is concluded that professional attempts to innovate should not only stress the importance of the technical aspects of reform, but should pay attention to hidden (and not-so-hidden) agendas, and should not underestimate the power of key players, who can frustrate even the most technically perfect schemes.

Figueras focuses on the language policies of the European Union and the Council of Europe, and argues that a lack of transparency and detailed planning for implementation of such policies has been responsible for considerable confusion and ignorance on the part of language education professionals as to the aims and nature of many programmes and activities. In order to take advantage of the considerable resources devoted to language education it is essential to be an insider, able to interpret the dense and forbidding jargon of bureaucrats. Without inside knowledge and networking, knowing who to contact and who to believe, it is difficult to find one's way around the European labyrinth. The personal careers and agendas of bureaucrats, their interest and their willingness or otherwise to cooperate make knowing who is who and where an essential part of the micropolitics of European language education.

Alderson's final chapter discusses the difficulty in researching micropolitics and publishing accounts of micropolitical behaviour. By its very nature, micropolitics can be controversial and contested, and gathering suitable evidence to attest to events and motives is fraught with difficulty. Alderson presents a case study of attempts to publish an account of individual and institutional micropolitics in a professional journal and the reluctance of publishers to cooperate. He argues, however, that publication and discussion of the influence of micropolitics on various aspects of language education is essential if we are to reach a more mature understanding of the forces that promote and hinder developments in language education and that can help determine the very nature of language education policies, programmes, projects, activities and achievements.

J. Charles Alderson
Editor

References

Ackroyd, S. and Thompson, P. (1999) *Organisational Misbehaviour*. London: Sage.
Alderson, J.C. (1999) What does PESTI have to do with us testers? Paper presented at the International Language Education Conference, Hong Kong Institute of Language Education.
Buchanan, D.A. and Badham, R. (1999) *Power, Politics and Organisational Change: Winning the Turf War*. London: Sage.
Fullan, M. (2001) *The New Meaning of Educational Change*. London: Routledge.
Henrichsen, L.E. (1989) *Diffusion of Innovations in English Language Teaching: The ELEC Effort in Japan, 1956–1968*. New York: Greenwood Press.
Kennedy, C. (1988) Evaluation of the management of change in ELT projects. *Applied Linguistics* 9 (4), 329–342.
Markee, N. (1997) *Managing Curricular Innovation*. Cambridge: Cambridge University Press.
McNamara, T. (2001) Language assessment as social practice: Challenges for research. *Language Testing* 18 (4), 333–349.
Pennycook, A. (1994) *The Cultural Politics of English as an International Language*. London: Longman.
Phillipson, R. (1996) *Linguistic Imperialism*. Oxford: Oxford University Press.
Richards, J.C. (1984) The secret life of methods. *TESOL Quarterly* 18 (1), 7–23.
Rogers, E.M. (1995) *The Diffusion of Innovations*. New York: The Free Press.
Shohamy, E. (2000) *The Power of Tests: A Critical Perspective on the Uses of Tests*. London: Longman.

Chapter 1
Setting the Scene

J. CHARLES ALDERSON

Introduction
Vignettes

At recent conferences in the UK, around the presentations of papers, over coffee breaks, in bars and at dinner tables, I heard the following stories, all allegedly true:

> A famous language pedagogue and head of department is frequently invited to exotic places to deliver lectures. He writes one new lecture per year, which he delivers wittily in a myriad of places. Meanwhile, back home, his colleagues have to substitute for him, decisions are deferred until he returns, students are unsupervised, and the Centre is out of control as factions, both external and internal to the Centre, tear it apart.

> When a colleague who had run a successful local project attempted to make a proposal for a continuation of the same project on a geographically much wider basis, the proposal was hijacked by her superiors, presented by them (unchanged) for funding and they then took all credit for the success of the bid. The original proposer was then obliged to implement the new project: all the work and none of the praise.

> A researcher is investigating the admissions process at his university, and interviews the admissions officers. He discovers that although the process normally follows explicit guidelines, exceptions are occasionally made, either because a particular candidate has an important position back home, and he could influence whether more students come from his institution, or because the student is recommended by colleagues, and it is awkward to challenge a colleague's claim that the student is sufficiently qualified and experienced to be admitted

to the course. Another student has received a scholarship from the British government, and there is pressure to admit the student because he is a useful contact for the British Council and Embassy in that country.

A British Council Country Director decides, shortly before leaving his post, that the staff should work in open offices to enhance communication, so, without consultation, he arranges for the walls to be torn down and open offices to be created. The new incoming Director dislikes open offices and arranges for the walls to be rebuilt (at tax payers' expense). Another British Council Director arranges, at considerable expense, for the refurbishment of the reception area of the building. Within two years the new Director turns the reception area into a computer centre, at considerable expense to the UK taxpayer. One year later, the British Council vacates the building and opens new premises elsewhere.

Such tales are not unfamiliar in language education; they are never published, yet they remain part of the folklore of the field. Other scenarios are well known, yet often accepted as a normal part of life in language education:

A new three-year teacher training programme was set up in a European country, which was by all accounts highly successful, which devoted far more time than traditional preservice programmes to teaching methodology and teaching practice. However, after a few years, the traditional language departments managed to have the three-year programme closed, and all budding teachers had to attend the traditional five-year literature and linguistics programmes, with only a bare minimum of teaching methodology and teaching practice.

An international organisation was set up by a group of language examination providers to promote their language exams. One key rule of the organisation was that each language could only be represented by one sole examination provider testing its national language, unless that examination provider did not object to another national language provider joining the organisation. The national providers of French and German exams had no objection to other French and German examination providers joining, but the provider of English exams has to date not allowed other English exam providers to join, despite the fact that English is by far the most widely tested language in Europe, and virtually every nation has examination bodies that test English.

Expatriate 'expert' teachers clash with principals and colleagues in their institution, causing great recrimination and hurt, but are easily able to take up a post in another country, which they have never visited and whose culture they know nothing about.

University experts in applied linguistics jet into language education projects in exotic locations, deliver several lectures on the need for more up-to-date methods of teaching, both inspiring and frustrating the local audience in equal measure, and then fly back to their universities never to be seen again.

In one Southern European country, where certificates in English are generally regarded as a passport to university entrance and to good employment, public education in English is in a lamentable state, and parents prefer to send their children (from ages as young as seven or eight) to private language schools, since the state system is widely believed to be terminally inefficient. Yet many of the teachers in the private language schools also teach in the state system, and the suspicion is that they teach quite differently in the two systems.

The language textbook industry, especially for English, has a huge market, and publishers have no scruples in claiming that products developed for one part of the world are equally relevant and useful in completely different societies. Since the Common European Framework of Reference (Council of Europe, 2001) has become almost the standard European reference for curriculum development, exams and textbooks, publishers have wasted no time in claiming that their textbooks are suitable for learners at B1 or A2, without any evidence whatsoever that their content has changed, much less been aligned to the Common European Framework of Reference.

A major non-governmental organisation (NGO) involved in language education claims that it 'values people', is 'a valued partner for the provision of English', and 'people are its greatest asset'. It is currently involved in making radical cuts in its staffing levels, without consultation, but the posts that are most costly – those of expatriate directors and assistant directors – are protected, and only relatively low-paid local staff are to lose their jobs.

The language education literature

In language education, especially in such a commercially successful enterprise as English language education, we hear and read more about the positive, the exemplary, the success stories, than about the negative, the normal, the failures. We hear much more about the Good Language Learner than we do about the Bad Language Learner. We certainly hear more about The Reflective Teacher than we do about The Unthinking Teacher, and we read more about the Communicative Syllabus and the Communicative Classroom than we do about the Confused Syllabus or the Confusing Classroom. Our 'professional' literature prefers not to deal with the 'unprofessional', other than implicitly, by contrast.

We hear much less, if anything at all, about those individuals who are not innovators or original thinkers, those who do not lead, those who are not paragons. Just ordinary human beings: the barely competent, those who resist change, the lazy, the less than ambitious, those who just want a quiet life and want to be with their family, to earn enough money to live on, and a bit on the side to brighten up an otherwise normal, maybe dull, certainly normal, life.

Similarly, there are many 'normal' institutions, with their weaknesses and foibles, their sins and their 'dirty linen'. Yet again, we rarely read about such institutions in the literature. We do not read about unprofessional or dubious behaviour, unscrupulous practices, ruthless treatment of rivals, competitors or clients. Yet surely they exist.

In many walks of life, we know that there are conspiracies, there is wilful negligence, there is incompetence, there are hidden agendas, there is unethical behaviour. Indeed, there is even criminal behaviour. Laws and the justice system exist to deal with such anti-social (albeit quasi-normal) behaviour, just as codes of practice and codes of ethics exist to define acceptable behaviour (even if such behaviour is not normal). So, one might argue, unprofessional, unethical, dubious or even criminal behaviour is the province of the courts, or of the professional organisations that regulate their profession's behaviour and practices. Maybe, but where and when in our profession do we read or learn about such practices?

Often we read about unethical or dubious practices in other fields, in the media: investigative journalism, it is often called. History is full of biographies of politicians and their lust for and use of power. We even read about such characters in literature, where they are often fictionalised, to protect both the individual and the author. In our field there are not many examples of this, although the novel *Rates of Exchange* by Malcolm Bradbury is based on the life of a well-known applied linguist. But even that fiction does not directly address the dubious practices, the unprofessional, the negligent and the incompetent; it merely mildly satirises the vain, self-seeking itinerant charlatan.

It is my contention that in order to understand language education and its development and change, effectiveness or ineffectiveness, we need to scratch beneath the surface of the theory, the exemplary cases, the vaunted successes. We need to describe and understand the mass of ordinary human beings and their motivations and actions, for better or worse, and the agendas of the institutions that employ them.

Need for theory?

One might argue that we lack an adequate theoretical account of the politics of language education, as well as an adequate methodology for describing such politics (but see Alderson, Chapter 11). However, this view over-privileges theoretical accounts, especially in the present state of our knowledge, and it ignores the fact that many different theoretical perspectives are needed to understand the complexity of the issues which I argue should be investigated. Indeed, the need for a plurality of theoretical and disciplinary approaches is the main theme of this chapter.

Before we can develop a theory of the politics of language education, we need descriptive studies of the politics of language education, with an emphasis on developing suitable research and reporting methodologies. We cannot develop any theoretical understanding of phenomena without first describing them. We need to problematise the whole area first, before we can seriously attempt theoretical underpinnings. So what follows in this book is a series of such case studies. First we must admit what we do not know, then explore the area before attempting grand generalisations and theorising. And I am not alone in arguing this position of 'first research, then theorising'. Goldstein and Woodhouse in the context of criticisms of school effectiveness research in the UK that it lacks a theoretical base, argue:

> It is not incumbent upon every research endeavour to provide a strong theoretical basis of the kind that allows interesting predictions and shapes our interpretation of the world being studied. There is, for example, often an important period during which empirical evidence needs to be accumulated before coherent theories can be developed. (Goldstein & Woodhouse, 2000: 360)

In this chapter I do not present a coherent theoretical overview of approaches to politics in language education. Rather, the aim of this chapter is to explore briefly those aspects of relevant disciplines in the social sciences that might throw light on topics addressed in subsequent chapters, to offer insights from different perspectives in the hope that some will resonate with readers. Not all ideas will resonate with every reader or context, but I hope that all will be stimulating of thought, and that some aspect of some of the ideas might inspire readers to explore the field further in order to enhance our understanding of the unexplored field of the politics of individuals and institutions in language education.

In this chapter, I will first briefly deal with macropolitics and distinguish this from micropolitics. I go on to discuss those features of individuals – their personalities – which may contribute to politics. I next describe the individual in groups, leadership and management theory. I then describe social and cultural influences that may also play a role in the politics of language education. Finally I address the nature and role of politics in commercial and quasi-commercial organisations, the topics of change and resistance to change and the nature of micropolitics in educational contexts.

Macropolitics vs Micropolitics

Issues to do with the macropolitics of English language education have been discussed in applied linguistics since the early 1990s at least, although Pennycook shows that English has played a dominant role in many countries for over 400 years.

> Whereas once Britannia ruled the waves, now it is English which rules them. The British empire has given way to the empire of English. (Pennycook, 1994: 1)

As the English language has spread globally, local varieties of English have developed, which Kachru and Nelson (1996) have characterised as the Inner Circle/Outer Circle/Periphery of English as an International Language. Debates rage about standards of correctness of World Englishes and the role of the non-native in teaching and using English (McKay, 2002; Medgyes, 1994; Phan, 2008). A 1979 brochure for a chain of private language schools – International House, cited in Medgyes, (1994: 3) claimed 'Once we used to send gunboats and diplomats abroad; now we are sending English teachers'. The British Council Annual Report, 1968–1969, proclaimed 'There is a hidden sales element in every English teacher, book, magazine, film-strip and television programme sent overseas' (Medgyes, 1994: 10–11).

Some see in this an imperialist conspiracy. Phillipson (1992), for example, argues that English has committed linguistic genocide by dominating the world's languages, as a tool of linguistic imperialism, of colonial, then neo-colonial and latterly commercial hegemony. Although Pennycook is somewhat critical of Phillipson's argument, seeing it as too deterministic, nevertheless he uses a similar rhetoric of colonial expansion, British domination of trade, and Anglicist and Orientalist attitudes to language to explain the colonial and post-colonial global role of English.

This volume is less concerned with the macropolitical role that English has played (and still plays) and with issues to do with English as an International Language. We do not address the acceptability or otherwise of local standards of English, except insofar as it affects the issues surrounding native/non-native English speaker individuals. Unlike Pennycook, we are not directly concerned in this volume with free markets, international relations, poverty, multinational companies and the global diffusion of certain forms of knowledge, culture and thinking, although clearly these are important issues that impact on a global language like English and which are themselves affected by the role of English in the world. Indeed, we are not in principle concerned with English language education but with language education more generally, since, although most examples in this volume do indeed concern English language education, we believe that in principle the issues addressed are generalisable beyond any particular language. However, we would be foolish to claim that matters like the claimed dominance of English for science, medicine and commerce, or the role of English in gate-keeping and in economic success do not play some part in the politics that we are interested in – micropolitics and the role of the individual, and individuals in institutions, in such politics. Nevertheless, in several of the case studies that follow this chapter, it is evident that macropolitics often provides an important context for micropolitical behaviour, and this is especially true in the area of development aid, and projects in language education. Inevitably, macro and micropolitics are frequently intertwined.

Blase defines micropolitics as follows:

> Micropolitics is about power and how people use it to influence others and to protect themselves. It is about conflict and how people compete with each other to get what they want. It is about cooperation and how people build support among themselves to achieve their ends. It is about what people in all social settings think about and have strong feelings about, but what is so often unspoken and not easily observed. (Blase, 1991: 1)

Furthermore, Tollefson (1995: ix) claims that 'power and inequality are central to language teaching and learning. What happens in the language classroom is intimately linked to social and political forces and practitioners must understand these links if they are to be fully effective in their work'. Each article in his edited volume 'examines ways in which language policy and language education around the world are linked with the distribution of political power and economic resources' (Tollefson, 1995: 1).

However, the social and political reality he and co-contributors refer to is more the politics of language planning, the role of English in the world, the sorts of issues addressed by Phillipson and Pennycook. In this volume we are much less concerned with such macro issues, and more with the issues of how individuals relate to each other within groups, across groups and within organisations, an aspect of micropolitics that has not been addressed in our field to date.

We acknowledge the importance of English as a global language and we have argued above that many institutions have vested interests in promoting the teaching and use of English (as well as other world languages). For example, although the British Council was originally set up explicitly to promote British culture, language and political systems, in order to counter the spread of fascism, alongside its linguistic and cultural work the British Council has developed a clearly commercial role, seen in the setting up and promoting of its own English language services (often to the detriment of British-based English language services, or to British-owned private language schools abroad). Thus the British Council has increasingly become a competitor to other commercial interests, rather than an even-handed facilitator of English language services.

It is instructive when considering the role of commercial and quasi-commercial institutions to remember the size of the second and foreign language learning market – estimated at 12,000 million USD in 2007 (http://www.phrasebase.com/blog/second-language-acquisition-market-forecast.html, last accessed 10.2.07).

Yorio argues

> Second language programs can be viewed within a marketing framework. It is clear that we are suppliers of a product (or services) which consumers need and avail themselves of. Students are consumers who pay for our product directly (from their own pocket) or indirectly (through subsidies given to them or us). (Yorio, 1986: 670)

Indeed, we will in this volume consider the politics of individuals and institutions also from a commercial/managerial perspective and not merely an educational one.

Although we do not necessarily believe that language education should model itself on commercial practice, we agree with White (1987: 217–218) that 'all of us in ELT can benefit from the experience and theories derived from the commercial sphere, with whom we may be surprised to find that we have more in common than we thought', for the simple reason that behaviour in organisations has been much more thoroughly studied in the theory of management than in language education.

The commercial nature of the ELT business per se, however, and the implications for cultural and macropolitical influence, if not dominance, are not primarily the concern of this volume, not only because the ground is now fairly well trodden already and the issues are familiar to most ESL professionals in the West in the 21st century, but because they are not directly related to matters to do with the conflicts experienced in schools, projects, groups and institutions in many parts of the world. We need to explore other as-yet-unexamined, unproblematised issues, and it is my hope that this chapter and this volume will make clear what other matters need critical inspection.

In examining the dynamics of groups and of conflict of the various actors in schools, Ball maintains that micropolitics is not confined to schools:

> I take schools, in common with virtually all other social organisations, to be arenas of struggle: to be riven with actual or potential conflict between members; to be poorly coordinated; to be ideologically diverse. I take it to be essential that if we are to understand the nature of schools as organisations, we must achieve some understanding of these conflicts. (Ball, 1987: 19)

Whilst one would naturally prefer to avoid conflict, and much writing about society, organisations and innovation is aimed at removing or avoiding conflictive situations, it is naïve to think that this can be done without understanding the nature of the conflict, potential or actual, and the nature of the subcultures themselves, as well as of the individuals within those cultures. The thesis of this book is that applied linguistics and language education in particular, has so far largely ignored an understanding of the nature of the politics of institutions and of individuals within them.

The Individual

I begin by looking at what is known about individuals: their personalities, what motivates them, and their various roles in organisations, including leadership. I will turn not only to psychological and social psychological theory, but also to management theory, since it is there that most studies have been undertaken of behaviour in organisations. This is not to assert that management theory can be transferred lock, stock and barrel to language education, but language educators can learn a great deal from management theory that is relevant to language education. Management theory is especially relevant to commercial organisations within language education, including publishers and examination bodies, private language schools and NGOs like the British Council and other cultural agencies. In the final section of this chapter we will see how applicable it may be to educational institutions which typically have more autonomy of staff and flatter hierarchies.

Psychology as a discipline has a great deal to contribute to understanding how individuals relate to each other inside and outside institutions. An individual's personality, in particular, has an important influence on others and on activities, achievements and attitudes. However, this is a vast and complex topic and we will only be able to skim the surface here. The complexity of the issues can be seen in the fact that Allport (1961, cited in Fontana, 2000: 100) identified 18,000 terms for personality traits (like 'friendly', 'calm', etc.) used in the literature to describe people and personalities, and as many as 4500 of these terms were in frequent use! Not surprisingly, psychologists, who attempt to bring some order and theoretical understanding into the study of people and personality, disagree among themselves as to the description, nature and stability of personalities and personality types.

However, the following account should suffice to suggest relevant aspects of individuals' personalities that affect the politics of organisations. It is common, for example, to characterise one's colleagues as 'aggressive' and 'competitive', 'adaptable', 'easy-going', 'lazy', and so on, and such personality features are believed to influence how groups work, how conflicts arise, and how goals are achieved or missed, as illustrated in some of the opening vignettes above. Yet the literature fails adequately to account for the effect of such personal characteristics when examining the process of projects, the workings of organisations and the development of guidelines for management. As I will discuss in the final chapter, it is often difficult to provide adequate evidence for the effects of such characteristics, which in turn then inhibits the production of full and frank accounts of project and management failures. The result is unfortunately a distortion of reality, and leads either to an unduly rationalised and optimistic view of how organisations operate, or to a cynical rejection of such texts as being 'motherhood and apple pie', divorced from reality and achievable only by paragons or tyrants.

Personality

Trait psychologists seek to identify relatively permanent features of personality. Wundt (1832–1920) took ancient classifications of humans into four types ('melancholic'; 'phlegmatic'; 'choleric'; and 'sanguine') and explained them by positing two basic traits – *strength of emotion* (strong and weak) and *speed of emotional change* (volatile vs stable). A person can be placed at any point on these two continua of strength and speed. Eysenck (Eysenck, 1983, 1990; Eysenck & Eysenck, 1969) took this further, and developed a highly influential theory of personality with two dimensions: *extroversion–introversion*, and *neuroticism–stability*. The extreme extrovert makes social contacts readily, likes change and variety in life, is easily aroused emotionally but not very deeply and tends to be materialistic, tough-minded and free from social inhibitions. The extreme introvert is the opposite of this. Neuroticism, or instability, means one is likely to be excessively anxious, whilst stability indicates relative freedom from anxiety. Eysenck was at pains to stress that these are stereotypes and most people will fall towards the middle of each of these scales. Nevertheless, it is clear that one's degree of extroversion/introversion can impact on one's colleagues in organisations.

One personality dimension frequently encountered in the psychological literature is that of *inferiority* and *superiority* complexes. Complexes are associations that we have about ourselves and the world. If we have an inferiority complex, we believe that we are less effective than those around us, and this belief can affect our whole life and how we relate to the world. Those with a superiority complex, on the other hand, assume, without sufficient evidence, that others are less able or are worth less than they are, and they fail to judge people on their merits. Sometimes a superiority complex hides insecurity, where the person concerned is unable to face the reality that he or she may not be as good as they believe themselves to be. One defence for such fragile self-esteem is to ignore criticism. An inferiority complex may lead us to expect failure rather than success when tackling tasks, which itself leads to lowered expectations.

Self-esteem, its protection and a lack of self-esteem would appear to be behind many behaviours which are seen as conflictive or negative. Personality characteristics associated with low self-esteem include aggression, depression and hostility to others (Fontana, 2000: 27). The role of the peer group in the development and maintenance of one's self-esteem is important, but it is also important to note that one can have high self-esteem (and acceptance) in some groups in which one participates, for example, at work or in clubs, yet low peer acceptance and hence low self-esteem in other groups. It is also generally accepted that one's self-esteem can change over time.

Self-esteem is an important component in Maslow's (1968, 1987) well-known definition of needs, which he divides into deficiency (maintenance) needs and being (growth) needs. He sees needs arranged in a hierarchy, represented as a pyramid with seven layers, where the bottom four layers (the deficiency needs) are subdivided into (from the bottom upwards) basic physiological needs, need for safety and security, need for interpersonal closeness and need for self-esteem. The higher being or growth needs are also subdivided, into cognitive needs, aesthetic needs and, at the highest level in the pyramid, self-actualisation.

The first (lower) four layers relate to a person's biological or psychological balance, including the need for food and water, sleep, the absence of pain, and include self-esteem and security. If these needs are not met, Maslow argued, it would be difficult or impossible to fulfil needs further up the hierarchy. The top three layers relate to the fulfilment of individual potential, but few people reach the level of self-actualisation because needs at some lower level remain unsatisfied.

Williams and Burden point out an interesting apparent contradiction between the two sets of needs:

> Whereas deficiency needs require a safe, secure environment which is aimed at producing a state of equilibrium, being needs can drive the individual into territory where a degree of tension and stress can be most productive. (Williams & Burden, 1997: 34)

Clearly if one's workplace, one's home environment, or one's relationships, do not meet one's needs at one or more of these levels, there will be problems for individuals and this may well result in attitudes and behaviours which we might call political. Maslow's theory has been highly influential in the study of behaviour in organisations and has to be taken into account in a study of the politics of individuals in language education.

Achievement motivation is an important feature of personality, and relates in part to Maslow's hierarchy of needs. Once one's basic needs have been fulfilled, we are more motivated by social acceptance and status. People who have high levels of achievement motivation – need for achievement or N'Ach (McLelland, 1961) – set themselves higher goals than average, and usually have more than average success in achieving their goals. Those with low N'Ach either set themselves very easy goals which they know they can reach, or they set very difficult goals which are clearly impossible and so they cannot be blamed for failing to reach them.

A related concept is *locus of control*, which refers to how individuals view the reasons behind their successes and failures. An external locus of control attributes failure to external circumstances – 'the exam was too hard', 'my luck ran out' – whereas those whose locus of control is internal accept responsibility for their successes and failures – 'I didn't try hard enough'. A tendency always to blame others can be a way of ignoring one's own inadequacies and always blaming oneself can lead to an inferiority complex. Clearly, how one is motivated and how one attributes failure and success will have an important impact on one's relations with others in one's social and professional lives.

Cognitive style has been shown to be an important trait related to personality. Some people are *focusers* and others are *scanners*, such that focusers tend to delay hypothesis-making until they have enough evidence to make a decision or act, whereas scanners tend to jump to conclusions on the basis of little evidence. Scanners may make up their minds about other people quickly, whilst focussers wait until they have enough evidence to make up their mind. Some people are *reflective*, others are *impulsive*. Researchers have also identified an *authoritarian* cognitive style, characterised by rigidity, intolerance of ambiguity – as seen, for example, in a tendency to dismiss alternative arguments. Such people tend to be conventional, intolerant of nonconformity, deferential to authorities and antagonistic to those who oppose authority, as well as tough-minded, even bullying, dominating, destructive of others and their ideas, and a tendency to stereotyping.

Research (Friedman & Rosenman, 1974; Friedman & Ulmer, 1984) has also identified two different managerial styles, known as Type A and Type B personalities. Type A personalities respond to pressure by intense activity, become competitive, hasty, find it hard to delegate and drive themselves hard. Type B people are more relaxed, willing to delegate, see problems as obstacles to be overcome rather than challenges or competition. They also seem to experience less stress.

Optimism–pessimism is another dimension along which people vary, and which characterises their reactions to problems and difficulties. It appears that the more control we feel we have over our lives, the less likely we are to experience pessimism (Fontana, 2000: 186).

In a large organisation we may not be able to change the macro events around us, but there are many micro ones that lie within our power and often it is the feeling that small things are on top of us that produces much of our pessimism – the sense that life is so difficult that we cannot even deal with its minor irritations (Fontana, 2000: 186).

And, indeed, it is often because people do not feel in control of their lives at work that they misbehave (Ackroyd & Thompson, 1999).

Individuals in groups and leadership

How one relates to being in a group is an important aspect of personality. Individuals who tend to conform to group norms tend to be defensive, rigid and moralistic, and intolerant of ambiguity (Crutchfield, 1955), as well as anxious for social approval, to have low self-esteem and tend towards authoritarianism, offering unquestioning obedience to superiors and the group and demanding unquestioning obedience from their subordinates (Fontana, 2000: 87). Pressures for conformity to the group are increased when individuals feel incompetent or insecure when operating independently; when the group consists of three or more people; when the rest of the group are unanimous in their decisions; when the individual's opinions are public to the group; and when the group has prestige in the eyes of the individual (Myers, 1998).

The study of group dynamics and group decision-making is valuable in understanding how organisations work. Research has shown that good group decisions depend on the presence of group cohesion (members share common aims and a common desire for a successful outcome), group participation (each feels heard and able to contribute), group communication and good group leadership (is acceptable to members, protects members' self-esteem, keeps the group focused, operates democratically and delegates responsibilities) (Fontana, 2000: 85). Poor group decision-making is the opposite in some or all aspects. One has to beware group pressure on individuals who may disagree with the group but find it difficult to express that disagreement for fear of expulsion. Groupthink can make life difficult for individuals and can also lead to poor decision-making, especially if the group is confident of its superiority of judgement. Group decision-making can also lead to tension between groups and to conflict, since the creation of strong group identity and loyalty can lead to rivalry and antagonism to other groups – the essence of micropolitics.

From the above it is clear that group dynamics are very important. Some people are more disruptive than others, some are more dominant in discussions, and groups develop their own cultures and subcultures, with subgroup rivalries and hostilities, group values, norms and hierarchies. Different groups will vary in all these features and how individuals relate to the different groups of which they are members (social, leisure, work, religious, etc.) will also vary, such that some can be leaders in one group but submissive in others.

However, most group leaders have the confidence and ability to define the group and give it direction, identity and values. Thus the study of leadership is an important aspect of understanding organisations and individuals within those organisations. It is common to distinguish leadership styles, in particular *task leadership* and *social* or *relationship-focused leadership*. The former is task-centred and directive and the latter is more mediatory, democratic and concerned with building team spirit. Most management texts consider that both styles are appropriate in different contexts and for different purposes, although the latter is generally better for morale. Interestingly, there is thought to be a gender difference here, such that women are more inclined to social leadership while men are more oriented to task leadership. Men are more likely to talk more assertively, interrupt others, express opinions and smile infrequently, whilst women are more likely to hear out others, express support and encourage others to express their views (Fontana, 2000: 90).

Management textbooks, for example, Adair (1983), have a long history of seeking to understand what makes a good leader, but recent thinking, in particular Goleman et al. (2002), Birkinshaw and Crainer (2002) and Taylor (2002) has moved beyond the stereotypical command-and-control view of leadership to stress that there are many different leadership styles suited to different organisations at different times.

In particular, the leadership style of the former coach of the England football team, Sven-Göran Eriksson, is held up by Birkinshaw and Crainer (2002), not only as typical of Swedish management styles – which are held to have a strong work ethic, a strong belief in equality, to seek consensus and harmony – but also as reflective of modern approaches to leadership, which display a concern for people and relationship issues embodied in the 'emotional intelligence' often attributed to women rather than men.

Eriksson is said to create an atmosphere of trust and commitment among his team, to have good one-to-one person skills, yet to be a strong decision-maker who has great skill in handling talented individuals. He is the very antithesis of the dictator or tub-thumping bully of the caricature manager who is all too real in many organisations, including, no doubt, within language education.

Management theories

Leadership is, of course, a focus of management studies. Many traditional management theories – so-called scientific management – explicitly assume that management behaves rationally to establish clear goals and minimise economic costs.

Theory X (McGregor, 1960) holds certain assumptions about man, such that management acts in accordance with the view that they prefer people to be under control. Theory X assumes that employees do not like work, will avoid work when they can and will behave badly at every opportunity if forced to work. Theory Y, on the other hand, holds that people do like work and are naturally active and creative. They can be allowed to decide for themselves how to order their work and are sufficiently responsible as to be able to work without supervision.

Theory Y has had much less influence in practice than one might hope and it is much more common for management to act in line with Theory X. However, as Argyris (1972) shows, much more sophisticated views are needed of the internal workings of organisations, since research has consistently shown that human factors inhibit acting according to norms of rationality. Argyris' work had its origin in a belief that sociological approaches to understanding organisations 'apparently ignored much of the research in personality, interpersonal relationships, and group dynamics' (Argyris, 1972: viii). He argues that we need both a psychological and a sociological view of man to understand how organisations work. When studying humans, it is important to be aware that people can have wants and expectations that are deviant from, and inconsistent with, the social culture.

Research of top management groups suggests that the amount of conformity, risk-taking, openness, destructiveness, intergroup crisis, management crisis and trust are all critical in the way individuals search, understand, and ultimately manipulate the system to adapt it to its environment (Argyris, 1972: 25).

Many management textbooks are written in abstract, theoretical terms that are probably off-putting to the average language teacher or applied linguist, which may be one reason why the management sciences are not consulted as often as perhaps they should be. Another reason may be that language educators feel that the business world is alien to their thinking and values (despite the thriving private language school business throughout the world). It is therefore refreshing when one comes across a readable, down-to-earth book about entrepreneurs that also has relevance to language education. Southon and West (2002) present a common-sense approach to management. What makes their work relevant to a consideration of the politics of language education is the emphasis they place on the importance of people, of communication, of cooperation and trust, in a business (and, by implication, the effect of absence of communication and trust, and the presence of difficult personalities, in organisations).

They characterise entrepreneurs as being confident – they know they can achieve their goals, however irrational that may be – and charismatic – they attract and inspire people. Entrepreneurs have a great deal of energy, are obsessed with work, ambitious and want to change things in a hurry. The down-side of their confidence is that they are also often arrogant – they know they are good – and manipulative. They cannot complete things and keep coming up with new ideas – they get excited by new projects, and consequently often lack focus. They can be impatient, mercurial as well as ruthless, and are often obsessed with the competition.

Many ventures in language education have similar characters to the entrepreneur: the charismatic textbook writer, the persuasive lecturer, the head of an academic department, a Minister of Education, and so on. Indeed, many have turned into entrepreneurs, setting up their own businesses, academic departments or centres, publishing houses, software companies and the like. Such people, like entrepreneurs, need supportive teams, both to help them realise their dreams, their plans and projects, their policy or their research, and to advise, restrain and calm them.

Southon and West argue that management in small enterprises is similar to how sportsmen and women are motivated by the best team captains, managers and coaches. Good leaders of sports teams do not criticise people for failure, but get them to learn from their mistakes. 'Blame cultures encourage people to put their own safety before the welfare of the group, to score cheap points off one another and generally to avoid risk.' Teams are encouraged to celebrate success, and individuals are praised in public, in order to get across the message that excellence is encouraged and celebrated. Leaders, in short, have to generate enthusiasm, and lead from the front. The analogy with educational settings is obvious, and bad micropolitics are often the result of poor leadership and lack of motivation.

However, Southon and West also argue that as organisations get bigger than 20 people, they change again (and it is interesting to note that sports teams very rarely are bigger than 20). Once an organisation goes beyond 21 people or so, it requires formal bureaucratic management. It is in such large organisations that most management science and textbooks are applicable, but, as Southon and West argue, some things are constant, particularly the notion that business (and management) is about people. However, in large companies and institutions, people are employees and are unlikely to feel as much loyalty to the organisation. They are selling their skills and whilst they need to be treated fairly, one cannot expect the same sort of commitment as one can from a smaller organisation or a sports team. Their motivational hierarchy will be different, with the higher needs being met outside work, and money and conditions will be more important in the workplace. The same may well apply to larger educational organisations.

The Influence of Society and Culture

Language education is an international business and activity. It is inevitable, therefore, that the influence of the culture of the society in which language education takes place will play a significant role in communication and miscommunication, in cooperation and conflict; in short, in politics. It is, moreover, important to recognise that language education is by its very nature cross-cultural, by virtue of the fact that it deals with a language not spoken by the learners, and this problem is heightened when speakers of one language teach or work in an environment, either where their own language is not spoken, or where the language of the learners is not that of the environment.

Hofstede and Trompenaars both address the issue of cultural diversity. Hofstede (1980) identifies four dimensions on which national cultures in relation to work can be distinguished. These are:

- Individualism-collectivism – The relationship between the individual and the collective in society. In high individualism countries everyone takes care of themselves, and society values individual achievement and initiative. In low individualism countries, one's identity is socially based and group decisions are important.
- Power-distance – The amount of inequality among individuals. High power distance countries typically have tall organisation pyramids, more centralised power, and large wage differentials. Low power distance countries have flatter, more decentralised organisations and smaller wage differentials.
- Uncertainty avoidance – The ease with which individuals cope with uncertainty about the future. High uncertainty avoidance countries show resistance to change, higher job stress and less risk-taking. People prefer to work in large, stable organisations that create order and structure. Low uncertainty avoidance countries exhibit greater openness to change, and more risk-taking. People are comfortable working in smaller, more entrepreneurial organisations, with relatively few rules.
- Masculinity–femininity – The extent to which people of both genders exhibit typically masculine or feminine qualities. In high masculinity countries people are more assertive, more work-focused and more concerned about recognition for their contribution. In low masculinity countries people are more concerned about relationships and the quality of their work environment, and they see work as less central in their lives (Birkinshaw & Crainer, 2002: 23–24).

Trompenaars (1993) emphasises that we each live in different sorts of cultures: cultures of work, cultures of origin and cultures of organisations (and, of course, it is clear that within any one culture of origin there will be different cultures of religion, family, leisure, etc.). Authority, bureaucracy, good fellowship, accountability, are all experienced differently in different cultures. Essentially, understanding culture means understanding what values mean to people in different cultures, since culture patterns the whole field of social relationships, be they business, personal, religious or other.

However, much of culture and cultural values is hidden from the observer, at least initially, and Trompenaars talks of the onion rings of culture, where the more explicit features of culture like artefacts, food, houses, monuments, language, fashions, and so on, can be peeled away to reveal more implicit layers, which include norms – the sense a group has of what is 'right' and what is 'wrong' ('this is how I should behave') – and values – the definition of 'good' and 'bad' ('this is how I desire to behave'). Finally, underneath this are the core basic assumptions about existence, which are not consciously questioned, which are self-evident to the group, because they are a result of routine responses to the environment. 'Culture is the means by which people communicate, perpetuate and develop their knowledge about attitudes towards life. Culture is the fabric of meaning in terms of which human beings interpret their experience and guide their action' (Geertz, 1973).

Cultural differences are not simply a matter of exotic cultures in faraway places, but they apply even in apparently homogeneous places like Europe, where north-west European culture is said to be analytic, logical, systematic and rational, whereas Euro-Latin cultures are more person-related, with more use of intuition and sensitivity. Even the Belgians and the Dutch show cultural differences, with Belgians respecting authority, accepting it as paternalistic and hierarchical, and the Dutch distrusting authority, which the Belgians see as overly democratic and unduly consultative, according to Trompenaars (1993: 8).

Although cultural differences have been empirically established for different countries, it is worth noting that these are tendencies and do not necessarily apply to individuals within any given country. Moreover, and equally importantly, it is not necessarily the case that culture is co-terminous with nation or state. Cultures can cross borders (there are Hungarian speakers from Hungarian cultures in Austria, Croatia, Romania, Serbia, Slovakia, Slovenia and the Ukraine), and there are subcultures within any nation. To assume that the Welsh, Scottish and Northern Irish have the same culture as the English within the UK is clearly naïve. Equally, even within England, there are significant differences between Southern and Northern cultures. There are also class and educational distinctions, such that the middle and upper middle classes, especially if they have been to public school (private schools in the English system) are more likely to conform to the Southern culture than to the Northern one, even if they come from the North. Thus the matter of cultural differences is complex and never static. What is important is to be sensitive to the possibility that our interlocutors and partners may have quite different, and unexpected, values to our own, and we need to be prepared to negotiate through possible misunderstandings. Conflict in a work or social situation is often the result of such misunderstandings, and such conflict can give rise to micropolitical differences.

In comparison with Hofstede or Trompenaars, Scollon and Scollon (1995) present a much more nuanced view of culture, which they prefer to call discourse systems, to emphasise their view that discourse is the means through which culture is communicated. They emphasise that just as individuals in modern societies have multiple identities, as members of different groups – a mother, daughter, wife, teacher, church worker, member of a sports team and more – so too are they engaged in multiple and often cross-discourse discourses. Indeed they prefer the term 'interdiscourse communication' to 'intercultural communication'.

Scollon and Scollon also explore different discourse systems, two of which they call voluntary systems: the corporate and the professional, and two of which they call involuntary: the generational and the gender discourse systems. They make the point that because we are all involved in different discourse systems, we face the problem of conflict among these, which they see as inevitable, because language is itself ambiguous, can never be wholly explicit, and therefore inferencing meaning from discourse is inevitable, varies from person to person (because of different knowledge of the world and cultural expectations and norms), and yet inferences are reached rapidly and are rarely tentative, because of the pressures of communication. Thus misunderstanding is inevitable, and one can never know enough about other discourse systems to avoid it. Rather, one needs to be sensitive to possible misunderstandings and their sources, to question one's own immediate interpretations, probe them via others to check that these interpretations are correct, and to monitor communication constantly to beware of misunderstandings as they occur.

The problem of misunderstanding is exacerbated for a global language like English, of course, because of its use in many intercultural, interdiscoursal communications, among individuals who are members of a myriad different groups and discourse systems. Scollon and Scollon are at pains to stress, in addition, that the problem in communication for 'non-native' speakers of English is typically not so much problems of pronunciation, pronouns or faulty grammar, since these are usually obvious, and can be compensated for or tolerated, but differences in patterns of discourse, which are much more hidden. One example given is the difference between Westerners and East Asians in how information is presented. Asians prefer to present the background to a topic, reasons for or against a position, before the main point or action is presented, whereas Westerners first nominate their topic and then present the reasons why a particular action is proposed. The former style is labelled 'inductive' or 'topic-delayed' and the latter 'deductive' or 'topic first'. Westerners are said to see the Asian style as inscrutable or shifty, whereas Asians see the Westerner as rude and blunt.

Thus, to understand the politics of language education we need to study the way in which the various discourse systems at play actually work and interact. The details of this are well beyond the purview of this chapter, but as language professionals, it behoves us to use our professional knowledge about communication when seeking to understand politics. Scollon and Scollon (1995) is a useful reference point. Chapter 9 in particular, in which they examine the profession of ESL teaching, is relevant to this volume and is worth quoting from at length. Scollon and Scollon point out that, as an ESL teacher, one is both a member of a profession and a member of a corporate culture (an educational institution). Some will identify themselves more with one than the other, which can create conflicts of identity, especially as ESL teachers work in many different institutions (Scollon & Scollon, 1995: 195).

Scollon and Scollon contrast two different types of ESL professionals: native speakers and non-native speakers. The former typically have considerable experience of travel and other cultures, whilst the latter will typically have studied ESL in school, and they may even see themselves as nonmembers of their own home societies. Often among the most outward-oriented members of their cultural group, the non-native speakers may well have greater cross-cultural experience than their non-English-teaching colleagues, which can lead to conflicts within the institution. Non-native speaker teachers tend to be rather well educated, whereas native-speakers may only have a first degree, may have entered teaching as a result of international travel during a gap year, or as a result of native-speaker schemes like those in operation in Japan (JETS) and Hong Kong (NETS), and are likely to have little formal knowledge about the language, unlike their non-native speaker colleagues.

Scollon and Scollon point out that for many ESL teachers, especially native speakers, there may be a conflict between the professional and corporate discourse systems. 'Professional discourse is goal-oriented, emphasises individual success over organisation goals and is highly relativistic. The discourse system provides support, contacts and connections and resources in pursuit of individual career development' (Scollon & Scollon, 1995). However, professional identity is often at cross purposes with the organisational discourse system in which the native speaker works (although this conflict is much less likely to be true for the non-native speakers).

> (The native ESL teacher) is more likely to draw a comparison with another English teacher who is in a country across the world than with a history teacher who is teaching down the hall. The ESL teacher is more likely to engage in correspondence with, to join in research projects with and to read of the research of another ESL teacher in some other country than to be aware of the work of colleagues in the same institution who teach in other fields. Because of this outside primary reference group, the ESL teacher is likely to be somewhat resistant to internal pressures to conform to the corporate culture of his or her own employing institution. (Scollon & Scollon, 1995: 197–198)

As a result of job mobility and experience of different working environments, the native-speaker ESL teacher may have a highly relativistic, anti-ideological stance and may not be supportive of the corporate ideological position. Such teachers tend to be rather sceptical of the university or school's discourse system, which they can leave relatively easily, unlike non-native speakers. This mobility is likely to lead to a difference in values, commitment, discourse, and may create considerable resentment.

Undoubtedly, in language education institutions and projects there is all too often a clash, overt or covert, between natives and non-natives in terms of beliefs, practices, degree of security and insecurity, often made worse by differences in pay, mobility and willingness to insist on change.

Medgyes (1994) also discusses the difference between native and non-native English teachers and asks 'Who is worth more?' He sees non-native speakers as norm-dependent, since they do not have the confidence to set norms: they depend on native speakers to tell them what is wrong and what is right. This can turn into stress which may be made worse by fear of looking a fool or being judged as having low foreign language proficiency, especially in front of native speakers, and having their authority undermined in front of learners.

Medgyes argues, however, that non-native speakers almost certainly know their learners' problems and cultures far better than do native-speaker teachers. Native speakers may be good language models, but if they are monolinguals, as so many are, they are certainly not good learning models. And since native speakers of English have not grappled with learning English, they have much less insight into learning difficulties specific to English. Too often, native speakers ignore the cultural context of their learners and seek to impose an alien learning culture.

The issue of cultural differences in education systems is explored in some detail by LoCastro, Shamim, McKay and Cortazzi and Jin. LoCastro (1996) shows how policies for the reform of language education in Japan in the 1990s paid lip service to the then prevailing orthodoxy in Anglo-American applied linguistics, but the content of the curriculum bore little resemblance to communicative theory, emphasising very traditional approaches. She argues that the power-coercive (Kennedy, 1987; White, 1988) approach adopted by the Ministry of Education actually reflects traditional Japanese values of hierarchy, of the importance of conforming to social norms, of the role of education in Japanese society of maintaining social order, of de-emphasising individualism. She claims that an important part of Japanese culture is the belief that the Japanese cannot learn foreign languages (a belief reminiscent of that of many English-speaking countries), that students must learn languages 'in the Japanese way' and that too much access to other ways of thinking is dangerous. This is reflected, she argues, in views of the appropriate nature of language learning (grammar-translation, recitation), of the importance of examinations, of appropriate behaviour in classrooms (exhibiting what she calls pseudo-conversational patterns, where the teacher answers and assesses his/her own questions, where there is very little student questioning or interactions), and so on.

Shamim (1996) illustrates in the Pakistani context the danger of an imposition on one educational system of ideas taken from an alien system, a phenomenon common in Hong Kong and elsewhere, and shows how teachers are not the only participants who may resist change. She encountered fierce resistance on the part of students to her attempt to introduce 'communicative methodology' into her class, in the hope that students would abandon their customary silent, note-taking, non-contributory role. Instead, the students boycotted her classes, to the extent that, as exams approached, she felt obliged to become less 'communicative', more teacher-centred, more 'authoritarian' and students were more satisfied with her teaching. She argues that 'there were parallels between learners' beliefs and assumptions about the definition of knowledge and learning and the norms of appropriate classroom behaviour, on the one hand, and on the other, the culture of the larger community, whose norms they share as members of the community' (Shamim, 1996: 106).

The 'culture of learning' (Cortazzi & Jin, 1996) is part of the hidden curriculum, and learners and teachers may be unaware of its existence or influence, especially where the language teacher is a native of the language being taught. The culture of learning is exemplified by the Chinese tradition of Intensive Reading, which is the core of the English language syllabus and methodology and which has the same structure, content and method throughout China (Cortazzi & Jin, 1996: 181–184). This Intensive Reading is both the product of China's isolation from much of the rest of the world from the late 1940s to the early 1970s, and also of a centuries-old Confucian tradition of learning through the close study of words and texts memorised by heart (Cortazzi & Jin, 1996: 184). There are culturally determined expectations of what a good teacher is: Chinese learners are reported to value deep knowledge of the subject, above all else, with patience, humour and being a good moral example coming higher than good teaching methods or arousing the students' interest. 'Western teachers make me think I have one more friend, but not one more father or mother' (cited in Cortazzzi & Jin, 1996: 188). Phan (2008) makes a similar point in relation to Vietnamese teachers of English.

However, we should beware of the trap of believing that there is such a thing as a national culture (e.g. 'Japanese' culture, 'Pakistani' culture, 'Chilean' culture) which is homogeneous across all the various groupings which make up a society. Muchiri (1996) reminds us that societies have many subgroupings, each with their own subculture, and such subcultures are often in conflict, rather than in harmonious co-existence.

Whilst recommending that the local culture of learning should be taken into account when devising curricula, textbooks and tests for English as an International Language, McKay (2002) acknowledges that this is not necessarily so simple, because there will be different views within that culture as to what is appropriate. She gives the example of Chile in the late 1990s, where the Ministry of Education introduced a curriculum reform intended to be relevant to the local context, including a focus on receptive skills, and a textbook focusing on the use of English in Chile, using local content. Teachers appeared to support this reform (although support may have been conditioned by the provision of the materials free of charge), but preservice educators argued that they were in a better position than the Ministry to know what students needed in terms of an appropriate methodology (whilst other teacher educators had never seen the textbook, and knew very little about the curriculum reform). Thus it is probably naïve to believe that just because the reform is instituted by local educators, they will agree on what is appropriate. Who decides who the local educators are? Will they always all share the same opinion? Rationally, no doubt, all the stakeholders should be involved fully in decision-making, but given that each group may decide it knows best, and given the likelihood that each group will have different and competing vested interests and hidden agendas, agreement on action will necessarily involve institutional and individual struggle: micropolitics.

Politics

Rational behaviour, misbehaviour and politics

Ackroyd and Thompson (1999) are critical of much management theory for assuming that human beings are rational, that individuals and groups will respond to appeals to reason, and that organisations can be managed in such a way that confrontational politics are removed. Even modern management theory that advocates changing the corporate culture, such that individuals and teams become self-regulating on the basis of trust, fairness, caring and empathy, empowerment, career-enriching opportunities, equitable pay and benefits, and so on (Boye & Jones, 1997), has failed to show that politics and misbehaviour are eliminated.

Ackroyd and Thompson show that organisational misbehaviour is manifested in a variety of forms, from the more obvious extremes of sabotage, pilfering and absenteeism to more subtle forms of resistance to managerial power like joking, irony and satire, sexual misconduct and sexual politics. Misbehaviour is a weapon in the politics of work, where managers traditionally seek to control, and employees resist such control by being recalcitrant. They argue that 'misbehaviour' results from the suspicions that employees have about management's intentions, from their desire to extract the maximum of benefit with a minimum expenditure of effort, and from their scepticism about the claims of many managers that changes in work practices and relationships are in the employees' best interests.

Ackroyd and Thompson argue that one of the reasons why managers have problems with misbehaviour, and why employees are cynical about managers' attempts to remove misbehaviour is that managers themselves often misbehave, since they are also individuals with their own goals and weaknesses.

Management has the ability (the power) to move the goal posts – to evaluate the same behaviour in different ways at different times – changing the operative criteria of good practice and misbehaviour as they go. 'My boss has vision, whilst I lack attention to detail; my boss's disrespect for bureaucracy is my failure to follow procedure; my boss's concern for change and innovation is my lack of consistency' (Ackroyd & Thompson, 1999: 12).

Misbehaviour is resistance to use and abuse of power, as well as itself an abuse of power. An important aspect of misbehaviour is that it comes about as a result of the formation of groups within the organisation. This is in part in reaction to management, creating a 'Them and Us' attitude, but in part as a natural result of social forces at play in the organisation. Whereas traditionally misbehaviour was seen as the behaviour of deviant individuals, Ackroyd and Thompson argue that it is essentially a social phenomenon, albeit often created by particular strong or determined individuals.

Organisational politics

Buchanan and Badham (1999) argue that organisational politics are inevitable, especially in times of change, and therefore it is important to understand political behaviour and political agents.

Political behaviour plays a more significant role in organisational life than is commonly recognised, or than is openly admitted. We perhaps like to think of our social and organisational culture as characterised by order, rationality, openness, collaboration and trust. The reality is different. Competition sits alongside cooperation. Informal 'backstaging' supports public action. We see self-interest, deceit, subterfuge and cunning as well as the pursuit of moral ideals and high aspirations ... initiatives are pursued, decisions are taken and changes are introduced to preserve and extend the power bases and influence of individuals and groups. Major decisions and significant changes are particularly liable to heighten political activity. Organisational behaviour cannot, therefore, be understood without a knowledge of the role of political behaviour (Buchanan & Badham, 1999: 1–2).

However, it is common to condemn organisational politics:

> Politics refers to individual or group behaviour that is informal, ostensibly parochial, typically divisive, and above all, in the technical sense, illegitimate – sanctioned neither by formal authority, accepted ideology, nor certified expertise (though it may exploit any one of these). (Mintzberg, 1983: 172)

Others have written at length about political behaviour in organisations. One particularly extreme view of political behaviour is presented by von Zugbach's (1995) 'Winner's commandments':

1. Me first. Nobody else will put your interests before theirs.
2. There are no absolute rules. Other people's ideas of right and wrong do not apply to you.
3. The organisation is there to serve your interests, not the other way round.
4. You are on your own. Nobody is going to help you become a winner.
5. Be paranoic. Watch out, the bastards are out to get you.
6. Suck up to those who matter and suck up well. Identify the key people in the system who will help you.
7. Say one thing and do another. You need to pay lipservice to the organization's cherished notions of how things should be done.
8. Be a team player, but make sure you beat your fellow team members.
9. Remember that the truth is not always to your advantage. Those who control your future do not necessarily want to hear the bad news.
10. Manipulate the facts to suit your interests. Even when things are bad you should come up smelling of roses.
11. Get your retaliation in first. When there is blood on the organisation's carpet, make sure it's not yours.
12. Blow your own trumpet – or better still, get someone else to do it for you.
13. Dominate your environment or it will dominate you.

(von Zugbach, 1995: 1–2)

Lest one is repelled by the apparent cynicism of such a set of guidelines for political behaviour, von Zugbach presents the contrasting behaviour of 'the losing manager':

Do you attend meetings where no political decision will be made?

Do you regard the organisation's rules with sanctity rather than contempt?

Do you perform tasks that could have been delegated?

Do you do things for which the team gets the credit?

Do you make yourself available and allow others to interrupt you?

Do you regularly volunteer when asked?

Do you read carefully every memo, letter, report and every other document which lands in your tray? (cited in Buchanan & Badham, 1999: 29–30)

However, political behaviour cannot be wished away and it is therefore preferable to understand how politics are done in organisations, in order, as Buchanan and Badham put it, to 'emancipate through exposure', and to help individuals to learn how to respond to political behaviour by understanding its nature. Power, politics and change are inextricably intertwined.

Buchanan and Badham define power and politics neutrally, as follows: '*power* concerns the capacity of individuals to exert their will over others; *political behaviour* is the practical domain of power in action, worked out through the use of techniques of influence and other (more or less extreme) tactics' (Buchanan & Badham, 1999: 11).

Power can be treated, not as a property of an individual but as a property of the relationship between an individual and others. Importantly, sources of power depend on the beliefs and perceptions of others, since our perceptions shape our behaviour as much as does 'reality' – giving much scope to the possibilities of impression management. What matters is what other believe one's source of power to be.

As in national party politics, virtuosity in 'spin', or in presentation of people, of policies, of actions, of events and outcomes, has become increasingly significant. Management skill becomes the ability to simulate appropriate attitudes, values, beliefs and emotions in an opportunistic manner to suit the circumstances (Buchanan & Badham, 1999: 36).

Buchanan and Badham contrast what they call 'the political entrepreneur' with other possible roles in the politics of organisational change (see Table 1.1).

The main theme of Buchanan and Badham (1999: 18) is that 'the change agent who is not politically skilled will eventually fail'.

Buchanan and Badham discuss at length aspects of political behaviour, which they label 'the turf game' and define as 'a game in which individuals and groups seek to defend and extend their turf' (Buchanan & Badham, 1999: 15). 'Turf' can concern areas of influence and power; status and reputation; access to and control over resources, or it can simply be to keep

Table 1.1 Perspectives on politics

The puritan	Does not get involved at any level because politics means 'dirty tricks', and is unethical and damaging.
The street fighter	The 'pure politician' for whom playing the game, to win, by whatever means, is the end in itself – and is enjoyed
The sports commentator	Understands the game and can pass appropriate comment and judgement, but does not become personally involved in the play
The political entrepreneur	Adopts a creative, committed, reflective, risk-taking approach, balancing conventional methods with political tactics when the circumstances render this necessary, appropriate and defensible

Source: Buchanan and Badham (1999: 32).

doing what they currently do and enjoy. Turf can be either personal, or collective – groups act to protect their collective turf.

The 'tactics' (Table 1.2) are presented by Buchanan and Badham as examples of the moves and tactics of the turf game in the context of organisational change.

Change and politics

A typical rational problem-solving management approach for implementing change is as follows: identify problem; gather data; analyse data; generate solutions; select the solution; plan for implementation; implement and test; continue to improve (Buchanan & Boddy, 1992: 10).

Project management models assume that change develops in a logical and planned sequence, key actors have clearly defined responsibilities and there is a clear completion date. Such models also assume that conflict is due to failures in interpersonal communication – which is naïve and ignores sources of resistance. Most importantly, 'planning and decision-making and communicating in the real world are socio-political processes not rational-empirical. It is not "the information" that reaches decisions but the players with their competing interpretations, and different values, interests and preferences' (Buchanan & Badham, 1999: 189).

Nevertheless, as they point out, 'despite what we know about the untidy realities, change has to *appear* in our culture to be rational and

Table 1.2 Turf game tactics

Image building	Actions which enhance reputation and further career; appropriate dress, support for the 'right' causes; adherence to group norms: air of self-confidence
Selective information	Withhold unfavourable information from superiors: keep useful information from your competition: offer only favourable interpretations; overwhelm others with complex technical data
Scapegoating	Make sure someone else is blamed: avoid personal blame: take credit for successes
Formal alliances	Agree actions with key people; create a coalition strong enough to enforce its will
Networking	Make lots of friends in influential positions
Compromise	Give in on unimportant issues to create allies for subsequent, more important issues
Rule manipulation	Refuse requests on the grounds of 'against company policy', but grant identical requests from allies on grounds of 'special circumstances'
Other tactics	The more covert and ruthless aspects of political infighting

Source: Buchanan and Badham (1999: 27–29).

linear' (Buchanan & Badham, 1999). Buchanan and Badham (1999: 155–156) argue that failures in implementation of change are due to the political difficulties which are inherent in change, especially change which is complex, rapid and that threatens vested interests and privileges. Change that takes place slowly over time is less problematic, although, since effective change often requires the commitment of senior management, the turnover of senior management – which is often more rapid than the time needed to implement major changes – can result in new management not being committed to the change instigated by their predecessors, because they wish to make their own mark on events.

In fact, this desire of newcomers to make their mark on projects is also often true of language education, where newcomers may disparage the work of predecessors, or fail to support it and instead promote new projects and activities, or actively undermine the work on ongoing projects.

However, it is also important to take account of likely resistance to change:

> Changes will always be contested, championed by one set of interests over another and, ultimately, represent the triumph of particular groups and interests over others. (Buchanan & Badham, 1999: 171)

They detail the following sources of resistance to change (Table 1.3).

Clearly, change will never be easy or straightforward. Buchanan and Badham suggest (see Table 1.4) that change may proceed in different phases, where different strategies may be appropriate at particular phases in the 'change implementation life cycle'.

Failed innovations can also be seen as being phased: enthusiasm; disillusionment; panic; search for the guilty; punishment of the innocent; praise and rewards for the non-participants (Buchanan & Badham, 1999: 185).

Table 1.3 Sources of resistance to change

Ignorance	Failure to understand the problem
Comparison	The solution is disliked as an alternative is preferred
Disbelief	Feeling that the proposed solution will not work
Loss	Change has unacceptable personal costs
Inadequacy	The rewards from change are not sufficient
Anxiety	Fear of being unable to cope in the new situation
Demolition	Change threatens destruction of existing social networks
Power cut	Sources of influence and control will be eroded
Contamination	New values and practices are repellent
Inhibition	Willingness to change is low
Mistrust	Motives for change are considered suspicious
Alienation	Alternative interest valued more highly than new proposals
Frustration	Change will reduce power and career opportunities

Source: Buchanan and Badham (1999: 199).

Table 1.4 A phase model of political strategy and tactics

Phase	Political strategies/tactics
Conception	The politics of project presentation, selling, positioning, justifying
Launch	The politics of project definition, recruiting support, coalition building
Delivery	The politics of driving, steering, keeping momentum, blocking resistance
Completion	The politics of termination and withdrawal, reporting back and moving on
Afterlife	The politics of representation, takes and myths of problems and success

Source: Buchanan and Badham (1999:196).

Buchanan and Badham (1999: 203) advise that, when innovations fail, it is important 'to construct an account that will be believed and honoured. The problem is that secondary goals of truthful representation and avoidance of blame may often conflict'. They present the following different ways of accounting for failure (Table 1.5).

Table 1.5 The construction of accounts

Category	Construction
The excuse	Admit that damaging behaviour has occurred but that you are not responsible; negative consequences were unforeseen, you were under considerable pressure at the time, the damage was actually caused by something or someone else
The justification	Admit responsibility but claim the behaviour was justified in the context; because no harm was done, because positive outweighs negative consequences
The concession	Admit to the offence, expressing apologies and remorse, and offer restitution; may seek to deflect censure and blame as well
The refusal	Deny that the damaging behaviour ever happened; claim that the challenger's version or perception of events is incorrect; or deny that the challenger has a right of reproach, because they are not involved, suffered no damage themselves

Source: Buchanan and Badham (1999: 203).

The politics of schools

Much of the previous section applies to organisations like publishers, examination bodies, NGOs like the British Council, and private language schools. We can expect that there will be some variation across different cultures, but it is highly likely that some version of organisational politics takes place in most settings. What is not yet clear from the literature we have surveyed is to what extent politics is important in educational establishments. Yet the definition of micropolitics as being about power and the use of it to influence others suggests that it operates in all organisations, including educational institutions.

Micropolitics arose partly in reaction to the rationalist perspective of school management theories, which emphasise structural aspects in accounting for behaviour, stressing authority rather than power, making assumptions of rational efficiency, effectiveness in decision-making and collegiality and consensus among school members. However, Pfeffer (1981) argues that organisational structures are themselves the result of political actions among individuals and groups. Micropolitical activity is undertaken to deal with resistance or opposition (Blase, 1991: 7). Rational school models 'ignore individual differences in values, ideologies, choices, goals, interests, expertise, history, motivation and interpretations – factors central to the micropolitical perspective' (Blase, 1991: 3).

However, micropolitics is not necessarily about conflict. Factors such as compliance patterns and socialisation processes are closely linked to political processes, and even stable organisations have political regimes.

Micropolitics is best perceived as a continuum, one end of which is virtually indistinguishable from conventional management procedures, but from which it diverges on a number of dimensions – interests, interest sets, power, strategies and legitimacy – to the point where it constitutes almost a separate organisational world of illegitimate, self-interested manipulation (Hoyle, 1986: 126).

Gronn (1986) considers that there are different types of conflict: not only open conflict but also covert conflict (where a group may suppress its tendency to dissent); latent conflict (where problems are seen as 'personal troubles'); inaction through self-censorship (where groups do not engage in conflict because of the power of others) and inaction due to a tendency to accept a potentially conflictive situation as normal.

However, school-level politics are frequently submerged, subtle and covert, and may frequently be obscured by organisational routines – and therefore may not be easy to study. Strategies to control others include the manipulation of language, information, roles, committee structures and membership, agendas and teacher participation in decisions. A commonly reported political tactic to stack the odds in favour of those in a superordinate position is to hire staff who are expected to be sympathetic to their own ideology. This is not unknown in higher education also.

Ball and Bowe (1991) show how micropolitics can affect the implementation of change and how external forces for change affect micropolitics. The process of change should thus be seen as political rather than technical, and as collective rather than individual. 'Implementation (of change) for us is taken to be a matter of struggle and conflict with material, vested and self-interests at stake. Policy is not just something that is done to people – it is essentially contested both in its formation and its implementation' (Ball & Bowe, 1991: 24).

Although it is frequently argued that teachers' attitudes need to change before an innovation can be successful (Hargreaves & Fullan, 1992), it is also the case that change of attitude does not guarantee change of behaviour (Kennedy & Kennedy, 1996). Teachers are more likely to change their behaviour (use a new textbook or classroom technique, prepare for an exam differently, use a new methodology) if they believe that others are also in favour of the change, especially those who have power and influence over them, like Heads of Department, School Principals, colleagues, and even parents. If they believe that those others do not favour the behaviour to be changed (regardless of whether their belief is accurate) then they are unlikely to change their behaviour. This Ajzen calls their 'subjective norms' (Ajzen, 1991; Bandura, 1991, 1998). Such subjective norms are clearly influenced by power and therefore politics: politics play a crucial role in whether a change will happen or not.

In addition, however, it is also important that teachers believe that they have control over their behaviour. If they do not, they are unlikely to change. Behavioural control can be internal or external: the skills and abilities that teachers have to implement a change, the amount of information or understanding they have of the change; or the influence of the examination, timetabling, lack of suitable equipment or materials, time, size of class or institutional support and cooperation of colleagues – again, a matter in part of politics of groups. Favourable *attitudes* to change (essentially an individual matter) need to be accompanied by an *intention* to change before change can happen, and this intention is itself influenced by subjective norms and perceived behavioural control, both of which are psychosocial in nature – perceptions about how others, including the local culture, will react to the proposed change. However, need for achievement (NAch) and adequate motivation are also important, without which the teacher is unlikely to face the discomfort that almost always accompanies change.

Thus, individual personality issues, as well as cultural, social and political matters all combine to influence behaviour, and favourable attitudes, or even cognitive beliefs about the outcome of an action, will be inadequate on their own.

In many respects, a view of teaching that is defined largely in technical terms may be seriously misguided. Teaching styles, materials and purposes, it seems, are significantly affected by political considerations (e.g. parental expectations) that typify life in public schools. Everyday political factors and the use of power by individuals and groups, in particular, affect the quality of teaching and learning in schools (Blase, 1991: 204).

We thus end this chapter with Blase's (1991) 'working definition' of the complex organisational phenomenon that is micropolitics:

> Micropolitics refers to the use of formal and informal power by individuals and groups to achieve their goals in organisations. In large part, political actions result from perceived differences between individuals and groups, coupled with the motivation to use power to influence and/or protect. Although such actions are consciously motivated, any action, consciously or unconsciously motivated, may have political 'significance' in a given situation. Both cooperative and conflictive actions and processes are part of the realm of micropolitics. (Blase, 1991: 11)

In this chapter we have discussed a range of different approaches to understanding micropolitical behaviour, from individual personality types to individual needs and how individuals act within groups, including aspects of leadership. We have briefly touched upon aspects of management theory before addressing the topic of the influence of society and culture on behaviour, beliefs and attitudes. Finally we examined in some detail the nature of behaviour and misbehaviour in organisations and organisational politics. This exploration of relevant issues and theories is intended as a backdrop for the case studies in the following chapters.

References

Ackroyd, S. and Thompson, P. (1999) *Organizational Misbehaviour*. London: Sage Publications.
Adair, J. (1983) *Effective Leadership*. London: Pan Books.
Ajzen, I. (1991) *Attitudes, Personality and Behaviour*. Milton Keynes: Open University Press.
Argyris, C. (1972) *The Applicability of Organizational Sociology*. Cambridge: Cambridge University Press.
Ball, S.J. (1987) *The Micro-politics of the School: Towards a Theory of School Organisation*. London: Routledge.

Ball, S.J. and Bowe, R. (1991) Micropolitics of radical change: Budgets, management and control in British schools. In J. Blase (ed.) *The Politics of Life in Schools* (pp. 19–45). London: Sage.

Bandura, A. (1991) Social cognitive theory of self-regulation. *Organizational Behavior and Human Decision Processes* 50, 248–287.

Bandura, A. (1998) Health promotion from the perspective of social cognitive theory. *Psychology and Health* 13, 623–649.

Birkinshaw, J. and Crainer, S. (2002) *Leadership the Sven-Goran Eriksson Way: How to Turn your Team into Winners*. Oxford: Capstone Publishing Ltd.

Blase, J. (ed.) (1991) *The Politics of Life in Schools: Power, Conflict and Cooperation*. Newbury Park: Sage Publications.

Boye, M.W. and Jones, J.W. (1997) Organisational culture and employee counter-productivity. In R.A. Giacalone and J. Greenberg (eds) *Anti-social Behaviour in Organisations* (pp. 172–184). London: Sage.

British Council (1969) *British Council Annual Report, 1968–1969*. London: The British Council.

Buchanan, D. and Badham, R. (1999) *Power, Politics and Organisational Change: Winning the Turf Game*. London: Sage Publications.

Buchanan, D. and Boddy, D. (1992) *The Expertise of the Change Agent: Public Performance and Backstage Activity*. Hemel Hempstead: Prentice Hall.

Cortazzi, M. and Jin, L. (1996) Cultures of learning: Language classrooms in China. In H. Coleman (ed.) *Society and the Language Classroom* (pp. 169–206). Cambridge: Cambridge University Press.

Council of Europe (2001) *A Common European Framework of Reference for Learning, Teaching and Assessment*. Cambridge: Cambridge University Press.

Crutchfield, R.S. (1955) Conformity and character. *American Psychologist* 10 (5), 191–198.

Eysenck, H.J. (1983) Human learning and individual differences. *Educational Psychology* 3, 3–4.

Eysenck, H.J. (1990) An improvement on personality inventory. *Current Contents: Social and Behavioural Sciences* 22 (18), 2.

Eysenck, H.J. and Eysenck, S.B.G. (1969) *Personality Structure and Measurement*. London: Routledge and Kegan Paul.

Fontana, D. (2000) *Personality in the Workplace*. Basingstoke: Macmillan Press Ltd.

Friedman, M. and Rosenman, R.H. (1974) *Type A Behaviour*. New York: Knopf.

Friedman, M. and Ulmer, D. (1984) *Treating Type A Behaviour – and Your Heart*. New York: Knopf.

Geertz, C. (1973) *The Interpretation of Cultures*. New York: Basic Books.

Goldstein, H. and Woodhouse, G. (2000) School effectiveness research and educational policy. *Oxford Review of Education*, 26, 353–363.

Goleman, D., Boyatzis, R. and McKee, A. (2002) *The New Leaders*. London: Little, Brown.

Gronn, P. (1986). Politics, power and the management of schools. In E. Hoyle (ed.) *The World Yearbook of Education 1986: The Management of Schools* (pp. 45–54). London: Kogan-Page.

Hargreaves, A. and Fullan, M. (1992) *Teacher Development and Educational Change*. Basingstoke: Falmer Press.

Hofstede, G. (1980) *Culture's Consequences*. London: Sage.

Hoyle, E. (1986) *The Politics of School Management*. London: Hodder and Stoughton.

Kachru, B. and Nelson, C.L. (1996) World Englishes. In S.L. McKay and N. Hornberger (eds) *Sociolinguistics and Language Teaching* (pp. 71–102). Cambridge: Cambridge University Press.

Kennedy, C. (1987) Innovating for a change: Teacher development and innovation. *English Language Teaching Journal* 41 (3), 163–170.

Kennedy, C. and Kennedy, J. (1996) Teacher attitudes and change implementation. *System* 24 (3), 351–360.

LoCastro, V. (1996) English language education in Japan. In H. Coleman (ed.) *Society and the Language Classroom* (pp. 40–58). Cambridge: Cambridge University Press.

Maslow, A.H. (1968) *Toward a Psychology of Being*. New York: Van Nostrand.

Maslow, A.H. (1987) *Motivation and Personality*. New York: Harper and Row.

McGregor, D. (1960) *The Human Side of Enterprise*. New York: McGraw-Hill.

McKay, S.L. (2002) *Teaching English as an International Language*. Oxford: Oxford University Press.

McLelland, D.C. (1961) *The Achieving Society*. Princeton: Van Nostrand.

Medgyes, P. (1994) *The Non-Native Teacher*. London: Macmillan.

Mintzberg, H. (1983) *Power In and Around Organisations*. Englewood Cliffs, NJ: Prentice Hall.

Muchiri, M. (1996) The effect of institutional and national cultures on examinations: The university in Kenya. In H. Coleman (ed.) *Society and the Language Classroom* (pp. 122–140). Cambridge: Cambridge University Press.

Myers, D.G. (1998) *Psychology*. New York: Worth.

Pennycook, A. (1994) *The Cultural Politics of English as an International Language*. London: Longman.

Pfeffer, J. (1981) *Power in Organisations*. Marshfield, MA: Pitman.

Phan, Le Ha (2008) *Teaching English as an International Language: Identity, Resistance and Negotiation*. Clevedon: Multilingual Matters.

Phillipson, R. (1992) *Linguistic Imperialism*. Oxford: Oxford University Press.

Scollon, R. and Scollon, S.W. (1995) *Intercultural Communication: A Discourse Approach*. Oxford: Blackwell.

Shamim, F. (1996) Learner resistance to innovation in classroom methodology. In H. Coleman (ed.) *Society and the Language Classroom* (pp. 105–121). Cambridge: Cambridge University Press.

Southon, M. and West, C. (2002) *The Beermat Entrepreneur: Turn Your Good Idea into a Great Business*. London: Pearson Education.

Taylor, D. (2002) *The Naked Leader*. Oxford: Capstone Publishing Limited.

Tollefson, J.W. (ed.) (1995) *Power and Inequality in Language Education*. Cambridge: Cambridge University Press.

Trompenaars, F. (1993) *Riding the Waves of Culture. Understanding Cultural Diversity in Business*. London: Nicholas Brealey Publishing.

von Zugbach, R. (1995) *The Winning Manager: Coming Out on Top in the Organisation Game*. London: Souvenir Press.

White, R. (1987) Managing innovation. *ELT Journal* 41 (3), 211–218.

White, R.V. (1988) *The ELT Curriculum: Design, Innovation and Management*. Cambridge: Blackwell Publishers.

Williams, M. and Burden, R.L. (1997) *Psychology for Language Teachers: A Social Constructivist Approach*. Cambridge: Cambridge University Press.

Yorio, C. (1986) Consumerism in second language teaching and learning. *Canadian Modern Language Review* 42 (3), 668–687.

Chapter 2
Professional Advice vs Political Imperatives

ALAN DAVIES

Introduction

Micropolitics is a term that the right-wing think tank, the Adam Smith Institute, claim to have coined in the 1970s (Pirie, 2005) to describe the process of examining the exercise by interest groups of 'strategies such as power, coercion, cooperation, cooption and influence to obtain resources and achieve goals' (Ehrich & Cranston, 2004: 21). I attempt a micropolitical approach in this chapter to describe two case studies, the longer one in Nepal and the shorter one in West Africa, both reporting events that took place some 30 years ago in an attempt to uncover what was personal in the policy decisions that were taken. Such an attempt is made easier by the distance of the events referred to, bringing into sharper focus than was evident at the time the actions and above all the attitudes of the main actors. In order to characterise these attitudes, I use the distinction Sentimental–Instrumental (Kelman, 2006; Mejias & Anderson, 1988). The sentimental role concerns values that are traditional and cultural, while the instrumental role has to do with economics and job-improved possibilities. While both sentimental and instrumental roles may be observed micropolitically, that is in individuals or in interest groups, sentimental is more micro and instrumental more macro, in that the sentimental attachment is more about identity and the instrumental more about conformity and normative expectations.

With regard to language and language education, the instrumental role concerns the value of language learning for job and other economic prospects while the sentimental role emphasises the importance of a language (often a heritage language such as Irish Gaelic in Ireland or Basque in Spain) to maintain group traditions and culture and to demonstrate differentiation from other groups. In some settings, the sentimental can become instrumental, thus Welsh in Wales today and Catalan in Catalunya now have an instrumental role since they control access to employment.

The comparison by Scollon and Scollon (1995) of two different types of ESL professionals, native speakers and non-native speakers referred to by Alderson (this volume) is pertinent to the Nepal Survey described below. Over the course of the Survey, what became clear to the three expatriate members of the Survey team was that our view of English was different from that of our Nepalese colleagues on the Survey team. For us, English was a means to communicate with the world outside; for them to have English on the curriculum was a mark of being modern whether or not much learning took place. After all, they might have thought, who needed to communicate in English in Nepal since everyone spoke Nepali? For them English was largely symbolic. That meant that, for the English native-speaking Survey members, change in method, in textbooks, in examinations was necessary and expected, but for our Nepalese colleagues (as Alderson, this volume, points out in a different context) it was irrelevant. They saw themselves as teaching a subject rather than a language.

In many settings language policy decisions have to do with schooling. In my Nepal example, as we see below, the argument was about the optimum starting age for English. In West Africa, again as we discuss later, it had to do with how to examine English attainment. What each of these settings reveals is the influence of key players. No doubt, we should rejoice that decisions are not faceless, that opinions of individuals matter. Indeed, when these are informed individuals their opinions and advice should matter. But for the purposes of this chapter, as for the volume as a whole, our contention is that our understanding of language policy decisions must take into account the role of key individuals and interest groups.

I begin the chapter with a brief consideration of the goals of language in education, by reference to Kaplan and Baldauf (2005).

Goals of Language in Education

Kaplan and Baldauf (2005) begin their study of language in education by insisting that it is a political activity. To illustrate their argument, they discuss language in education policy in three very different polities: Japan, Sweden and North Korea. 'Given the political nature of much language in education planning...and its contextual embeddedness in the language ecology of particular situations, this chapter is organized around an examination of the situation in three polities...' (Kaplan & Baldauf, 2005: 1015).

Their discussion leads them to the conclusion that there are 12 general issues which, they claim, 'are implicated for language-in-education goals' (Kaplan & Baldauf, 2005: 1032). Given the central role Kaplan and Baldauf accord to politics in language in education decisions, it is hardly surprising that on analysis most if not all these issues are at bottom political. What is more, they all exemplify the thesis of the chapter van Els contributes to the same volume (van Els, 2005) that there is always a tension – perhaps we should call it a systematic tension – between the political and the professional views of language in education decisions.

> There are signs of a growing awareness of the need for a rational approach to curricular change. But the normal practice in second language learning and teaching planning ... still is for uninformed laymen to develop policies without any recourse to empirical findings or expert advice. (van Els, 2005: 989)

The ambition of political actors is to make a sentimental language choice (such as Nepali medium under the New Education System Plan and English when that Plan was abandoned) also instrumental. If they do not succeed in making it instrumental, support for the sentimental choice will lessen as parents and other stakeholders come to realise that the choice they have been accorded does not provide modern opportunities for their children.

van Els also reminds us that such policy choices are necessarily – and properly – attempts to reconcile the needs of society with those of the individual. These two sets of needs cannot, van Els maintains, be kept apart.

From a planning point of view, such divisions are not very useful, as societal needs cannot be separated from individual needs – societal needs are always transferable into, that is, have been derived from, the individual needs of (a number of) members of that society. In essence all educational needs are individual. On the other hand, not all individual needs are also societal; they only take on a societal dimension when society declares needs of (groups of) individuals important enough to take them into account when formulating a national educational policy (van Els, 2005: 977).

Trite adages such as 'what is good for society is good for individuals' hold good only for benign societies. Language in education choices are political in that they are about the general welfare of that society and (in benign societies) they are generally acceptable to individuals. But what about van Els's complaint that it is 'uninformed laymen' who make these decisions? Three of Kaplan and Baldauf's general issues, Nos 9, 10 and 11, are of particular relevance to my case studies.

No. 9: 'continued prominence of colonial languages'. Surprise and indignation are sometimes expressed at the continued hold of the colonial languages on former British and French colonial territories as though this was somehow a recent phenomenon. It is not. History is in part the story of conquest by empires which, with the due effluxion of time, withdraw and fade away but often leave behind their customs and their language. This is as true of Latin, Chinese and Arabic as it is of Spanish, French and English. *Pace* Phillipson (1992), the prominence of such excolonial languages does not necessarily kill off local languages, as we see, for example, in India and Africa today. However, while the decision in favour of the former colonial language may well be the political choice, there is a strong body of professional opinion in favour of promoting one or other (or more than one) local language. Some success towards that end has been achieved in Malaysia, Indonesia and East Africa. But the decision is not easy, either way, whether for the colonial or the local language. Indeed, in most cases some compromise using both seems to be achieved. And curiously neither decision is politicised since both are likely, in different ways, to achieve the same political end, that of national unity. The choice is essentially a professional choice and, as one might expect, professionals differ as to which choice to make.

No. 10: 'increasing impact of English on educational systems'. This is an extension of No. 9, whereby English is not just the colonial but the global language. And, of course, more general globalisation of communications tends today to increase the interest in and demand for English. Some polities – countries such as France – may object to this apparent take-over, but it is unclear whether the increasing grip of English has any effect at all on the status and role of French in francophone polities. What is very clear, however, is that English has more and more become the first foreign language in many educational situations. This does indeed have an effect on the status of other languages (and the extent to which they are widely studied) and, as with all such dynamics, on the future provision of teachers of other languages. But what is less often discussed is how far different Englishes, sometimes called World Englishes (Davies *et al.*, 2003), are being made use of. And indicative both of the increasing spread of English and of its possible fragility is the attention now being given to the study of English as a lingua franca (Elder & Davies, 2006; Seidlhofer, 2004). The attention being given to English as a lingua franca can be regarded as an acceptance of the instrumental role of English in business and other work-related settings in which many language functions, such as social and creative uses, are stripped away.

No. 11: 'inadequacy of training for many teachers (both in terms of language and methods)'. No doubt this is the case; see below in my discussion of Nepal. What this inadequacy of training seems to represent is not so much a tension between the political and the professional in the sense that those on the political side want one solution and those on the professional another. Rather it represents a lack of interest by the political in the importance of language education. Lip-service may be given, but in spite of the advice – and the protestations – of the professionals language education has lost out in the general expansion of secondary education. This is not the case in every polity, of course. But even in the Netherlands, a particularly language-aware polity, where general proficiency in English is very high indeed, there is a professional view that the very success of English should mean that the state can withdraw its efforts. The argument is that the need for English is so self-evident to everyone that the Dutch require few external incentives. And so de Bot (2000) proposes that, since English will be learnt anyway, it would make sense to teach other important EU languages which at present are neglected.

Instrumental and Sentimental Roles

A superposed language of wider communication, for example French, Arabic, English within a polity represents a deliberate choice, whether that language is national, official or medium of education. The choice itself may be conscious or unconscious but that it is a choice is clear, both operationally and institutionally. In sociolinguistic terms, the choice of which language(s) should carry functional load and should be armed with formal credentials is of interest because it compels a balance between the sentimental or symbolic and the instrumental roles all such language situations must achieve if they are to be successful (Kelman, 2006). It may be that in much early or initial second or foreign language teaching the role for most learners is largely sentimental or symbolic.

Foreign language (FL) teaching in schools is mounted by the state and welcomed by the public not because much actual language learning takes place nor because it represents a necessary basis for subsequent language learning, since most children opt out at the end of two or three years, but because it is necessary to fulfil the sentimental role as an indication of awareness of and attendance to traditional cultural and status values which require that a foreign language should be being learnt. The requirement that it should actually be successfully learnt represents attachment to the instrumental role. To be in the process of learning a foreign language (or even to be seen to be learning) is to be a member (or to seek to become a member) of the literate, educated, professional and business middle classes. Language teaching thus has some correspondence with various curriculum choices which emerge from time to time as liberal, humane, nonvocational (e.g. learning to play a musical instrument or do ballet) as opposed to the scientific and the vocational.

In England, it has recently been announced that foreign language teaching (FLT) is to be made compulsory from age seven in all primary schools. This decision accords with the widespread view that language learning should start as early as possible in spite of the discrediting of an earlier version of that view (Burstall, 1974). Meanwhile, children in secondary schools are permitted to opt out of language learning after two years. These two policy decisions seem contradictory, suggesting an attempt to compensate for inadequate secondary foreign language teaching (FLT) by a lengthy primary school FLT. But the reality is that unless there is an easy continuity between primary and secondary FLT, primary FLT provides only a shaky foundation for a seriously instrumental secondary FLT.

In situations of relative abundance of resources (such as the UK) the importance even at early learning stages of maintaining a balance biased in favour of sentimental role values can be tolerated and accommodated. In difficult circumstances, in developing countries particularly, resources may be too scarce to tolerate such a balance and only one role may be achievable. Even in such cases, however, strong sentimental attachment may endure and obscure the problems of providing for the instrumental role. The official view may well be that both roles are important or indeed that the sentimental provides a necessary grounding for the instrumental. But given, in such circumstances, the massive language learning loss through withdrawal from school[1] after the early years, it is not cynical to conclude that the reason for the large scale enrolment in education and therefore in language learning is sentimental and that officials may regard drop-out as actual sentimental achievement, that is that the sentimental goals have been early achieved. In a resource-poor society we might expect official policy to take an instrumental view of FLT, embracing it for its role in their country's modernisation programmes. But if half the cohort of Primary 1 students leave school at the end of Year 1 and if, as happens, there is thereafter a haemorrhaging of the student population year by year, it is doubtful whether the policy of embracing serious FLT for the whole school population is in any way instrumental (Williams, 2001).

Case Studies

I now cite two examples of language situations where there has been conflict between the political, widely interpreted and the professional. The first, which is discussed in some detail, is that of an English Language Teaching Survey (ELT) in Nepal in the 1980s. The second, dealt with more briefly, looks at the School Certificate English Language examination in 1960s Anglophone West Africa. In both cases, the advice of the professional consultants was at odds with the requirements of the state. In Nepal the state was represented by the Ministry of Education and in particular by the Permanent Secretary of that Ministry who himself had once been my colleague at Tribhuvan University when I worked in Nepal. Then he had been professional rather than political but in the intervening years he had become a senior bureaucrat in the Ministry and thus viewed policy more as a political than as a professional. In West Africa the state was represented by the West African Examinations Council (WAEC), a parastatal organisation which had hired the consultant whose advice it had accepted, failing to notice that the radical change in the examination, which the consultant recommended, required an equally radical change in the syllabus. Since the state has overriding authority, it is reasonable to enquire whether there is any purpose in inviting and receiving professional advice, which may well be rejected if it does not accord with macropolitical policy. My view is that such advice does have a role but that professionals, who are typically focused on instrumental ends, need to recognise the sentimental appeal at the micropolitical level.

Survey of ELT in Nepal

I provide data from a 1980s ELT survey of Nepal (Davies, 1987, 1990; Davies et al., 1984). Although this language teaching example is concerned with English language teaching, I consider that my remarks have implications for other language teaching situations.

Background

Nepal is an example of a resource-poor society. The country is landlocked and among the poorest in terms of GDP. In 2006, the literacy rate was about 24%. For historical reasons English occupies the position of first foreign language in the state system and educational medium in the private schools. English has been taught as a foreign language in Nepal since the mid 1850s when Nepal first came under the hegemony of British India. Before 1970 English was introduced in Grade 3 of the Nepalese Primary school. The few private schools were all English medium. Then in 1971 the New Education System Plan (NESP) made large scale changes, aiming at 'counteracting the elitist bias of the inherited system of education' (NESP, 1971: 8). English, seen as part of that elitist bias, was started a little later, in Grade 4, and private schools were required to switch to Nepali medium.

But before the NESP had properly got under way it had already become clear that there were problems of implementation. There were complaints by academics about the standard of English at Tribhuvan University, the national university. In a small country, professionals can exercise an important influence as a lobby. At the same time, more and more middle-class parents, especially in Kathmandu, were sending their children to English medium schools in India, mainly to the Darjeeling area (which is largely Nepali speaking), although whether it was primarily for the sake of access to the English language was not clear.

Official concern that these India-educated children of the middle classes might never return to Nepal, as well as middle-class parents' lobbying in Kathmandu for the reopening of the private English medium schools led to the early repeal of the NESP. Private schools were encouraged to use English as medium again and permitted to do so if they considered they had adequate resources: indeed all schools were permitted to become private if they so wished. The intention was clear: to attract back to Nepalese private schools those children currently attending private schools in India and, at the same time, and as a necessary corollary, to encourage and promote English teaching generally in the state system. Already by 1984, 13 secondary schools in the Kathmandu Valley had been privatised and private colleges were also being set up. The population had increased dramatically by about 50% in the previous 15 years and the number of pupils in schools had also increased: between 1976 and 1980 the increase in Grades 6 and 7 (lower secondary) was 100%, indicating a problem for the Ministry of Education in finding enough teachers with adequate English even for the existing NESP start in Grade 4.

The Ministry of Education decided in 1982/1983 to set up a Survey of English Language Teaching (ELT) to provide information about the state of English in the educational system and to make recommendations particularly about the optimum starting age for English, about the aims, content and so on of the current teaching materials and about the adequacy of levels of English proficiency among teachers. Three external consultants, Eric Glendinning, Alan MacLean, and the present writer were selected by the British Council and three Nepalese counterparts, Niranjan Kumari Bajacharya, Jaya Raj Awasti and Arun Pradhan were appointed by the Nepal Ministry of Education. The team spent 36 person weeks (the bulk by the three counterparts) together in Nepal at the beginning of 1984, carrying out the Survey of ELT for the Nepal Ministry of Education. Maclean, Glendinning and I had each spent between two to five years in the 1970s working in ELT in Nepal and were therefore somewhat familiar with the situation. The results referred to in this chapter come from the report of the Survey. In particular I discuss here the interviews with officials and teachers and the results of the proficiency tests we conducted.

Interviews

Officials and teachers involved in ELT were interviewed. One of the recurring themes was that of the 'right age' for starting formal language learning (Hyltenstam & Abrahamsson, 2003). There was, we found, considerable support by individuals and officials for starting English at the beginning, in Grade 1. Parents seemed to remember that English used to start there – in the days of many fewer schools and many fewer pupils. It also makes sense to lay opinion that if a skilled behaviour (such as language learning) is not being adequately acquired what is needed is more practice. Hence, it seems sensible to start English earlier and to teach it, and therefore practice it, longer. This essentially 'political' attitude was countered by us with the available research evidence, that there is no optimum age for starting language learning, that adults can learn as efficiently as children and indeed more quickly and that what matters is the local situation in which the language is being taught. But that was a mistake on our part: our appeal to the saliency of the local situation was used against us: if the local was what mattered, then in Nepal the earlier the better. Here was a clear example of a possibly irreconcilable clash between political and professional – especially since the leading political advocate was Principal Private Secretary to the Crown Prince, and therefore virtually unchallengeable. This man, like the Ministry of Education Permanent Secretary, might have been expected to take a professional perspective. After all, they were both former English teachers. But the Crown Prince's Private Secretary, like the Ministry Permanent Secretary, had moved from the professional to the political and both saw themselves not just as embodying authority but also as having the interests of the masses at heart. That, plus their credibility as former professionals, made them very powerful opponents to our professional arguments. These two men, representing as they did, the Crown and the Ministry of Education, were key stakeholders: even if their arguments could be challenged (as they were), their views would still carry the day. What we as consultants had to do was to admit to ourselves the significance of their role and then ask ourselves not whether we should compromise against our will but just what merit there was in their position. For those responsible for making the decision, the political was bound to weigh more heavily than the professional argument, if only because in a country where most children who started school did not continue beyond Grade 1 any impression of excluding most children from the opportunity to learn English was bound to be unpopular, given that English was widely viewed in Nepal as the key to modernisation. School leavers with little or no English were condemned to traditional – and poorly-paid – roles. The fact that, even if they were permitted to start English, most would still drop out was somehow ignored or brushed aside: what mattered was that the opportunity was given. Or, perhaps more sceptically, that all were allowed to participate in a sentimental education.

The counter claim of professional advice is not strong, given that it remains uncertain and indefinite. Our professional advice was that a start in Grade 1 would give too much attention to the early years and lead to distortion, essentially an argument against an over emphasis on the sentimental role. And with the existing English teaching force (as will become apparent later) three more years of English would not necessarily improve learning.

Another favourite topic was the 'decline of English' which meant that existing members of the establishment considered that new recruits (to the Civil Service for example) were less proficient in English than used to be the case at that stage of training. We tried to make two issues clear: first, the difficulty of such comparisons over time, given that strict comparability is unachievable; second, the romance with which most of us look back at some better time, some prelapsarian Eden, more innocent, almost perfect. We all do it: standards are always thought to be slipping. We talked this over with many people. Our results suggested that there was no evidence that standards had declined.

Proficiency test

The major instrument used by the Survey team for assessing English language proficiency was an adaptation of the so-called Proficiency Test. This test, constructed in the 1970s by Clive Criper, then of Edinburgh University, while attached to the Malaysian Ministry of Education, consists of 13 short graded reading passages each containing a number of blanks for filling in. The total number of blanks in the test as a whole is 147. Here are some of the passages which include the example provided, the first passage (the easiest) and the last (the most difficult). Although the test is open-ended, correct answers are severely restricted to a small set of acceptable answers provided on the mark-scheme.

Proficiency test example passages

Example passage
 Swami is a boy. He is a small ... (1) ... His sister is Lolita. She is a girl. She is a tall ... (2) ... Swami has a ball and Lolita has a ... (3) ... Swami has a cap and Lolita has a ... (4) ... but they do not have new caps.

Passage 1
 Swami has a ball. It is a big red ... (1) ... He throws it to Lolita ... (2) ... she does not catch ... (3) ... The ball falls into the pool ... (4) ... Swami can't get it out. '... (5) ... Tata to go and get it ... (6) ... 'says Lolita. 'Tata, good dog, ... (7) ... my ball,' says Swami to ... (8) ... dog. Tata jumps into the ... (9) ... He catches the ball in ... (10) ... mouth and swims back ... (11) ... Swami. 'Clever Tata! Good dog!'

Passage 13
 His features were not good nor yet too ... (139) ... He had rather full round dark ... (140) ... which might have been called pretty ... (141) ... they had been set in a lady's ... (142) ...; a fairly large nose which ... (143) .... have been masterful and ... (144) ... was not; a small still babyish ... (145) ..., usually open and revealing ... (146) ... big and irregular teeth and a drooping ... (147) ... than retreating chin.

 Students were given one hour to complete the test. Scores are reported in percentages and related to word counts in simplified reading schemes. In order to reach an independent reading ability (i.e. coping with non-simplified texts) a percentage score of 60 is needed. The passages are very steeply graded and as a result the test was particularly useful for our purposes because it enabled us to compare on the same instrument pupils from Primary to College level and to include English teachers. Results for students and teachers and their related reading levels are given in Table 2.1.
 Two very clear conclusions are to be drawn from these data. The first is that students' reading levels (which we claim are an indication of their overall English proficiency) are always very weak. They improve very slowly and in Grade 10 are still quite inadequate to cope either with the Nepal School Leaving Examination (SLC) or with the demands imposed by higher education. This conclusion is driven home by the correspondences provided in the last column to vocabulary levels. What these show is that even in Grade 10 (the last year of the secondary school) students in Kathmandu are only at a 750 word level[2] and outside the urban centres of the Kathmandu Valley they are still at the 500 level. This makes the

Table 2.1 Proficiency test results and related graded reading levels

Students	n	Mean	SD	Reader vocab count
Valley of Kathmandu Grade 10	278	12	12	750
Out of Valley Grade 10	34	8	6	500
Budhanilkantha School Grade 10	20	65	10	Unsimplified
Amrit Science Campus Year 1	44	41	16	1800
Mahendra M Camus Biratnagar				
First Year A	39	16	10	750
First Year B	25	4	3	300
Valley Teachers Secondary	6	51	12	2200
Out of Valley Teachers Secondary	43	37	13	1500
English Supervisors	5	65	6	Unsimplified

teaching and learning of English over seven years a largely vain effort. Even in prestigious Amrit Science Campus (which accepts only first class SLC diploma holders) the mean score is 41%. True, some students there are able to operate at the unsimplified text level as shown by the wide range of scores. But others are well below. For effective work in science and technology it is essential for students to be able to read ordinary text books (which are not simplified) in English with understanding. In Amrit Science Campus, for most students that is not possible, and for no students at all in our sample from Mahendra M. Campus in Biratnagar down on the Indian border. Only in Budhanilkantha (Grade 10) does a school reach an adequate level, but then that must be expected given the unique and atypical resources of such a well-endowed institution. (Budhanilkantha was established under a British Aid programme to be a centre of excellence. The school was English-medium, staff were largely expatriate, fees were high, all students were boarders. It was not in any way typical of local secondary schools, not even of the private schools.)

The second conclusion is that teachers' English – while better than their pupils' – is just not good enough. The specialist English supervisors alone, but no teachers, even in the secondary system, reach the level of operating at an unsimplified level of reading text; while outside the Kathmandu Valley, the secondary level is especially weak. This is in our judgement among the more important findings of the Survey since it explains so much else, the frequent use of Nepali in the English language classroom, the nonflexibility of the English teachers actually use, the lack of use of supplementary materials (because teachers, let alone students, cannot understand them), the reliance on rote memorising and the dependence on the School Leaving Certificate (SLC) previous examination papers as 'guides'. Teachers of English lack confidence in their own English and therefore cannot be expected to teach English effectively.

Recommendations

We reported that in our view ELT in Nepal should be more intensive and that it would make sense for it to start at Grade 8. Why did we take up this position? For three reasons:

- there was no incremental learning through the grades;
- teachers' proficiency was inadequate;
- the instrumental role of English needed maximising.

We recognised that such a solution was elitist in that it excluded the masses from educational opportunity to which in Nepal English had the key. We also recognised that the private English medium system would flourish and that the promises we might make to improve the teaching in Grades 8–10 so as to make it better than the present system were only hopeful. At the same time the present system was already effectively very elitist. The private system was flourishing. English language teaching in Grades 4–7 was largely sentimental and possibly hindered a necessary emphasis on serious language learning later. The policy decision to start English in Grade 1 biased still further the emphasis on the sentimental role, in two ways, first by making the appearance of reform more important than the substance and second by laying a more frail learning foundation because of the inevitable increase of teachers with inadequate English. The Ministry of Education was, we recognised, on the horns of a dilemma. As indeed were we. We could insist that from a professional, research-informed position English should not start until Grade 8 where it would be well resourced and could in three years, by the end of the secondary school, reach satisfactory levels of achievement. But we knew that politically this extreme position, however well intentioned and professionally respectable, could never be accepted by the Nepalese authorities. The planning imperatives required a compromise and therefore realising this we proposed that English not start in Grade 1 but in Grade 4, as was already the case, and then continue for seven years. No additional English teachers would be needed which would provide some relief for the overstretched system.

The Grade 4 start was in due course accepted by the Nepal Ministry, not, I suspect, so much because we recommended it but for reasons of inertia. It was just easier to leave things as they were. Parents would not complain that modernising opportunities were being denied their children. Teachers would be left to carry on as before, with no demand to work harder because English would not be starting earlier. The Ministry of Education would not have to find money for new teachers in the first three grades. Indeed, it was becoming clear to us that our Survey itself had been mounted as a quasi-sentimental project. No instrumental outcomes were expected or required. What mattered was the public fact (reported on radio and in local newspapers) of appearing to be doing something to improve English language teaching in the state system. No-one ever intended to initiate change. But it was a good compromise. In other words, we accepted that both sentimental and instrumental roles had their parts to play and what we wished to achieve was a lessening of the importance of the sentimental role. Concentration on teacher training for secondary teachers would mean that upper secondary school entrants should be regarded as false beginners after their sentimental journey through the primary and lower secondary school classes.

Therefore, our major recommendation was for a concentration of available resources for ELT over the following five-year period on in-service teacher training for Grades 8, 9 and 10, first to improve teachers' English and second their methodology. What false beginners need is better teachers, better at English and better at language teaching, who can adapt their teaching (and thereby their materials) to the levels and problems of the individual students in normal classrooms. Course design for training teachers to be flexible in this way could be a major contribution of applied linguistics to Nepal's ELT problems. In the 20 years or so since the Survey was carried out, the starting age for English has indeed been brought down to Primary One. We do not know whether teacher provision has been improved. What is clear today is that the severe political problems that have racked Nepal in this period will have to be resolved before serious innovation is possible in education and ELT.

Need to Compromise

I have argued so far in this chapter that in situations of limited resource, although professionals argue for the instrumental role of ELT they also need to recognise that all professional advice is given in a micropolitical context where compromise is necessary. Even in resource-poor situations, sentiment matters; it may well be that the sentimental decision makes pragmatic sense. Since the political imperative in such societies is for government to seem to be acting in the best interests of the masses, thereby avoiding political unrest leading to confrontation and violence, it may well make sense to give the masses what they claim as their right, which in Nepal meant open access for all to ELT rather than restricted later access for a limited meritocracy. Most people are unaware that unless adequate resources are available such open access in itself is meaningless, it leads nowhere because the open access is in the present, its emptiness in the future. Our support for the Ministry decision recognised that it is important politically that opportunity appear to be equally distributed and that the instrumental choice (starting in Grade 8) would in practice be little better in terms of success in English because the able students would succeed under either system. And the instrumental choice would alienate large numbers of parents whose children had been denied a precious opportunity, even though that opportunity would in practice be quite empty. In such societies the elites are indeed influential but they are not the target of the policy we are discussing since in general their children attend private schools. The population of interest are the parents of children at state schools, that is, most parents. They need to believe that their children are on track to modernity.

WAEC School Certificate

I turn now to my second example, that of Anglophone West Africa in the 1960s. What this example suggests is that the professional's instrumental advice may be misjudged by focusing too narrowly on one variable in the situation, in this case the examination. At that time, the West African Examinations Council (WAEC) conducted school examinations in all four former British territories (Nigeria, Ghana, Sierra Leone and the Gambia). In all cases, the medium of instruction in the secondary system was English. With the increase in school numbers after independence, there was a widespread feeling that standards of English were declining, as we saw in the Nepal case. The West African Examinations Council (WAEC) accepted the advice of a professional consultant, that, in order to effect change quickly, the lever for change (Pearson, 1988) was the examination. In giving this advice the consultant was taking up what appeared to be a sensibly instrumental position, that what mattered for effective education in West African secondary schools, all of which were English medium, was an examination based on a state-of-the-art grammatical description of English which both teachers and students could easily draw on and use to improve their reading and writing skills. Adopting such an examination would, the consultant seems to have believed, lead to improved outcomes in English language at the School Certificate level, committed, as he was, like the consultants in the Nepal example, to the instrumental role of English. For a time, his view triumphed, indicating how important is the powerful individual in policy decisions. What the consultant did not recognise was that the existing examination, which he dismissed as wholly sentimental and which was in due course, restored, had its own instrumental validity.

Now introducing a new examination for an existing syllabus is revolutionary enough. Introducing an examination for a nonexistent syllabus was a lever not for change but for disaster. The consultant's apparent inability to recognise that his new examination was just inappropriate without proper education of teachers in understanding and operating his preferred grammatical description of English based on Hallidayan systemic linguistics and without the production of student textbooks and an adequate lead-in time of several years, suggests to me that his ostensibly instrumental approach was misjudged. What I mean by that is that his attachment to Hallidayan theory was so strong that he persuaded himself that it was important for its own sake to impose it in the examination on the assumption but with no evidence that it would lead to an improvement in the teaching and learning of English.

For the consultant, the whole system needed to be changed rapidly. That the existing syllabus, the teachers and the examination did not provide students with the proficiency they needed and deserved after so many years' study, would be difficult to dispute. The problem needed radical action. The examination was rewritten and put into immediate operation. But for teachers and students there was no obvious connection between the new examination and the existing School Certificate syllabus (which they had been working on). For teachers and students, the new examination lacked validity: the English it tested was not the English they had studied.

The appeal of the new examination to the consultant was that his English language model of choice (systemic grammar), on which the examination was based, was precisely that it was not traditional but modern, and therefore superior, a more valid representation of English. But for teachers and students this was of little interest. English for them was represented by the criterion instantiated in the existing School Certificate examination. If the new examination was to be successful it had to forge a compromise with the training students had received: this required rewriting the School Certificate syllabus and at the same time re-educating the teachers. This was done but too late: the new examination was quickly abandoned and the system reverted to its former state.

And, as it happens, there was serious dispute as to whether the English language model represented by the new examination was indeed state of the art or just an interesting and somewhat quirky heresy. In Australia, systemic linguistics (Martin, 2005) has been hugely influential in teaching English as a mother tongue in the school system. But it has had much less impact on the teaching of ESL.

Conclusion: Balancing Political Constraints and Professional Advice

The notion that language is always political is compelling: 'language teaching and learning are political in the sense that they always involve two languages with differing cultural prestige in the world at large and in the particular situation in which the teaching and learning are taking place' (Joseph, 2004: 348).

That language is always political explains why states' language policies (both L1 and L2) may come under attack by nationalist groups (e.g. the English First movement in the United States) and their conservative supporters because those policies are thought to be insufficiently interventionist. But even when they are not interventionist, there is always a state policy: no country allows students or their parents to choose any language medium they wish. And the same is true for the second/foreign language option. Schools may have a choice but that choice is always restricted, if only on practical grounds (teachers, materials, examinations). The two cases discussed in this chapter, that of Nepal and, more briefly, that of West Africa, both show that the role of professionals is always limited, and perhaps properly limited. Unless professionals recognise that they are operating in a political context and are therefore prepared to compromise (as they were, I have suggested, in the Nepal example), their advice is likely to be rejected.

Both in Nepal and in West Africa the professionals needed to accept a compromise between the sentimental and the instrumental. In Nepal, the professionals' insistence on a late start for English (in Grade 8) was eventually tempered by the requirement that a sentimental choice was politically necessary. The professional focus on instrumental ends had to accept the political imperative of a concern for current (sentimental) process. In West Africa, the professional's unequivocal recommendation of an instrumental option, proved to have been misguided.

Professions are increasingly being required to take account of the views of non-professional stakeholders, These may well be what van Els (2005) calls 'uninformed laymen'. Uninformed laymen aside, one of the under-researched influences on policy, both from the political and the professional sides, is the role of key individuals, people who bring conviction, sometimes ideologically based, to the case in hand and are therefore not open to argument and persuasion. In the examples I have discussed, in Nepal and West Africa, the key individuals may have been misguided and yet all three had back stories which gave them what Kaplan and Baldauf (2005) refer to as the 'contextual embeddedness in the language ecology of particular situations'. They could not be ignored. While it is indeed necessary that those in political power are ready to take advice from professionals, it also behoves professionals to recognise that their evaluation and their advice must take account of the difficult political choices and ask themselves if they really have gone deep enough into the 'contextual embeddedness in the language ecology of particular situations' (Kaplan & Baldauf, 2005: 1015).

Notes

1. In Nepal in the mid-1980s some 50% of those entering Grade 1 did not continue to Grade 2.
2. A vocabulary level of 3000 is considered unsimplified.

References

Burstall, C. (1974) *Primary French in the Balance*. Windsor: NFER.
Davies, A. (1987) When professional advice and political constraints conflict: The case of Nepal. *Focus on English*. Madras: British Council.
Davies, A. (1990) *Principles of Language Testing*. Oxford: Blackwell.
Davies, A., Glendinning, E. and McLean, A. (1984) *Survey of English Language Teaching in Nepal*. Report presented to HMGN Ministry of Education and Culture.
Davies, A., Hamp-Lyons, L. and Kemp, C. (2003) Whose norms? International proficiency tests in English. *World Englishes* 22 (4), 571–584.
De Bot, K. (2000) An early start for foreign languages (but not English) in the Netherlands. In R. Lambert and E. Shohamy (eds) *Language Policy and Pedagogy: Essays in Honor of A. Ronald Walton* (pp. 129–138). Philadelphia: Benjamins.
Ehrich, L.C. and Cranston, N. (2004) Developing senior management teams in schools: Can micropolitics help? *International Studies in Educational Administration* 32 (1), 21–31.
Elder, C. and Davies, A. (2006) Assessing English as a lingua franca. *Annual Review of Applied Linguistics* 26, 282–304.

Hyltenstam, K. and Abrahamsson, N. (2003) Maturational constraints in second language acquisition. In C. Doughty and M. Long (eds) *Handbook of Second Language Acquisition* (pp. 539–588). Oxford: Blackwell.

Joseph, J. (2004) Language and politics. In A. Davies and C. Elder (eds) *The Handbook of Applied Linguistics* (pp. 347–366). Oxford: Blackwell.

Kaplan, R.B. and Baldauf Jr., R.B. (2005) Language-in-education policy and planning. In E. Hinkel (ed.) *Handbook of Research in Second Language Teaching and Learning* (pp. 1013–1034). Mahwah, NJ: Lawrence Erlbaum Associates Ltd.

Kelman, H.C. (2006) Interests, relationships, identities: Three central issues for individuals and groups in negotiating their social environment. *Annual Review of Psychology* 57, 1–26.

Martin, J. with D. Rose (2005) *Genre Relations: Mapping Culture*. London: Equinox.

Mejias, H.A. and Anderson, P.L. (1988) Attitude towards use of Spanish on the South Texas border. *Hispania* 71 (2), 401–407.

NESP (1971) *National Education System Plan for 1971–1976*. Kathmandu: HMGN Ministry of Education.

Pearson, I. (1988) Tests as levers for change. In D. Chamberlain and R. Baumgardner (eds) *ESP in the Classroom: Practice and Evaluation* (Vol. 128) (pp. 98–107). London: Modern English Publications.

Phillipson, R. (1992) *Linguistic Imperialism*. Oxford: Oxford University Press.

Pirie, M. (2005) On WWW at http://www.adamsmith.org/blog/archives/000902.php. Accessed 19.11.08.

Scollon, R. and Scollon, S.W. (1995) *Intercultural Communication: A Discourse Approach*. Oxford: Blackwell.

Seidlhofer, B. (2004) Research perspectives on teaching English as a lingua franca. *Annual Review of Applied Linguistics* 24, 209–239.

van Els, T. (2005) Status planning for learning and teaching. In E. Hinkel (ed.) *Handbook of Research in Second Language Teaching and Learning* (pp. 971–992). Mahwah, NJ: Lawrence Erlbaum Associates Ltd.

Williams, E. (2001) Testimony from testees: The case against current language policies in sub-Saharan Africa. In C. Elder, A. Brown, K. Hill, N. Iwashita, T. Lumley, T. McNamara and K. O'Loughlin (eds) *Studies in Language Testing: Experimenting with Uncertainty: Language Testing Essays in Honour of Alan Davies* (pp. 200–210). Cambridge: UCLES and Cambridge University Press.

Chapter 3
Micropolitical Issues in ELT Project Implementation

TOM HUNTER

Introduction

This chapter tells the story of how politics and personality combined to influence the delivery of a large, complex, aid development ELT project (here referred to as PELT). As the team leader of this project, I was both puzzled and frustrated by the behaviour of stakeholders in the project process. Some were, at best, neutral in their support for the work of the project, while others seemed to conspire against its success. Similarly, factions were in conflict with each other. Any notions of 'the greater good' or 'for the sake of the country' were a long way down the list of priorities for many stakeholders. I, therefore, resolved to explore the issues involved in more detail. It was clear to me that current literature on change management and conflict resolution did not adequately explain the place of affective factors in the political decision-making of stakeholders.

The chapter begins by exploring what is meant by aid development projects and describes issues in the 'Projectisation' of aid development. These issues relate to projects specifically designed for English language development. They include the effects of internationally agreed development goals on ELT and the importance of process management in ELT projects. The role of consultants in the project process is investigated, with examples from projects I have known. The chapter then goes on to define political psychology as a field of enquiry and its relevance to the analysis of politics and personality in projects. PELT is then described and a concluding commentary examines issues in political psychology which are important in understanding the story of the project.

The ELT Project in Aid Development

The definitions and descriptions of project features outlined in this section are provided by the Project Management Institute (2003). These include the definition of a project, the historical development of the project, the characteristics of project management responsibilties and the development of the ELT project.

A project can be defined as a collection of activities undertaken within a fixed period of time designed to bring about a change of some kind (a new product or service or perhaps new parameters or goals). Project management organisations vary, but are usually nongovernment organisations (NGOs) of various kinds or quasi-independent government agencies. Some typical players in international aid development are the British Council, the Centre for British Teachers (CfBT), Carl Bro and the Agha Khan Foundation. Each will bring a certain 'flavour' to their work. For example, Carl Bro, a Danish organisation which manages a wide range of projects in education, engineering, agriculture, and so on, declares in its website the following 'five commandments':

> Our Mission, Vision and Core Values form the basis of our Five Commandments for successful project management. The Five Commandments act as a daily guide in our project-related work.
>
> (1) Communication and information. A good project manager is a listener, and communicates information at all levels in the right place and at the right time.
> (2) Planning (inc. time and economics). A good project manager conducts the project in the right direction and achieves the set goals.
> (3) Proactivity and dedication. A good project manager seeks insight and understanding, and keeps abreast of the situation.
> (4) Responsibility and credibility. A good project manager takes responsibility and ownership, and turns up well prepared and in good time, every time.
> (5) Respect in mutual relations. A good project manager creates a positive atmosphere in the team by respecting the differences between co-workers. (Carl Bro website)

Most project management organisations would claim to adhere to similar declarations. Donors can be of two kinds: 'gifters' (such as the British Department for International Development [DFID] or the Canadian International Development Agency [CIDA]) or 'lenders' (such as the World Bank and the Asian Development Bank [ADB]). Although quite disparate organisations with often self-serving political vision, most of the big donors now adhere to the Millennium Development Goals or MDG (UN Millennium Declaration, 2000), which seek to achieve the following eight goals by the year 2015:

Goal 1: Eradicate extreme poverty and hunger
Goal 2: Achieve universal primary education
Goal 3: Promote gender equality and empower women
Goal 4: Reduce child mortality
Goal 5: Improve maternal health
Goal 6: Combat HIV/AIDS, malaria and other diseases
Goal 7: Ensure environmental sustainability
Goal 8: Develop a global partnership for development

Although the goals underpin all aid development in all sectors worldwide, by 2005 problems began to arise in the achievement of the goals – particularly in relation to the notion of conditionality. Most donors had been in the habit of placing conditions on bilateral aid (i.e. aid based on a contract between two countries – one the donor and the other the recipient). This might commit the recipient, for example, to tackling corruption or undertaking to develop transparent financial procedures. Concerns have been, to give just two examples, that such conditions have not in fact reduced poverty or made the work conditions of women any better, but may indeed have contributed to their worsening states (DFID, 2005). Similarly, donors themselves have not always been the most honourable of partners. There have been cases when domestic pressures have led to contracted aid being withdrawn. This was the situation, for example, following the end of the Cold War and the diversion of resources from Africa to Central and Eastern Europe. Most donors, therefore, prefer to talk in terms of partnership with recipients. Aid will be forthcoming, it is argued, where recipients are seen to be planning for MDGs. Donors will then form partnerships with largely recipient-driven initiatives and programmes.

Aid development projects (Kerzner, 2003) were exploited for propaganda purposes by both sides during the Cold War but in recent years tighter fiscal controls have led to the development of monitoring and descriptive instruments (e.g. logical framework analysis). This projectisation has meant the advent of the accountant's grip on projects which has not always sat well (see Kerr, this volume). This has especially been true when project outputs are not concrete, tangible or timely – the case with many human development projects.

Projectisation, therefore, has generally resulted in a less flexible framework for development to flourish. It has meant a greater attention to the achievement of, and accountability for, outputs. It has meant at times placing fiscal considerations above those of developmental ones. Notions of ownership and sustainability, part of the mantra of project management, often belie local context where achievement of independence in technical competence is not easily compartmentalised into project cycles. In recent years, this has been recognised and has resulted in a 'sector wide approach' (SWA) to development, that is, holistically dealing with the development needs of a whole sector. However, old habits die hard and many a SWA is simply a series of individual, finite and self-contained projects collected under a thematic umbrella. Thus, the art or science of project management, design and delivery is still highly relevant. Projectisation, therefore, underpins the Sector-Wide Approach.

It will be clear to members of the English language teaching (ELT) community, that none of the eight MDGs directly involve ELT. None of them justify, for example, committing scarce resources to a large multi-faceted project designed to improve the national delivery of English language teaching at secondary school level in a developing country. Such projects were quite common in the 1970s and 1980s, when British aid in particular supported many such projects around the world under the Key English Language Teaching (KELT) scheme. Through this scheme, ELT specialists were assigned to institutions and ministries in developing countries to deliver projects designed to reform English language teaching. Almost certainly, they were conceived of as instruments of the donors' national interests. They were also popular with recipients' ruling elites, who saw (and continue to see) English language as an exclusive attribute carrying both prestige and material rewards.

It must also be clear, however, that none of the MDGs can be achieved without partnerships with donor institutions and personnel and that such partnerships are more conveniently and more effectively conducted through a common language, which usually means the English language.

This instrumental need for ELT is complemented by a more developmental consideration. Uniquely, the medium of the ELT project is its message. The product is its process. This requires a unique project methodology and while such a process-focus may be desirable, or even compulsory, in non-ELT projects, it is actually necessary in ELT ones. The kind of people, therefore, who have to manage and deliver ELT projects must be accomplished process managers and the following section investigates what roles consultants play in the successful delivery of such projects.

Roles of Consultants in ELT Projects

Key to the successful delivery of a project is the notion of consultant. The term is used to describe the technical experts temporarily appointed to a project and charged with delivering the outputs of the project.

Consultation, according to Schein (1969: 11), is 'a set of activities on the part of the consultant which helps the client to perceive, understand and act upon process events which occur in the client's environment'. A client can be either an individual or a group or an organisation.

Huffington (1996: 104) defines consultation as a *process* involving an individual who is invited to help a *client* with a work-related problem. In different ways, Schein and Huffington together make the following general observations.

In the consultation process:

- The client is responsible for the *fulfillment of the task*. The client has to live with the consequences long after the consultant has departed.
- The consultant is responsible for the consultation *process*.
- The consultant uses her skills and knowledge about the *change process* to engage in a joint investigation of the meaning of the problem for the client.
- The consultant has a *different perspective* to that of the client. This can allow the consultant to inject new concepts and ideas which could lead to the creation of a new set of meanings for the client.
- The difference between consultation and other activities such as *supervision, counselling, teaching, advising, training, inspecting,* and so on, is the notion of responsibility. All of these activities could be considered to be part of consultancy work if the person undertaking the activity is **not** ultimately responsible for fulfillment of tasks. Negotiation is often required between consultant and client to establish these parameters of responsibility.
- A key skill for a consultant is to be able to play many roles (such as those expressed in the activities above) according to the client's request, the stage of the process, and so on. Always implicit is a training role (either as facilitator or direct trainer) on the part of the consultant in order to pass on process skills to the client.

Consultant activities range from nondirective, client-centred activities (such as listening and reflecting) through to directive and consultant-centred activities (such as recommending and planning implementation) (Schmidt & Johnson, 1970). Choices as to whether to be directive or nondirective may be decided by the client in negotiation with the consultant, or they may grow out of what is appropriate at a given time in the process (i.e. whether a consultant is listening or diagnosing or recommending, etc.).

Selection of consultancy styles is a question of experience and personal awareness. On ELT projects, selection of consultant style and focus is likely to reflect the relative linguistic and technical competence of the client's target group. However, these decisions might also be political in nature. There may be sound professional reasons to have a consultant who recommends or plans implementations but who is excluded from doing so because the client considers it to be politically unacceptable or inappropriate.

Style and focus imply a methodology. For example, a non-directive consultant would employ a form of consultancy which would characterise how to conduct the consultancy in a nondirective way. Three forms (or models) of consultancy – each with its own implicit methodology – have been identified by both Brunning et al. (1990) and Stewart (1996). Table 3.1 summarises the two views of these models.

The form of consultancy which often seems most appropriate to the majority of ELT projects is 'Process Consultancy'. This is because such projects are almost always engaged in the change process and/or in organisational development. There is invariably a training role and tenets of sustainability and local ownership would suggest a client-centred, facilitative, advisory role on the part of the consultant. However, conflicts can arise between consultants and clients and these are explored below.

Potential Areas of Client-Consultant Conflict

Firstly, confusion and conflict can occur between client and consultant over the notion of *responsibility*. The client often assumes that a service is being purchased and that therefore some kind of redress is possible in the event of shoddy workmanship. However, serious negotiating needs to take place to tease out this assumption. The consultant should have control of the process but should engage the client frequently as to where the process is going (i.e. the end product). Good lines of communication are essential.

Conversely, the client may be tempted to view the consultant as a deputy and withdraw from the whole project process. Clear delineation is required through explicit Terms of Reference. These should be frequently re-examined.

Secondly, the consultant is not a manager or an extension of a manager. Consequently, the consultant will look at issues from a different point of view to a manager. The consultant must be prepared, for example, to challenge the perceptions of the client and even to be critical, where appropriate.

Table 3.1 Consultancy models

Characteristics and methodology	Brunning et al. (1990)	Stewart (1996)
The client 'buys' information, services, advice, etc. Content-oriented. Success depends on clients defining their own problems and matching the consultant to the problem. The consultant is an expert who is expected to propose solutions. Consultant dependant.	The Purchase Model	The Lawyer-Client Model
The client knows there is a problem but does not know the causes. The consultant must diagnose the problem and give a course of treatment. Success rests on whether the client (patient) can describe her symptoms (problems) and whether the consultant (doctor) can diagnose the problem and prescribe the medicine. Consultant dependant.	The Doctor-Patient Model	The Doctor-Patient Model
More concerned with the processes by which problems are solved than the content of a problem. The consultant helps clients to help themselves. The consultant is a change agent. This form of consultancy is appropriate in chronic change situations and in organisational development (OD). Client centred. A developmental, training and advisory role for the consultant.	The Process Consultancy Model	The Process Consultation Model

In this sense, the consultant is independent, but point of view must be negotiated and agreed between client and consultant.

Thirdly, the consultant can often be expected to solve the problem(s) of the client by producing solutions and either administering them or training people to administer them. However, the consultant's perspective is different. The consultant is mainly concerned with helping the client *understand* what the problem(s) mean in terms of the process of change needed, what its effects will be on routines, personnel, resources etc.

Negotiation can draw these two points of view together but will lead to tensions and conflicts if left undefined.

Next, the style adopted by the consultant (directive vs non-directive) is more a matter of personality than any external project factor. Conflict can occur between client and consultant over choice of style. Some clients want a diplomatic approach (the 'soft' consultant) while others require a more authoritative style (the 'hard' consultant). Conflict occurs not so much over differences in personality (good consultants are supposed to offer a range of styles for different occasions), but rather in failing to agree a style. There may also be genuine disagreement over what constitutes an appropriate style in a given context – in which case, further negotiation is required.

Likewise, choosing an appropriate model of consultancy (i.e. 'lawyer-client', 'doctor-patient' or 'process consultation') must be seen as a shared responsibility between client and consultant. In particular, the first two models assume the client having a grasp of the background issues and problems, although in the case of the doctor-patient model, this may not extend to knowledge of how to cure the problem. Conflicts occur when client and consultant assume different types of consultancy models for the same set of project issues. Similarly, difficulties may occur when the client defines a set of problems/issues, and the consultant has different opinions.

Finally, conflict can occur between *local* and *international* consultants over the expectations of the client. This is illustrated in the following case study:

> Local consultant Y was one of three local consultants employed on a project in Country S. Funding for project activity was through a World Bank loan, but the project was managed directly by the Ministry of Education of S. There were also two international consultants on the project. From the outset, consultant Y (along with the other two local consultants) had been subjected to seemingly random summons by the Ministry of Education (MoE) to attend various activities. Such activities were outside of the consultants' Terms of Reference. However, the consultant acquiesced (i) because she sought re-employment, (ii) because of prevalent attitudes towards authority, (iii) it made her feel valued, and (iv) because she altruistically wanted to make a contribution to the national good. In the meantime, mainstream project work was postponed or slowed down.

Dealing with this case, the client needed to see a difference in roles between a consultant and a project officer; the local consultant needed to examine more closely motives for undertaking consultancy and also needed to learn self-assertion (in an appropriate cultural manner). The international consultant needed to take a lead in raising awareness of what consultancy work entails without alienating parties; and the donor should have laid down stricter guidelines on the roles of local consultants.

Such conflicts are seen where the client is a government ministry or a local educational institution. Even when the client is a BANA (i.e. British, North American, Australasian) organisation (Holliday, 1994), the pressure on the local consultant to conform to local 'wants' is enormous. Indeed, the very notion of negotiation itself may be fraught with difficulties for local consultants engaged in unequal encounters with clients.

These conflict factors may occur singly or collectively in the crucible of a real project. The following section describes such a real setting and explores conflict potential further.

Describing PELT: A Case Study

This is a description of a real project (referred to here as PELT). This project had an initial life of three years and a combined budget of some $8 million ($5.2 million of which was provided by an international donor). The purpose of the project was threefold: (i) to provide INSET for some 12,000 ELT secondary teachers through a network of local trainers based in resource centres set up by the project, (ii) to work with examination boards on reforming ELT national examinations in line with new syllabi, (iii) to write textbooks for Grades 9–12 in line with new syllabi.

PELT personnel

In all, there were to be seven international consultants from the donor country working with 11 local counterparts. These counterparts were, themselves, to act as line managers to a network of up to 56 trainers in 28 satellite resource centres.

A team of five local consultants (professionals of standing in the community) was appointed to the project in monitoring, research and impact study roles. Similarly, a team of eight textbook writers was recruited and trained to write books for Grades 9–12. Short-term consultancies to the project were provided by a UK institute of higher education.

Design dysfunction

Even before commencement of the project, conflicts emerged over its design. It is quite normal for project details to be negotiated prior to the signing of a final contract. However, a number of local factions were instrumental in the negotiating process and each had claimed ownership of features of the project. Commonly, if more than one final draft version of documentation is in circulation and if senior managers do not make available concluded documents, then some stakeholders could easily be working to the wrong documents. Put simply, papers get buried in various corners of a large government bureaucracy. This was the case with PELT. Three outcomes were identified:

First, early draft documents expected many more thousands of teachers to be trained within the three-year period of the project. Simple arithmetic by the technical team indicated that this was not only physically impossible, but that there were not enough working days in each year to achieve targets. The final contract, therefore, settled on a figure of 12,000 teachers. This figure, however, continued to be contested even at quite high levels of local government despite the existence of a final bilateral version of the contract.

Second, local experienced staff was thin on the ground and so recruitment and training of trainers was identified as a risk to project progress. This reality meant that young, newly graduated teachers were recruited to become trainers. This seems to be common in development projects where local experienced professionals are reluctant to leave permanent civil service posts to join projects. This can usually be overcome by the temporary attachment of teachers to projects without loss of privileges. In reality, teachers often feel that their positions are under threat during their absences and so will not lend their considerable experience to what they see as here-today-gone-tomorrow projects.

Another common factor is that younger, less experienced local staff may be better agents for change than their older colleagues – less set in their ways. Where donors and management groups pressure, and are pressured, to achieve outputs and goals within project time-frames, the selection of malleable local staff is often the more attractive option for a technical team. Reactions in the education community can be mixed. On the one hand, the younger staff members can prove themselves and command respect, but equally, they can be the victims of professional jealousies and resentments. After all, they are the recipients of quality staff development and workshops, some even held overseas.

Third, initial documents suggested that the planned teacher-training provision should be in the form of a two or three days orientation. The focus of the orientation was to be on the new communicative approaches outlined in the new national syllabus. However, the final document settled on full training sessions of 75 to 80 hours with follow-up and activation stages and continued mentoring and supervision. This was at variance with initial planning and a number of initial planners resented having their ideas rejected.

The political and cultural environment

This continued adherence to a number of versions of the project design documents led to tension and conflict throughout the life of the project. Appeals to rationalism generally failed. The probable reasons for this are explored more fully later in this chapter, but might be summarised as issues of vested interest. Too many people would lose face if seen to have had their ideas rejected. Such political and cultural aspects of the project environment were important features of PELT's story. The political and cultural stew which made up the project's environment interacted with vested interests in a number of ways. The following three features were prominent in this interaction.

Firstly, this densely populated, low-income Asian country displayed a number of characteristics of its colonial past. It had also evolved a few new ones of its own: a top-heavy and inefficient centralised civil service, centralised education policies, high degrees of nationalisation, poor communications and transport infrastructures, an underdeveloped civil society maintained mostly by a thriving NGO sector, 'formal' (rather than 'substantive') democracy (Held, 1996), factional party politics characterised by confrontation rather than cooperation and compromise. Petty corruption was rife at all levels. Only 20% of all secondary schools were run by the government. Stories of ghost schools persisted (i.e. schools that appeared on official registers drawing salaries for teachers, but not in existence), per capita GNP was US$ 240 (compared to other regional neighbours of US$ 340, $460 and US$ 700). Female enrolments at secondary schools were a mere 12% as a percentage of age group, compared to 26% for males (World Bank, 1997).

Secondly, the status of English language showed many of the characteristics of post-colonial decision-making typical of other ex-British colonies (see Davies this volume for an overview of the prominence of colonial languages). At independence, English was replaced by local languages (although many elite private institutions continued to maintain English language teaching – a factor which soon led to considerable social status developing around English language use). In the PELT national context, this was further exacerbated by civil war and partition around the right to learn the mother tongue. Language policy had become, quite literally, a matter of life and death. Very soon, however, the pressure to reintroduce English as an official language and as the preferred second language of school learning, led to further education reform in the late 1970s. Textbooks were hurriedly written and syllabuses overturned. However, by now it was too late. A whole generation of school graduates had passed through the system without the need to learn English. The status of English as a second language was lost forever except to the elite 10% or so of the population. This made the defining of policy all the more difficult for planners. Was this an ESL or an EFL context? In a nation which called itself a people's republic, the principle of universal education was paramount and a policy could not be seen to favour one side or the other. And yet any national examination system which was to be fair to the majority, under-resourced EFL sector, immediately advantaged the minority ESL elite. The PELT team were always aware that commitment to universal ELT across the secondary school spectrum was not fully supported, even though political lip-service was constantly paid to the universality principle. Initially, it was thought that this position was simply a matter of lack of proper resourcing, but it soon became clear that a thwarting action on the part of the education status quo was in operation which sought to slow down, or even reverse, project progress. There were a number of reasons for this, not the least of them a fear of change. Universal access to English language would undermine the position held by the traditional ruling elite. Similarly, state identity and independence had been built on the establishment of the dominant mother tongue as the official language (this, following a bloody civil war) This resulted in a widespread reluctance at government policy-making levels to support the obvious, public spread of English language. Likewise, in a society where status and personal fealty still motivated political as well as social behaviour, the importance of maintaining current equilibrium would have produced a conservative approach to curriculum and methodology changes.

Finally, and of great concern to the English language consultants, was the English language teaching policy of the donor. Commitment to MDG internationally agreed targets on poverty alleviation had recently side-tracked ELT as a major recipient of the donor's aid. This followed more than two decades of major international aid to ELT. PELT was, itself, a throw-back to this explosion in ELT projects and should have been delivered some 10 years earlier. However, due to various political upheavals, postponements and changes of government, the project had been delayed until after the donor's change of policy. Feeling obligated to meet its commitments, however, the donor decided to proceed with PELT but always made it clear that the project was nonrenewable and that the budget was fixed and finite. This was an unusual situation for a development project of this size because tradition dictated that, major catastrophes notwithstanding, renewal or extension would always accompany success and that sustainability and ownership would not be possible to achieve within a three-year cycle. Pressure on consultants, therefore, was unprecedented at the commencement of the project. There could be no funded extension. Success must be achieved within three years. The recipient never really grasped this reality, choosing instead to see the donor's position as negotiable. This meant that the project team's attempts at instilling a sense of immediacy and urgency in the recipient towards project ownership and sustainability were largely unsuccessful. Such issues as, 'How will the Ministry of Education maintain the work begun by the project?' and 'How will the local personnel recruited and trained by the project be absorbed into official cadres?' were met with a disturbing lack of concern. Privately, ministry officials voiced their beliefs that all would be well after the donor extended the project for six or even nine years! They were to be bitterly disappointed.

Politics and Personality, or Political Psychology

In understanding PELT it is important to appreciate how politics and personality combined to influence behaviour which led to conflicts within the project. These conflicts are fundamentally different in nature to the conflicts of role definition explored above precisely because they have both political and psychological dimensions. According to Stein (2001: 108), Political Psychology 'analyses patterns of political thinking, feeling and identity, the interaction of these patterns and their impact on political choice and other forms of political behaviour'. It is concerned with the study of the psychology behind political behaviour and traditionally draws on various disciplines and fields of study within, and associated with, psychology. This might include 'diverse disciplinary sources including cultural and psychological anthropology, cognitive psychology, clinical psychology, economics, history, international relations, philosophy, political science, political theory, psychology of personality, social psychology, and sociology' (Feldman *et al.*, 2005: 1). It would seem appropriate, therefore, in considering the intersection of personality and politics to draw on ideas from the field of political psychology. In particular, this chapter makes reference to how personality is a function of social as well as political needs, how sociology, history and psychology combine to enhance our understanding of the project context and how culture affects political decision-making.

In political psychology, emphasis is not so much on the tortuous search for a definition of personality, but rather on 'how particular aspects of personality translate into political behaviour' (Cottam *et al.*, 2004). In this chapter, we are interested not so much in defining the personality types of the individual protagonists in PELT, but rather in how situation/context influenced individual differences to affect behaviour. Context seems to matter more than personality or leadership (Preston, 2001). For our purposes, individual differences in personality traits are seen as functions of

Micropolitical Issues in ELT Project Implementation　　77

an individual's striving to fulfil needs (Maslow, 1987). In many cases, such needs conflicted among the various project participants. Table 3.2 shows some of the more obvious polarities (Needs 1 and 2) with a description of the effects of each polarity.

Table 3.2 serves to demonstrate the effects of need (as a determiner of individual personality) on the politics of a project. The effect of individual traits should not be underestimated, particularly at bottlenecks (i.e. at points where project progress rests on the decision-making of one individual – a common occurrence in hierarchical bureaucracies).

Table 3.2 The effects of conflicting needs in the implementation of an ELT aid development project (PELT)

Need 1	Effect	Need 2
The need of international consultants to achieve targets, objectives and outputs within agreed timeframes and to create an organisation to do this.	Clashes between project and ministry over getting things done, particularly procurements, logistics and anything to do with spending money.	The need of civil servants to work only within the letter of civil service rules.
The need of international consultants to achieve sustainability as soon as possible.	Lack of synergy of effort. Ministry officials did not respond to project overtures of integration into government cadres.	The need of government officials to find extra money to fund activity to be sustained (and to keep donor money flowing where this is problematic)
The need of international consultants to achieve.	Conflicts arose at the deepest levels of cultural attitude. Western and Eastern motivators clashed. Many small, local conflicts were rooted here. The international team had to learn to adhere to the locals' hierarchies and protocols, while the local team had to learn that status in the eyes of the Westerners was earned.	The need of local participants to hold positions of status.

(Continued)

Table 3.2 *(Continued)*

Need 1	Effect	Need 2
The need of international consultants to implement a universal policy of English curriculum for all.	The ministry only gave tacit and conditional support to universal ELT. Support was largely verbal.	The need of the ruling political party to maintain a high profile for mother tongue education.
The need of the project to assess its impact.	The view of a project as a learning process was never understood or fully accepted by government officials. The production of outputs was paramount.	The need of government officials to show project progress to seniors.
The need of the project team to develop a reflective, open, transparent organisation built on the principles of a team approach to management.	Donor demand for transparency and models of good governance were at variance with the administrative culture of the government. This caused day-to-day as well as long-term sustainability and ownership issues. For example, the project was managed along team-building lines with open communication, shared responsibility and a process of organisational development based on reflection. However, in government circles, sharing responsibility and developing organisation spontaneously were not only frowned upon, but sanctions existed for their suppression.	The need of the civil service to maintain its traditional hierarchy and top-down management style.
The need of the project team to implement realistic, informed plans with targets agreed at the grassroots.	Conflicts arose over the difference between producing plans that could work technically and those that gave an appearance of activity in ministerial committees.	The need of ministry officials to produce and approve plans at ministry committee level.

Commentary and Conclusions

This commentary brings together many of the issues raised in this chapter, and expands, explains and/or qualifies them.

The delivery of an ELT project in aid development needs to focus on process. This is because English is the medium as well as the message of the project. It is also important that a project organisation is a learning organisation. Impact studies and reflective practices demand process data. Design document dysfunction, described above, emphasises the need for communication in a project. It seems that a point cannot be stated enough times and in as many different ways as possible. Project managers/team leaders complain about the number of times they repeat themselves with meetings, newsletters, project reports, various speeches and workshops, but in cultural contexts where people have cause to be suspicious of Officialdom and are only trusting of known interlocutors, frequent repetition is unavoidable. Such a reality needs an appropriate project methodology. This is a methodology that learns from doing: a process methodology.

Project methodology must be seen against the background of saving face. It has been suggested earlier in this chapter that one reason for design document dysfunction is that stakeholders engaged in early design had effectively been by-passed, excluded or superseded in their contributions. In many cultures, this could lead to serious loss of face and would need to be addressed. In PELT this could have involved a more inclusive policy towards stakeholders. This process of internal consultation slows down a project's progress but is, ultimately, time well spent. However, in the case of PELT, the sense of urgency instilled through the realisation that the project would never be renewed made it difficult to allow for such consultancy time.

Another strategy in helping to maintain face, is for project managers/deliverers to avoid singling out individuals and to commit to being non-judgemental. Implementation of this strategy has some important long-term implications for project methodology – not the least, an appropriate approach to reporting, impact studies and the development of an appraisal system. It also implies a well-developed cross-cultural strategy.

As the international consultant is invariably working in cross-cultural contexts, his/her job is to invite appropriate change in pursuance of helping the client to 'perceive, understand and act upon process events which occur in the client's environment' (Schein, 1969: 11). Cultural behaviour does not change overnight and even where such change is sought or desirable, the international consultant cautiously approaches such initiatives in partnership with all local stakeholders. The international consultant also has a unique relationship with the local consultant. This is at once a relationship of colleague and mentor. The local consultant has an informant's role to play, too, providing the international consultant with valuable cultural insights. When this relationship is allowed to develop, it can be one of the most productive partnerships in an ELT project. However, local consultants need to be aware of their own motivation for attaching to a project and ask whether this is in keeping with the aims of the project. A local consultant also needs to define closely with the client what consultancy roles, styles and models are appropriate. Ultimately, a local consultant can expect a satisfactory answer to the question: 'What will I be consulted about?' Should the local consultant feel obliged to assume final responsibility for project products, then a redefinition of roles is appropriate.

Unfortunately, clients are prone to fill management gaps within their organisations under the pretext of appointing local consultants to a project. ELT worldwide is under-resourced, particularly in the area of national specialists. It is therefore understandable that clients would see the opportunity to kill two birds with one stone and fill administrative gaps while appeasing project donor requirements. In the long term, however, such duplication is counter-productive because it is the client's responsibility to fulfill project tasks and the consultant's role to maintain a different perspective to the client. Such micropolitical considerations lie at the heart of successful ELT project implementation.

Such implementation can draw on the literature of political psychology in the same way that such areas as social psychology already contribute to our understanding of affective factors in learning English – particularly motivation, attitude and personality. However, attention to the political significance of factors in learning are less well documented. Take the example of 'Voice versus Exit' (Hirschman: 1970). Hirschman suggests that when members of an organisation (business, institution, state, etc.) feel that the organisation is failing them in some way, they have two possible responses: voice or exit. Through 'voice', members would vocalise their concerns, create text, hold meetings, complain, demonstrate, and so on. But through 'exit', members' efforts are geared towards leaving the organisation – resigning, emigrating, and so on. 'Exit' and 'Voice' can be seen as the connection between socio-economic and political action and are powerful indicators of the extent of decline of an organisation. In a project like PELT the terms also explain motives behind language policy and the EFL and ESL dichotomy. In this poor country, some people are educating themselves for 'exit' (even temporarily, e.g. attending a foreign university or undertaking overseas migrant work) while others are educating themselves for 'voice'. Hirschman suggests that a government would rather prepare its members for loyalty as this can reduce the numbers wanting to exit and is likely to lead to less confrontational voice. PELT needed to understand the relationship between exit and voice and the interplay of loyalty on both these in the national context. Indeed, all ELT projects need to do this as it can help towards unravelling the ESL/EFL debate in many development contexts, thus giving it a political as well as a socio-linguistic, dimension.

Maslow (1987) suggests that individuals require the fulfilment of a hierarchy of fundamental needs (e.g. moving from lower to higher levels: safety, love and respect, belongingness, esteem, self-esteem and self-actualisation) in order for their personalities to develop (see Alderson, Chapter One, this volume). This implies that personality is a function of need and so, in order to understand the effect of personalities in the workplace, we should first understand what needs motivate individuals. If we accept that the personalities of protagonists such as undersecretaries, ministers, vice-chancellors, directors, donor-advisers, project managers, team leaders, consultants, and so on, have an effect in the political arena of the project, then we should understand the needs of the various protagonists. This implies a commitment to maintain lines of communication throughout the project. It also places great onus on exceptionally good initial needs analyses and baseline surveys, as well as an efficient way to periodically up-date them.

Related to this is the proposal that personalities per se are not as influential as common sense would suggest. Rather, they seem to flex and bend according to changing contexts (i.e. shifting needs). The message for project implementers is, therefore, that personality clashes are not as destructive as is often believed. When lower level needs are not satisfied, this can lead to individual feelings of boredom, lack of energy, low self-esteem and personal and professional problems, and it is these that lead to so called personality clashes

As well as personality, other affective factors such as gender and age should be considered. The question of whether to work with young, fresh agents for change or to work with more experienced and established members of the system, is a universal issue in aid development. Sometimes, it is overtaken by the formal (and irreversible) appointment of local staff to a project, but on other occasions there may be room for the international consultants to have some say in selection. At the heart of the issue lies a fallacy: that all young participants are agents for change and that all experienced participants will resist change. This is patently not true. A project must find space for both kinds of stakeholders. Indeed, a good team should have a variety of role-players – among them sceptics as well as evangelists (Belbin, 1981). Donors probably need to be more understanding of the often long-winded processes of team building and adjust output targets accordingly.

PELT was deemed a success insofar as these things are measured. Teachers were trained (and a system of sorts completed what the project could not), books were written and examination procedures were overhauled. In this sense, the project products were sustainable and they became owned by the government. However, none of the educational processes were adopted by the government (e.g. team management, reflective evaluation, INSET methodologies, resource management procedures, etc.) The cadre of (eventually) highly skilled young trainers and resource centre managers was diverted, or left government service and joined NGOs where their skills are appreciated and utilised. Many of the reasons for this have been explored above. Time, in the end, ran out and the time needed to effect sustainable change was missing. The 'process of interaction, dialogue, feedback, modifying objectives, recycling plans, coping with mixed feelings, pragmatism and [politics]' (Everard & Morris, 1996: 220) was planned in to project strategy but always under pressure of time. The implementation team never lost sight of the fact that rational strategy has to be applied not only to defining the final change (end) but also how to get there (means). It simply ran out of time and this was due to a macropolitical decision far away from the context of PELT.

I began this chapter by stating my resolve to explore the issues which underpinned my puzzlement and frustration at the behaviour of stakeholders in the PELT project process. I attempted to achieve this through a micropolitical understanding of definitions of consultancy roles in projects as well as political psychology as a means to understanding motivation in project conflicts. It is my contention that personality (as a function of micropolitical motivation) in the causes of conflicts, as well as the notion of saving face, have played a large part in formulating these issues. However, the micropolitics of an aid development project are, I contend, always at the mercy of macropolitics.

Postscript

Recent developments provide a fitting postscript to the story of PELT and reinforce the importance of a political psychology perspective on aid development for ELT. Hilary Benn, the former UK Secretary of State for International Development, (DFID, 2005) writes as a preamble to DFID's rethinking conditionality (see above).

By supporting policy leadership in developing countries, donors will make their aid more effective. And by ensuring that aid is effectively used for reducing poverty, donors will give their own countries confidence that more aid will be worthwhile. (DFID, 2005: iii)

The effect of rethinking conditionality has been that in Country B a larger, more comprehensive project of realistic longevity has been proposed by the host government to tackle the unfinished work begun by PELT. This initiative has come about by locals effectively redefining the route to MDG achievement in Country B. I would also suggest that a change of leadership in DFID since PELT has had an effect on the previous policy of sidelining ELT in development programmes. Such a development is welcome to ELT professionals in general but will be understandably frustrating to those who participated in PELT and who can speculate at what might have been.

As to donors creating confidence in how worthwhile aid is, in this chapter we saw how a move away from conditionality is being mooted, but little or no indication is forthcoming as yet as to how illusive transparency-of-operations or the eradication of corruption as preconditions of recipient-driven development, will be dealt with to the satisfaction of voters in developed countries. It remains to be seen if countries like Country B will find the new donors' role of monitor as technically welcome as it might be politically.

References

Belbin, M. (1981) *Management Teams: Why They Succeed or Fail*. Oxford, Heinemann cited in K.B. Everard and G. Morris (1996). *Effective School Management* (3rd edn) (pp. 157). London: Paul Chapman Publishing.

Brunning, H., Cole, C. and Huffington, C. (1990) *The Change Directory: Key Issues in Organisational Development and the Management of Change*. Leicester: The BPS (DCP).

CarlBro website. On WWW at http://www.carlbro.com/en/Menu/HowWeWork/ProjectManagement/FiveCommandmentsProjectManagement/FiveCommandmentsProjectManagement.htm. Accessed 19.11.08.

Cottam, M.L., Mastors, E., Dietz-Uhler, B. and Preston, T. (2004) *Introduction to Political Psychology* (pp. 14). New Jersey. Lawrence Erlbaum Associates.

DFID (2005) *Partnerships for Poverty Reduction: Rethinking Conditionality*. Department for International Development, UK. Crown Copyright 2005.

Everard, K.B. and Morris, G. (1996) *Effective School Management* (3rd edn) (pp. 220). London: Paul Chapman Publishing.

Feldman, S., Huddy, L., Lavine, H. and Taber, C. (eds) (2005) *Political Psychology: Journal of the International Society of Political Psychology*. New York: Blackwell Publishing, preamble to website by C. Taber. On WWW at http://www.sunysb.edu/polsci/polpsych/index.html. Accessed 2.8.05.

Held, D. (1996) *Models of Democracy* (2nd edn). Cambridge: Polity Press, cited in Potter, D. *et al.* (1997) (eds) *Democratization* (pp. 24). Cambridge: Polity Press.

Hirschman, A.O. (1970) *Exit, Voice, and Loyalty: Responses to Decline in Firms, Organisations, and States*. Cambridge, MA: Harvard University Press.

Holliday, A. (1994) *Appropriate Methodology and Social Context*: Cambridge: CUP.

Huffington, C. (1996) Consultation and service development. In C. Jennings and E. Kennedy (eds) *The Reflective Professional in Education: Psychological Perspectives on Changing Contexts*. London: Jessica Kingly Publishers.

Kerzner, H. (2003) *Project Management: A Systems Approach to Planning, Scheduling, and Controlling* (8th edn). Chichester: Wiley.

Maslow, A.H. (1987) *Motivation and Personality* (3rd edn). New York: Harper & Row.

Preston, T. (2001) *The President and His Inner Circle*. Chichester, West Sussex: Columbia University Press.

Project Management Institute (2003) *A Guide to the Project Management Body of Knowledge* (3rd edn). Newtown Square, PA: Project Management Institute.

Schein, E. (1969) *Process Consultation*. London: Addison-Wesley.

Schmidt, W.H. and Johnston, A.V. (1970) *A Continuum of Consultancy Styles*. Unpublished manuscript.

Stein, J.C. (2001) Political learning and political psychology: A question of norms. In K.R. Monroe (ed.) *Political Psychology*. Mahwah, NJ: Lawrence Erlbaum Associates Inc.

Stewart, J. (1996) *Managing Change Through Training and Development* (2nd edn). London: Kogan Page.

UN Millennium Declaration, *8th Plenary Meeting*, UN General Assembly, New York. 8 September, 2000.

World Bank (1997) *World Development Report, 1997: The State in a Changing World*. New York: OUP.

Chapter 4
The Politics of ELT Projects in China

RON KERR

Introduction

In this chapter I consider *the politics of language education* and *language education as politics*, politics being here understood as the pursuit of interests by social actors (individual or collective) in institutionally defined areas of social action. The areas of social action that I address are (1) the UK government and its agencies and departments that were involved in international development in the mid-1990s and (2) the university departments in China that hosted UK language education projects during this period. In doing this I follow the example of Dezalay and Garth (2002), who, in their study of how US-developed approaches to economics were exported to South American countries in the post-World War II period, show how ideas and processes developed in the political context of one country (the donor of development aid) are taken up and used in political struggles in the context of another country (the recipient of development aid). In the same way, the preoccupations of British policy-makers in the mid-1990s with the reorganisation of the processes of government (or *governance*) around increased accountability and audit, a reorganisation known as the 'New Public Management' (Hood, 1991) or 'audit culture' (Power, 1997), are paralleled in the politics of the language education project in China that is the subject of the two-part case study that forms the latter part of this study.

I therefore pose the following question: How did changes in the way that development projects were managed by the UK development agencies translate into a Chinese academic department? In order to answer this, I begin by explaining my methodological approach. I then set out the socio-historical context of language education in international development in the mid-1990s, before looking at local effects by means of a two-part case study set in the context of one of the Chinese universities that hosted UK-funded language education (English Language Teaching) projects in the 1990s. In this two-part case study that forms the second part of this chapter, I try to show how the first period of local political manoeuvring in the English Language Teaching (ELT) projects in China was over the meaning of 'ELT methodology' and 'teacher training' in relation to the legitimacy of pedagogical practices, while the second part of the case study looks at the increasing emphasis on *management* over teaching and education within the project. The key agents in this case study were the actors in the Chinese university (the organisational hierarchy of departmental deans, professors, teachers, administrators) and the British experts, formally categorised as 'ELT Specialists'. Finally, I return to the politics of development in the UK to show how a change in public policy in the political and development fields in the UK, accompanied by an increase in the influence and authority of individuals associated with the new policy of 'basic education' (rather than 'ELT') as the way of advancing their personal and professional agendas, led after 1997 to the disappearance of both the ELT projects and the ELT Specialists from the field of language education in China.

Methodology

This study is historical and is situated in the contexts of the UK government and its agencies and of a university in Shanghai in the mid-1990s. The overall theoretical framework is that of Dezalay and Garth (2002, drawing on Bourdieu, 1998), and the research method used is case study (Yin, 1994). The case study itself is in two parts, reflecting the stages of internal project and departmental politics in the Chinese university. The first part tells the story of how the ELT Specialists attached to the project in Shanghai attempted to establish themselves as teacher trainers rather than as teachers, while the second part describes how the Specialists then attempted to establish their primary role as being that of managers. Following the approach of Dezalay and Garth (2002), each of these processes (from teachers to teacher trainers and from teacher trainers to managers) can be seen to correspond to changes in the way that international development was organised in London, where increased focus on *management* followed closely on the introduction of the New Public Management in the early- and mid-1990s.

The data that I draw on in the chapter include contemporaneous field notes, official documents and transcribed recordings of meetings and interviews. I also include data from other ELT projects in China, where these data serve to clarify the issues. The data were gathered by the author, who was at the time of the case study (1994–1997), an ELT Specialist based at a university in Shanghai. My own agenda in doing this was, first, to understand better the social and political forces in which my colleagues and I were implicated at the time; second, to use the data for my soon-to-commence PhD research and; third, to prepare an 'escape route' from ELT, given the then current rumours of a possible end of British support for the programme of ELT projects in China.

The two-part case study is followed by a section that relates the impact on the ELT projects in China of political and policy changes in the UK in 1997 following the victory of New Labour in the General Election of that year. But first I want to establish the role of projects and projectisation within the UK government and its agencies (particularly in the mid-1990s) in order to explain why projectisation became an issue in China, before, by means of the case study, looking at the politics of a particular project in one particular Chinese university department.

The Context

Language education and the politics of development

The two main British governmental or quasi-governmental agencies for promoting international development in the post World War II period were the British Council (BC) and the Overseas Development Administration (ODA). The ODA was, before the New Labour victory of 1997, a 'functional wing' of the Foreign and Commonwealth Office (FCO), funded and effectively controlled by the FCO, and headed by a Minister of State for Foreign and Commonwealth Affairs and Overseas Development. Before 1979 and again after 1997, the ODA had the status of a separate ministry and as recognition of this, in 1997 the ODA was renamed the Department for International Development (DFID). The British Council is a quasi-independent organisation, but one which has come to rely on the FCO for its core funding. The BC, during the period under consideration, administered various kinds of development aid on behalf of the ODA.

The macropolitical context of this study is therefore the end of the Cold War and the opening of the era of globalised markets in which the English language acted as a vehicle for the spread of management and marketing discourses (Fulcher, this volume; Kerr, 2008). The end of the Cold War period correspondingly meant that the focus of UK-funded international development moved away from Third World 'developing' countries (as Cold War proxies) to 'transition' countries, the post-communist states of Central and Eastern Europe and (in economic terms) China. The introduction of China's 'open door policy' after the years of isolation during the Cultural Revolution (1966–1976) thus coincided with a move in British development policy to promoting the English language as a vehicle 'to support the development of a free market economy' and 'to counter American influence and to gain commercial advantage' (British Council, 1990: 9).[1]

Thus the English language and its associated industries in the UK were believed to constitute 'comparative advantage' over competitors (by an ODA adviser: my field notes), while a concern to promote markets was also evident in the report on a seminar included in the 1992 collection of papers in Abbot and Beaumont (1997), where there is a coupling of, and grammatical equivalence between, promoting 'appropriate methodology and a market economy' (British Council, 1992: 88).[2]

In parallel to this concern to promote markets, the administration and delivery of development in the mid- to late-1980s involved a move away from the model of the *professional*, who embodied the ethical values and the practices of a profession and, based on an involvement in and understanding of the particular local context, enjoyed a large degree of undirected autonomy in judgement, towards a project model of control and accountability, where the technology itself externalised and transmitted the plans and intentions of the donor (Jacobs, 1996: 3). Thus a senior ODA adviser (British Council, 1986) described how in 1983, the ODA shifted its funding from the Key English Language Teaching (KELT) Scheme (which began in 1977) to 'the geographical funding on which virtually all of the ODA's other programmes rest' and therefore 'we are gradually moving from the old concept of the "KELT post" to the idea of the achievement of certain objectives by a number of methods which might include, *inter alia*, a fully funded British person who is an ELT specialist' (British Council, 1986: 126–127). It is worth noting here that these changes in the way that language education development aid was to be delivered were framed almost entirely in terms of the political needs of those involved in planning and delivering the aid (the donor). The possible effects of this kind of change at the recipient level and in particular how this one-way form of delivery might be accepted or resisted at the local level does not seem to have been considered by its proponents during this period.

At any rate, in the 1980s, as Jacobs (1996) confirms, this kind of development aid began to be delivered by way of time-limited projects (see also Hunter, this volume). The move to projectisation was indicative of a move from *professionalism* (which, as noted above, involves the exercise of autonomy and judgement) to *instrumental control*, a change that involved a shift in bureaucratic categorisation from 'KELT' to ELTO (project-based English Language Teaching Officer) (Markee, 1997), and in fact the ODA adviser went on to characterise the ELTOs as 'instruments': 'the ELTO post (is) perceived as only one instrument in the achievement of a strategy' (British Council, 1986: 128).

This period of projectisation that began in the mid-1980s might be termed the 'early' or proto-project era, and was retrospectively characterised (perhaps caricatured) by another ODA adviser as: 'ten years ago when I first joined ODA we would define projects as two specialists, five training awards, so much money for books' (policy speech 1996, my transcription). By this, the adviser meant that the early project was not operating as a full-blown accountability system. However, as we shall see, this early project era was superseded by the 'new' logical framework approach,[3] as accountability became an overriding preoccupation in the period of the New Public Management in the mid-1990s.

The impact of the New Public Management

The New Public Management (NPM) was a programme of reforms in the governance of the public services in the United Kingdom and a number of other countries in the 1980s and 1990s (Hood, 1991; Minogue, 2000; Sahlin-Andersson, 2001). The NPM was justified by the British government as increasing efficiency and effectiveness, providing value for money and, through compulsory competitive tendering, introducing a market element into the management of the public sector (Bislev et al., 2001). The main focus, however, was on accountability and audit, to the extent that, in this period, the UK government and its agencies created what has been called an 'audit culture' or 'audit society' (Power, 1997; Strathearn, 2001).

The effect of these reforms on the ODA was that (according to an ODA Adviser in 1996, my data): 'increasingly ODA operates like a commercial business'. This was further described by an ODA adviser as follows:

> we have a mission statement, we have business plans, we have policy papers, every official in ODA has a personal responsibility plan for the year which is reviewed every six months with your line manager and we're paid on how well we perform against our plan. (policy speech Wuhan, 1996, my transcription)

This introduces into a government department a schematic 'business model', the main features of which are, (1) *a mission statement*, (2) *business plans*, (3) *policy papers*, and (4) *a personal responsibility plan*. These entities are represented as existing materially not as practices but as documents: *statement, plans, papers*. So in *mission statement* and *business plan, policy paper* and *performance management*, we have a representation of a constellation of texts that integrates the NPM organisation – what Smith (1974) calls 'documentary reality'.

Another aspect of the NPM reforms relevant to this study was the organisational separation of functions between *conception* (or *policy*) and *execution* (or *operations*) or between *commissioning (principal)* and *contracting (agent)*. The question that this posed for the government and for the development organisations in particular, was, given the NPM's focus on accountability, how then to manage the accountability relationship between such functionally, organisationally and often geographically separated bodies.

One way of solving this problem of ensuring the accountability of geographically distant operations was to introduce, in place of the proto-project with its residual professionalism, 'full-blown' accountability systems, including project technologies such as the 'new style' *logical framework* (see Note 3). So the meaning of the term 'project' changed or expanded, from a time-limited intervention that could be negotiated locally and represented as successful in 'documentary reality' – to textually governed practices, controlled, predicted and centrally accountable. Of course this 'new' project approach meant that the role of the donor was strengthened *vis-à-vis* the local context in China: what an ODA Adviser in a policy speech in 1996 called 'moving authority to the centre' (i.e. London), with the intention that 'the centre is going to be much more proactive' and 'will define what are the major priorities' (my transcription).

In this same text, negotiating with the local institutions in China was denigrated as an old-style 'going to the Friendship Store' with a 'shopping list' (Friendship Stores were at that time hard-currency stores aimed at tourists), as in: 'we are no longer a sort of great big Friendship Store that sells everything ... we can't really go on with the old shopping list the "I've got an idea will you pay for it" sort of approach' (policy speech 1996, my transcription). Under this 'old shopping list' approach, the strategy for the local institution's representatives had often been to accept the donor's initial offer of aid and then try to wrest it to promote their own local (personal, departmental, institutional) interests, in many cases by treating the project primarily as a way of supplying foreign teachers. Thus, from their initiation, some of the ELT projects were subject to the competing agendas of the Chinese and British individuals involved and, in the case study that follows, I go on to describe in greater detail how the competing agendas worked out within the micropolitics of one project (a project that was based in a university in Shanghai in the years 1994–1998).

A Case Study of the Politics of Language Education in a Chinese University

Introduction

How was a language education project received in the Chinese context? To consider this in detail, I now introduce a two-part case study of how the UK Specialists attached to one project in China used *the project* to pursue their own professional/political agendas. The first part of the case study concerns the devaluing of Chinese pedagogical practices, the devaluing of *the teacher* and the establishment of the legitimacy of 'teacher training' on the western ELT model. The second part of the case study goes on to show how the role of *the manager* was then legitimised by means of the project's focus on accountability and how the role of the manager was valued by the UK agencies and Specialists over that of the teacher (a process of managerialisation). This is in part then a story of recategorisation that relates to the career paths of the Specialists (of whom the author was one). That career trajectory was, typically, from teacher (ELT) to MA in Applied Linguistics, to teacher trainer, to project manager, (and later) to generalist manager (or, as in my case, out of the field altogether).

Case study part one: From teachers to trainers

The case study is situated in a language development project at a university in Shanghai in the years 1994–1998, during which the university's Department of Language and Communication hosted an ODA language education project to which I was attached as one of two British ELT Specialists. The Shanghai project was intended to convert a cadre of Chinese teachers of English into teachers of 'Business English', who would use Communicative Language Teaching (CLT; alternatively 'communicative methodology') in their classrooms. This is the period of the 'proto-project', when professional educational expertise was still valued over managerialism, but this particular project was also intended to develop a financially self-sustaining business English school within the department by the end of its ODA funding in 1998, so management, marketing and budget management were also part of the project's remit (on paper). Thus when I arrived at the project in 1994, the main parts of the job were (on paper): teaching business English courses, project administration, teacher training, and the selection and training of Chinese counterparts who would subsequently be sent to the UK on Masters-level courses. The project director was an academic, a professor in the department. This Professor was (on paper) line manager of the two Specialists, but the project was closely monitored, on paper and by way of biennial visits, by two senior officials of the British Council, based in Beijing. The origins of the project were in the local context where there had been a negotiation between the local BC office in Shanghai and the university, with the former interpreting ODA criteria and priorities as follows: 'the Chinese wanted a translation project, we offered them a Business English project' (extract from my field notes).

But for many of the ELT projects in China, the main attraction for the Chinese departments was to obtain a native speaker of English. This was in order to benefit from the status gained by employing a native speaker, who could be used in attracting fee-paying students to foreign languages departments (the marketisation of Chinese universities was beginning in this period): thus 'the opportunity of listening and speaking to native speakers is something that participants ... frequently feel they benefit most from – and having native speaker teachers is accordingly a drawing card for a course' (Sunderland, 1990: 218). But although the foreign teacher's symbolic value was high, foreign teachers were often not considered serious by their Chinese colleagues and were restricted professionally to delivering the 'Oral English' or 'Conversation' classes (and thus used as a species of walking resource) and were not allowed near the serious courses, particularly 'Intensive Reading' (where Chinese was in any case the primary classroom language) (see Dzau, 1990 for an account of the ELT context in China). This meant that the first priority for the Chinese departments was to use the Specialists as direct teachers of Oral English, while the Specialists had to find ways of expanding or escaping from that role, because if they accepted this restricted teacher role, the Specialists were gaining status neither in the Chinese academic field nor in the BC/ODA development field, where teaching was not a particularly valued role. So for example, on being introduced to a British Council officer from Beijing, one of the Specialists was greeted with 'oh you're just a teacher' (the lowest category of British employee in the BC), with the force of 'you are not worth talking to'. But as the ELT Specialists attached to the projects were not intended primarily as teachers and were operating within the international development field (as employees of the ODA and the BC), their political/professional agenda was first to gain recognised status as teacher trainers (and this move to redefine themselves as teacher trainers can be seen as the first in a series of political moves by the Specialists to professionalise their position within the field of development by constituting a new category of *ELT project managers*, with an authoritative knowledge/expertise that could be recognised).

The first political move in this direction on the Shanghai project was to establish that the foreign 'Specialist' was not primarily a teacher, but was primarily a trainer (or, to introduce a term from another political/terminological debate: a 'teacher developer'). To do this, the Specialists first used the project as authority to delimit their teaching and this move was recorded in the project management team's weekly meeting minutes:

> Next semester the two classes at (the Vocational) College will be combined into one. (The specialists) said that as courses at (the Vocational College) were not part of (the project) and have no curriculum development or teacher training role, they would prefer not to be involved with teaching (Vocational College) classes next semester.

So the Vocational College where the Specialists had been teaching was defined by the Specialists as 'not part of the project' in order to restrict the amount of teaching they could be asked to do and also to define themselves as other than teachers (step one), and then (step two) the Specialists' job descriptions were written (by themselves) to minimise the overall amount of classroom teaching they might be required to do. In the following extract from my job description, point 3 is worded to do exactly that, while the other points cover managerial tasks and 'extending' 'teacher development' (a key move to legitimise this role instead of teaching). When writing the job description the BC asked the Specialists to 'provide a brief description of the main duties of the post'. In response, I wrote that these duties were:

(1) To maintain steady progress towards project objectives.
(2) To maintain records and produce reports relating to (1) above.
(3) To undertake a small amount of classroom teaching as deemed appropriate to the development of the project.
(4) To assist in the development of new courses and the evaluation and development of existing courses.
(5) To maintain and extend a programme of teacher development.
(6) To supervise the use of the (project) language centre and to develop a self-access centre.

However, this attempt by the Specialists to gain status within the projects as 'teacher trainers' initially ran into a difference of perception over the 'training issue', that is, over the meaning of 'teacher training', in that the Western aim was 'improvement of teaching skills', whereas the Chinese aims were 'language improvement, and *promotion*' (i.e. within the profession) (Sunderland, 1990: 226, quoting Morrison, 1988). The italicisation in the original indicates an awareness by the author (Morrison) of the importance of politics in gaining professional advancement for the Chinese, yet the comment ignores the fact that to be seen as a teacher trainer was also a matter of importance for the Specialists (although typically seen as politically neutral technologists). But as 'language improvement' here could be taken as 'listening to a native speaker', not only did the Specialists have to prove that they were not primarily teachers (for the purposes of the project) but they also had to try to redefine teacher training and have their definition accepted by the Chinese.

This could be done by, if necessary, bringing in the authority of the BC/ODA to define the legitimate activities of the project, where *conditionality* (that is, the provision of funding against the meeting of conditions) would be used to help to promote the BC's vision of the world. So (for example) in a letter to a Beijing university, where the Specialist was having difficulty in establishing a legitimate and authoritative role, the BC senior officer wrote to the Chinese project director that the Specialist was not to be used only or primarily as a teacher; that the project was primarily concerned with the introduction of CLT; and that therefore compliance with the ODA's conditions was advised. The senior officer concluded with a reference to conditionality:

> Substantial progress needs to have been made ... by December if the project is going to succeed in the envisaged timescale. Obviously the likelihood or otherwise of the ultimate success of the project is something which will influence the ODA when it comes to consider the extent of its future support. I would therefore very much like to be able to report to it by December. (extract from letter from BC officer, 1994)

However, for the Chinese academics teacher training had been based traditionally on the relationship between a *master* and an *apprentice*, so teachers tended to teach in the way that they felt that they themselves were successfully taught. This apprenticeship model (and the status of the academic master of content) was opposed by the western rational, technologised model, with its axioms such as 'student-centred learning', 'teaching English through English', 'no L1 in the classroom' and the reliance on lesson planning, lesson observations, and 'self-criticism' sessions after the observed lesson in order to inculcate its practices (similar in some ways to the methods used in the Cultural Revolution to identify heresy and impose orthodoxy).

So queries about the nature of language teaching from one project brought the following response from a BC officer in Beijing on the need to formulate an explicit 'model (or philosophy) of ELT' in order to establish orthodoxy and the need to identify teachers 'who do not properly understand' the orthodoxy: 'unless and until certain concerns are made overt through explicit consideration of them, there may well be some teachers who do not in fact properly understand what is expected of them and why, but whose misconceptions are not however immediately apparent'.

And the role of supervised practices in ensuring and judging compliance was emphasised, in that, as the BC officer stated: 'each teacher would be required to carry out the activity'.

However, for Chinese teachers the kinds of skills they could acquire through adopting this new way of teaching, although acceptable in the west and in commercial language schools (some of which, however, would not employ non-native speakers), were of little value in the academic field in China, where Western approaches and qualifications might in fact impede promotion (as noted by Morrison, 1988 in Sunderland, 1990). The Specialists, who had developed their teaching skills in English language schools and on Applied Linguistics MAs, not in Chinese universities, were therefore attempting to reproduce their own mode of teaching by converting the Chinese teachers to western ways of teaching English and western understandings of teacher training.

Of course, most of the Chinese teachers were resistant to this change, as for example in this interview, recorded in 1994 (my transcription), between two Chinese teachers ('H' and 'M'), who were discussing their feelings about 'student-centred' teaching and the role of compliance with the wishes of 'some foreign experts' (i.e. the Specialists):

M: when I teach College English[4] the students would ah expect you to do ah almost everything in class and the only thing let them to do is to review or if some good students they would like to preview, but ahm in the (project) it's not what the students require that you do everything or let them or let them do most of the things ... mmm (laughs)
H: yes
M: it is ah some foreign experts (laughs) would like you to let the students try most of the things in class.

But in the case of this teacher, the Chinese way of doing things overrides the western methods and M finds it difficult to comply:

M: I can erm I can organize the class better in fact I think so, sometimes before class I would erm be quite determined to try the learner centred way but in the class I would go back to the [teacher centred way]
H: [teacher centred]
M: erm not intentionally but erm I it's custom I think
H: yeah a tradition a custom it's difficult to change it

The western understanding of the role of learning as 'practice' rather than transferring 'knowledge' from teacher to student and therefore the authority and legitimacy of the western model are challenged:

M: Chinese students would sometimes or they would complain about
H: why?

M: they would say that the teachers do not say much, they do not teach the knowledge, so they would feel that the teachers do not have anything to say in class, just let them practise [and practise] and practise

H: [let them practise]

M: and they and they think that knowledge can be taught and they don't have to lea .ahm .s students may say they can learn after class they don't have to practise in class in class, they came to listen to the teacher.

But the process of inculcation of these teachers was planned to continue outside the local context and as the next step, in order to be converted to Western-style teachers and teacher trainers, these 'counterparts' (M and H) were to be sent to the UK to do Masters degrees in Applied Linguistics. On their return the counterparts would then be expected to take over most of the teaching and training on the project (thus again restricting the teaching role and the training role of the Specialists). This process did in fact take place during the two years left of the project after the return of M and H to Shanghai. However, when the British Specialists left and the project ended (in 1998), the Chinese teachers were reabsorbed into the department.

But for the Specialists, this process of gaining authority as trainers had to be achieved without alienating the political actors in the Chinese university, by seeking political alliances, maintaining face and accruing *'guanxi'* (i.e. credit gained through personal relationships and favours). Specialists who were unable to assert the legitimacy of their authority within their local political context and insisted on imposing the 'universal' model of CLT and its practices risked professional, political and personal isolation. This was defined by one Specialist as a lack of 'moral support'. In one of my transcripts there is a long discussion (in the context of a workshop on projectisation) between this Specialist and a BC officer as to whether moral support can be quantified. This discussion begins with the Council officer's assertion that: 'all inputs are cash based, resources have a cash value, people have a cash value'; to which the Specialist remarks: 'departmental support is an assumption you can't make, that sort of moral support thing, it's very important in a project'. Eventually the BC officer concedes: 'it's an important moral issue, an important issue personally or professionally, you can't legislate what people will give their support to'. By this I understood the BC officer to mean that, despite the remarks in which he seemed to be reducing the necessary support for a project to money ('cash'), he did, when challenged in this way, recognise the importance of personal and professional micropolitics within each particular project in gaining support for the project.

But as the politics of the development field was increasingly influenced by the New Public Management, the education professional (teacher and teacher trainer) began to decline in status compared to the manager. So having, as a first political move, asserted their status as teacher trainers over that of teachers, the second political move for the Specialists was to gain control of the authority of the project in order to represent themselves primarily as project managers. The second part of the case study goes on to describe this process.

Case study part two: From trainers to managers

The key to understanding the next political move by the Specialists is the changing valuations of the academic and the managerial: that is, the devaluation of the teacher in western societies and the increased social recognition of the manager (the process of managerialisation), with, in this case, the need for Specialists to be recognised as managers rather than as teachers in order to acquire status in the development field.

This new managerialism raised an issue of culture for the Chinese academics. In this period the Chinese academic field was still being materially and institutionally reconstituted after its destruction during the Cultural Revolution, when class background and class struggle replaced academic and intellectual status (Du Jinjiang, 1988; Sunderland, 1990). The academics had therefore been struggling to re-establish the legitimacy of a humanistic literature-based approach in the field of language education and the role of the cultured 'Confucian' intellectual, after their denigration and persecution during the Cultural Revolution. These academics did not regard language learning as an instrument of business but primarily as a cultural act by which they were distinguished from the *nouveaux riches* 'people of no culture'. But now the academics in the field of language education were again being challenged to 'change', this time first by western 'communicative methodology', legitimised by western rationalist and technologised pedagogies, and then by managerialism.

In this context, one of the hidden political aims of the ELT projects was to managerialise the Chinese academics as if through a process of conversion. As a senior BC official told me in September 1994, 'we're hoping the Professor's (i.e. the project Director's) stay in the UK will change him from an academic into a businessman'. And, during a visit to the project in September 1995, another BC officer stated: '(t)hey (i.e. the Chinese) don't realize yet what they've let themselves in for' (meaning that they had not yet understood this hidden aspect of managerialist convergence). A third officer, visiting the project in 1997, talked about the global processes by which teachers and academics were being forced to redefine themselves in relation to market forces (he gave British and Chinese examples). He said that he had had to do this himself in the context of the BC, converting himself from an educational to a managerial professional. Meanwhile the departmental Dean and the project Director showed by their body language – 'shrinking away' – how much they wished to distance themselves from this idea of becoming managers (recorded in my field notes).

This reluctance by the Dean and the Director to convert to managerialism meant that the day-to-day management of the project was left to the Specialists and increasingly so, as the accountability demands of the NPM began to influence the politics of the local and more time had to be spent on compiling reports and keeping project frameworks updated. The politics of the project then became, through reporting and monitoring and the provision of 'measurable' evidence, a matter of creating and controlling a 'documentary reality' directed at the BC and the ODA. That is, the project became a matter of managing the reporting system, rather than engaging with any interpersonal process of change (such as teaching or training). But this increasing preoccupation with the management of reporting also allowed the Specialists to use the authority of 'the project' to gain managerial status, a status which would be officially recognised by way of monitoring visits and reports filed in BC and ODA offices in London and Manchester.

Managing the project as a reporting system also taught the Specialists (and reminded the Chinese academics of) the lessons and rewards of compliance with the plans of an hierarchically superior authority. In my case this was done by learning the rules of the game from my colleague, a more experienced Specialist: that is, I had to learn how the political power hierarchy in which I was situated operated. Interestingly, this learning was done on an apprenticeship model of learning 'how to do projects': according to my colleague, the project should be treated as a 'game' that 'you play by the rules'. In this political game, the BC officers in Beijing were seen to play a key role, or rather two key roles: '(t)he BC officer is our enemy' in that she (the BC officer) monitors us and reports on us to the ODA, but also 'in a way she's our friend', meaning that the name and the authority of the officer (as the authorised representative of the BC and the ODA) could be mobilised in the local context to achieve our own political/professional ends.

Evidence of the use of the BC/ODA in this way to legitimise the Specialist as authorised representative can be seen in a meeting in the project office in the university. The main unstated reason for this meeting (its political agenda) was to convince the Chinese project staff of the importance of compliance with the reporting process. In my field notes I noted the following examples of *making the absent authority present* that were used by my colleague in talking to the Chinese during the meeting: 'this is what we've been asked to do when we provide this action plan'; 'to be able to say that we can increase the number of hours'; 'this is what (the BC officer) wants to see'; 'this is what they want for a project'; 'every year we write our report and say "this part has been successful"'; 'we can say that we have got a plan and we can modify it'; 'we have got a target'; 'if we send this, people can look at it and say'; 'this time next year we will be forced to do this again'; and 'in her letter (the BC officer) says'.

Here the grammatical (and social) agents are either excluded or obscured as 'they' or as 'people'. The geographically distant and physically absent authority is nevertheless invoked, made present: the one who has the right and the power to *ask*, to *want* – to *command* in effect. But these powers are presented in the speech of the Specialist, who thereby assumes the delegated authority of the office, becomes the official interpreter, the one who is present, whose job it is to write the reports, to constitute the documentary reality. And the response to the authoritative voice was eventually compliance, despite local resistance to the practices of monitoring, surveillance and reporting (familiar from Communist Party practices): lesson observation for example, was resisted by some of the Chinese academics as a form of 'Big Brother is watching you'. But the response from the Specialists to this resistance was again to evoke the absent authority to enforce compliance: 'we are supposed to know what's happening in these classes'.

The Specialists were thus accumulating managerial capital that they intended to convert into careers in the field of international development management. But the real political authority was with the centre (with London). The (at least in part) successful conversion of the Specialists to managers was followed by the dissolution of the Specialists as a social group when the politics of development changed after 1997 (Kerr, 2006). In the next section, I therefore move on from the case study to describe how this change in the political forces in London after the 1997 General Election, won by New Labour, affected the politics of language development and how this in turn impacted on the projects in China.

'The End of the World as We've Known it'

By 1997, 80 institution-based language education projects had run or were running in China (each with a three or four year time-limit). But the development field was about to be reconstituted by direct political intervention. The new policy imperative for Clare Short (as Secretary of State for International Development) after New Labour's election victory of

1997 was to focus development on 'the poorest of the poor' (for a perspective on how this policy change in the development field was linked to changes in the World Bank's politics, see Rose, 2006). This change in policy meant that the ODA (now renamed Department for International Development) would concentrate on improving basic education, which in turn meant the end of the tertiary-based ELT projects ('E-L-T is O-U-T', Clare Short is supposed to have told her advisers).

This change, the effective withdrawal of the ODA from projects in Chinese universities, was announced to representatives of the universities at a conference in Qindao in 1998. Platform speakers (representatives of the ODA, the BC and UK universities involved in projects) addressed the audience of Chinese academics and British Specialists in terms such as: 'it is the end of the world as we've known it'; and 'ruthless surgery (of projects) is now required' (from my field notes). The Chinese were informed that 'Father Christmas (i.e. the ODA) is going home and taking his bag of presents with him'. In more positive terms, other speakers said that: 'we have to build a new vision' for which 'we need a new style of management' (using e-networks for example).

But the pervasive feeling of the conference participants was a feeling of betrayal, abandonment and grief. It is worth noting that Maley in a high-profile report to the BC had tried (in his comments on proposed policy changes in 1995) to anticipate this reaction and, as a political intervention, to prevent it:

> Many people in the (Chinese) University world, for example, express feelings of abandonment and puzzlement at the policy decision to move away from institution-focused projects, leaving them with no apparent means of maintaining and developing relationships built up over the years. (British Council, 1995: 38)

I also think it is worth noting that this kind of insight into the affective side of development projects and the potential long-term effects of these feelings of grief and betrayal has never (to my knowledge) been taken seriously in the literature or by the development agencies.

As part of the Qindao conference, the Specialists were called to account by the ODA officers at individual interviews and were shown their own future insignificance: as one Specialist said after the meeting, 'I felt like a cockroach under their feet'. The Specialists were now dispensable; their accumulated capital (as teachers, trainers and as managers) was now valueless in China as the government agents operated to remake the field of international development. As a result, many of the Specialists subsequently returned to the classroom, others managed to move to project management posts (e.g. in Eastern Europe or the Middle East), some to specialised ELT posts (e.g. in testing), while some moved to academia, where they could use their experience (in the form of data) to pursue their individual agendas in other ways.

Conclusion

The study has addressed the question: how did changes in the way that development projects were managed by the UK development agencies translate into a Chinese academic department? In answering this question, I have tried to confirm Dezalay and Garth's (2002) findings, namely that the intended impact of a specific development intervention, based on political decisions by the donor country's government that reflect the internal agendas of that government, when inserted into the politics of the local recipient organisation, will be incorporated in unpredictable ways into the politics of the local and the agendas of the local social actors.

In order to answer this question, I first described how the introduction of the New Public Management in the 1990s changed the way that international development was managed in the UK. The consequent increased focus on management and accountability led to the introduction of an increased monitoring and control of geographically distant development operations by the UK-located agencies. I then described how these political and policy changes in the UK were translated into the politics of a particular project sited in a Chinese university department, and how these changes were co-opted by the ELT Specialists based in the Chinese university in order to promote their professional agendas.

The first part of the political agenda was for the Specialists to increase their status by being recognised as teacher trainers. The next political move by the Specialists was to shift their recognised expertise from Language Education (the content of the project) or to be more precise its methodologies, to the methodology of the project itself, a process that involved the Specialists trying to be recognised as managers.

The Specialists thus used their limited political agency to manipulate the political balance between the host department, its university, the BC and the ODA. But the ultimate and decisive power in this context was with the ODA, as was shown after 1997 when a change in UK government policy ended the programme of ELT projects in China. This final direct intervention in the local by the agents of the UK development agencies disbanded the Specialists as a social group. With a new policy focus on basic education, the ELT projects disappeared and as a consequence the language education Specialists also vanished from the politics of the local in China.

Notes

1. The role of the World Bank in promoting neoliberal market solutions ('economic imperialism') at the macropolitical level is covered in Jomo and Fine (2006).
2. The seminar was one of the 'Dunford' series of annual seminars at which representatives of the BC, the ODA and the academic community met in the UK to discuss matters of preoccupation in the language and development field.
3. The 'new-style' logical framework (originally designed by Team Technologies), has the form of a matrix of 16 boxes with categories that can be read, on the vertical axis, as activities, outputs, purpose, goal, and, on the horizontal axis, as narrative summary, measurable indicators, means of verification, important assumptions. It is a management technology that encodes a linear problem-solution approach to innovation based on an if-then logic.
4. College English was the standard series of textbooks produced in China for Chinese students of English.

References

Abbott, G. and Beaumont, M. (eds) (1997) *The Development of ELT: The Dunford Seminars 1978–1993*. Hemel-Hempstead: Prentice Hall.
Bislev, S., Salskov-Iverson, D. and Hansen, H.K. (2001) *Globalization, Governance and Security Management*. Copenhagen: Copenhagen Business School.
Bourdieu, P. (1998) *Practical Reason*. Cambridge: Polity.
British Council (1986) *Appropriate Methodology*. London: The British Council.
British Council (1990) *Know-How Fund for Eastern Europe: Report of a Joint English Language Teaching Mission to the German Democratic Republic*. London: The British Council.
British Council (1992) *Communication Skills in Development: The Role of ELT*. London: The British Council.
British Council (1995) *The Landmark Review of the Use, Teaching and Learning of English in the People's Republic of China*. Manchester: The British Council.
Dezalay, Y. and Garth, B.G. (2002) *The Internationalization of Palace Wars: Lawyers, Economists, and the Contest to Transform Latin American States*. Chicago and London: University of Chicago Press.
Dzau, Y.F. (ed.) (1990) *English in China*. Hong Kong: API Press.
Du Jinjiang (1988) Some reflections on advanced teacher training in China. *British Council ELT Newsletter*, Special Issue, Report on the 1988 ATTC Conference. British Council Beijing, 13–15.
Hood, C. (1991) A public management for all seasons? *Public Administration* 69 (1), 3–13.
Jacobs, C. (1996) *Institutional Strengthening and Technical Cooperation: Developing a Best Practice Model*. Manchester: Institute for Development Policy and Management, Manchester University.
Jomo K.S. and Fine, B. (eds) (2006) *The New Development Economics*. London & New York: Zed Books.
Kerr, R. (2006) Discourse and social actors: The unmaking of a social group. In A. Beverungen, N. Ellis, T. Keenoy, C. Oswick, I. Sabelis and S. Ybema (eds)

Organisational Discourse: Identity, Ideology and Idiosyncrasy (pp. 183–186). Leicester: The University of Leicester.

Kerr, R. (2008) International development and the New Public Management: Projects and logframes as discursive technologies of governance. In S. Das and B. Cooke (eds) *The New Development Management* (pp. 91–109). London: Zed.

Markee, N. (1997) *Managing Curricular Innovation*. Cambridge: Cambridge University Press.

Minogue, M. (2000) *Should Flawed Models of Public Management be Exported? Issues and Practices*. Manchester: Institute for Development Policy and Management, University of Manchester.

Morrison, B. (1988) Microteaching and teaching practice on ATTCS. *British Council ELT Newsletter*, Special Issue, Report on the 1988 ATTC Conference. British Council Beijing, 36–39.

Power, M. (1997) *The Audit Society*. Oxford: Oxford University Press.

Rose, P. (2006) From Washington to post-Washington consensus: The triumph of human capital. In K.S. Jomo and B. Fine (eds) *The New Development Economics* (pp. 162–183). London & New York: Zed Books.

Sahlin-Andersson, K. (2001) National, international and transnational constructions of new public management. In T. Christensen and P. Lægreid (eds) *New Public Management – The Transformation of Ideas and Practice* (pp. 43–72). Aldershot: Ashgate.

Smith, D.E. (1974) The social construction of documentary reality. *Sociological Inquiry* 44 (4), 257.

Strathern, M. (ed.) (2001) *Audit Culture: Anthropological Studies in Accountability, Ethics and the Academy*. London: Routledge.

Sunderland, J. (1990) Doing what the Romans don't do: Advanced teacher training courses in China. In Y.F. Dzau (ed.) *English in China* (pp. 222–249). Hong Kong: API Press.

Yin, R.K. (1994) *Case Study Research: Design and Methods*. Thousand Oaks: Sage.

Chapter 5
Teaching Immigrants the Language of the Host Community: Two Object Lessons in the Need for Continuous Policy Development

DAVID LITTLE and BARBARA LAZENBY SIMPSON

Introduction

This chapter is concerned with language education policy as it intersects with immigration policy. We present two examples of what can happen when policy decisions are taken as an emergency measure rather than as part of an ongoing process of policy development designed to anticipate and respond to changing circumstances. Interestingly, our experience was positive as well as negative; working in a policy vacuum brought us an unusual degree of autonomy as well as great frustration. There was no question of our having to work towards a compromise between educational principle and political expediency – we were financially accountable, but otherwise were left to our own devices. We have no doubt that this was a major factor underlying the success we achieved. On the other hand, we found it virtually impossible to break out of our policy vacuum and address new challenges; and in one case that led to the emergence of serious micropolitical problems. Reflecting on our experience as we have worked on this chapter, we have come to wonder whether there is a middle way that would allow us the freedom we have enjoyed but avoid the frustrations. Experiences reported elsewhere in this book warn against too much optimism.

Language and Immigration: An Area of Political Fudge

Large-scale migration poses perhaps the greatest single challenge to the social cohesion of European societies at the beginning of the 21st century.

The member states of the Council of Europe have adopted a policy of integration as their collective response to this challenge. By contrast with assimilation, which 'confines cultural or religious differences to the private sphere and shuns any consideration of "ethnic origins"' (Council of Europe, 2005: 11), integration

> aims at ensuring social cohesion through accommodation of diversity understood as a two-way process. On the one hand, immigrants have to accept basic values of European societies. On the other, host societies have to respect immigrants' dignity and distinct identity and to take it into account when elaborating domestic policies. (Council of Europe, 2005: 2)

The language of the host community clearly plays a crucial role in the processes of integration. This raises key policy issues for governments and generates a number of challenges for language professionals. How effectively the challenges are met is a function not only of professional competence but of the clarity, coherence and completeness of policy and its implementation. Unfortunately, politicians are as prone to fudge in this as in any other policy area.

The belief that immigrants should be granted citizenship only when they can demonstrate their proficiency in the language of the host community has been gaining ground in a number of countries, especially since the terrorist acts of 11 September 2001. On 9 December 2006, in a speech on multiculturalism and immigration, the British prime minister had this to say:

> [W]e should share a common language. Equal opportunity for all groups requires that they be conversant in that common language. It is a matter both of cohesion and of justice that we should set the use of English as a condition of citizenship. In addition, for those who wish to take up residence permanently in the UK, we will include a requirement to pass an English test before such permanent residency is granted.[1]

Since 2001 the common reference levels of the *Common European Framework of Reference for Languages* (CEFR; Council of Europe, 2001) have increasingly been used to define the proficiency levels required for citizenship. In terms of CEFR levels, what exactly did Tony Blair mean when he used the phrases 'share a common language', 'be conversant in that language' and 'set the use of English as a condition of citizenship'? Was he thinking of something like the Danish requirement of B1/B2 in spoken and B1 in written language, expected after a minimum of seven years' residence? Or did he rather have the example of France in mind, where the goal of language instruction for foreigners entering the country for the first time is the development of very basic oral skills, specified as A1.1, defined in detail by Beacco et al. (2006), and apparently based on a very different view of linguistic integration? We shall probably never know, but it will fall to language professionals to develop the tests that the British government has committed itself to introduce. They will have to reconcile professional standards of test construction with political goals that are likely to remain fuzzy; and when they have done so, they may find that their tests are exploited for unintended and inappropriate purposes. Hawthorne (1997) reports, for example, that since 1992 the Australian Department of Immigration and Ethnic Affairs has used the *access*: test of English to control the flow of immigration by raising the cut point in times of economic recession and lowering it when the economy is booming – something the designers of the test certainly did not intend. Buck (this volume) provides a comprehensive overview of the ways in which political and micropolitical agendas can compromise the integrity of language tests.

Another challenge that immigration generates for language professionals is the design and implementation of language learning programmes explicitly intended to support integration. This chapter is concerned with two such programmes that we have been responsible for in Ireland: full-time English language courses for adults with refugee status or humanitarian leave to remain, and the teaching of English as a second language to non-English/Irish-speaking pupils/students in primary and post-primary (secondary) schools. Both programmes arose from policy decisions taken by the Irish government in response to emergency situations; and both were conducted largely in a policy vacuum, which means that significant short-term gains were always at risk in the longer term. Our purpose here is less to blame than to draw attention to deficiencies in policy development and implementation that are certainly not unique to Ireland.

Example 1: Providing Intensive English Language Courses for Adult Immigrants with Refugee Status

Beginnings

Since the 1970s Ireland has received quotas of programme refugees under the terms of agreements between successive Irish governments and the United Nations High Commission for Refugees. Programme refugees enjoy most of the rights of citizenship from the moment they arrive in the country, and the government recognises an obligation to provide them with English language courses to facilitate their integration. The same facility is extended to asylum seekers who are granted refugee status or leave to remain in Ireland. In the mid-1990s in Ireland such courses were delivered by private language schools on the basis of competitive tender. The Refugee Agency was concerned, however, that this provision was not marked by obvious success. In 1995 its newly appointed chief executive invited David Little to write a discussion paper on the provision of English language courses for adult refugees, and in 1996 the Refugee Agency secured funding from the Department of Education and Science (DES) that enabled us to explore English-language provision for adult programme refugees from the perspectives established in the discussion paper. We identified a number of failings. None of the providers under contract to the DES had undertaken a needs analysis. Attainment targets tended to be those familiar to learners of English as a foreign language, in particular those implied by the Cambridge First Certificate examination. In an English-speaking country that was experiencing inward migration for the first time in its history, such tests were unknown to prospective employers and therefore had no currency for migrants. This did not matter, however, for we found no recorded case of an adult refugee taking and passing the First Certificate exam. The learning materials most commonly used were standard EFL textbooks, typically with a strong orientation to UK rather than Irish society and culture. Authentic materials of the kind adult refugees must quickly come to grips with – official forms of various kinds, information leaflets related to benefits and entitlements, public health notices, and so on – were not generally used. Teachers were given no special preparation to enable them to respond adequately to the learning and other problems their refugee clients were apt to bring with them to the classroom. None of the English language courses provided for programme refugees had been subject to formal evaluation. Finally, when refugees went on to enrol for skills and vocational training courses with FÁS, the national vocational training agency, their instructors – typically tradesmen: plumbers, carpenters, and so on – were not equipped to understand and help them overcome their language difficulties.

A number of factors were responsible for this state of affairs. From the beginning there had been no attempt on the part of the responsible agencies to identify or develop the kind of expertise needed to administer the provision of English language courses for adult immigrants; indeed, it seems likely that at first there was little awareness on the part of the DES or the Refugee Agency that this client group had specific needs. The private language schools mostly provided EFL courses for visiting foreigners and appeared to have little awareness of the difference between teaching a second and teaching a foreign language. They thus made little if any distinction between adult refugees and the teenagers who come from various European countries to take English language courses in Ireland each summer. On the other hand, it must be said that the level of funding invested in the courses was insufficient to make the development of an appropriately focused programme financially feasible. The weekly rate per student barely covered the cost of teachers' salaries.

The report we submitted to the Refugee Agency and the DES (Little & Lazenby Simpson, 1996) emphasised the importance of developing a fully professional, research-informed approach to the design, delivery and evaluation of English language programmes for adult refugees. After two years of deliberation the DES responded to the report by inviting us to establish a Refugee Language Support Unit (RLSU) as a two-year pilot project (1999–2001) attached to Trinity College Dublin's Centre for Language and Communication Studies, of which David Little was at that time director. In the meantime we had begun to collaborate with the Refugee Agency on an EU-funded project to develop and implement a 'prevocational' English language course for adult refugees – a course, in other words, designed to prepare adult refugees for mainstream vocational training. This may have given us semi-official status in the eyes of the DES; in any case there was no obvious alternative source of expertise.

Almost as soon as the RLSU was launched, in 1999, Ireland admitted a thousand refugees from Kosovo. Although they came to Ireland in the first instance for one year (and at the end of that time many of them returned home), their status entitled them to English language courses, and dealing with this entitlement became the RLSU's first major task. The Kosovars were dispersed around the country, housed for the most part in collective accommodation like disused army barracks and holiday camps. In some cases it was possible to contract local language schools to provide English classes; in others the RLSU had to recruit teachers and organise courses itself. The second major task, undertaken in 2000, was to launch a new tendering process for the private language schools. Two conditions were attached to the award of contracts: (i) that courses would be designed on the basis of needs analysis, and (ii) that the teachers of such courses would attend induction sessions provided by the RLSU. Some contractors complied with the second condition but none with the first. As a result the private language schools gradually disappeared from the scene, leaving the RLSU by default the sole national provider of English courses for adult refugees. In 2001 the RLSU became Integrate Ireland Language and Training (IILT), a not-for-profit campus company of Trinity College Dublin with charitable status (two of its seven directors were officials of the DES).

This move was necessary in order to separate IILT structurally and financially from Trinity College. It placed IILT firmly in the private sector, and although it was paid a core grant to meet central administration costs, its language courses were funded on the basis of a weekly rate per student, exactly as had happened previously with the private language schools. Its client population always comprised programme refugees and asylum seekers who had been granted refugee status or humanitarian leave to remain in Ireland.

Organisational framework

IILT's courses comprised 20 class hours per week and 10 hours of self-access learning and homework. This structure was determined by three factors: full-time courses offered by private language schools typically comprise 20 class hours per week; a total commitment of 30 hours was required by the Department of Social, Community and Family Affairs in order to secure learners' social welfare benefits; and common sense suggested that a maximally intensive time commitment was in the learners' best interests. This last consideration also explains why classes were continuous: the school closed only for Christmas and New Year.

Most students admitted to IILT's courses had some proficiency in English; in terms of the CEFR's common reference levels, the majority profile typically spanned the upper end of A1 and the lower end of A2. A small number of students came to us with no proficiency in English (and sometimes no literacy skills in their mother tongue), and an equally small number came with good general proficiency in English but a need to develop specific skills in order to access further or higher education or seek accreditation of professional qualifications acquired outside Ireland. As one might expect, students' general educational background was infinitely variable. In 2007 a total of 906 students attended IILT's classes, 478 in Dublin and the remainder at nine other centres around the country. They came from 93 countries in Africa, Asia and eastern Europe, so there was a rich mix of L1s, ethnic and religious backgrounds, and previous educational experience.

Basic pedagogical principles

The analysis of learners' needs, a strong emphasis on language learning through language use, and the development of learner autonomy were key to the proposals we made to the Refugee Agency and the DES in 1996. The emphasis on language learning through language use coincided with the reality of the teaching/learning situation. On the one hand, IILT provided its students with an immersion environment – English was necessarily the medium of teaching and the principal means by which students communicated with one another. On the other hand, students' motivation was likely to remain positive so long as what they learned in the classroom had an immediate impact on the ease with which they could manage their lives in the English-speaking world outside. The second emphasis arose from our belief that when learners of any age plan, monitor and evaluate their own learning, they are more likely than otherwise to meet their objective as well as their subjective needs. For adult refugees in Ireland objective and subjective needs coalesce in the imperative to learn as much English as they can in the shortest possible time so that they can deal with bureaucracy in its many different forms, access health care for themselves and their children, communicate with their children's teachers, apply for jobs, hold down jobs, and so on.

The analysis of students' communicative needs included the social, cultural and political dimensions and implications of language use. Given the diversity of our student population, needs analysis was necessarily specific to each class and underpinned teaching and learning on a weekly if not daily basis. As individual needs were negotiated and clarified, group needs began to emerge. Some of these could be addressed by the class as a whole – for example, all students seeking employment needed to know how to interpret their pay slip; while others were more satisfactorily dealt with by dividing the class into groups – for example, not all students needed to focus on the same domain of work. This highly individualised approach meant that there could be no pre-established learning goals, no single set of learning materials and pedagogical procedures, and certainly no textbooks. The absence of a fixed curriculum and a uniform set of learning goals also raised doubts about the appropriateness of conventional language tests.

As IILT's student and teacher numbers expanded and more teachers were employed, it made sense for teachers to share ideas, activities and materials. But it also made sense to devise a means of framing learning that could be used by all teachers and learners. We wanted to avoid unnecessary duplication of teacher effort, but also to make it easier for students to compile a detailed record of their learning: objectives and plans, vocabulary to be mastered, work in progress, work completed, reflection on the learning process, evaluation of learning outcomes. The Council of Europe's European Language Portfolio (ELP; Council of Europe, 2006) offered itself as an obvious way of meeting this requirement, especially as it is explicitly designed to support reflective learning in which self-assessment plays a central role. The setting of learning targets and the evaluation of learning outcomes depend on checklists of 'I can' descriptors that refer to listening, reading, spoken interaction, spoken production and writing and are scaled according to the proficiency levels of the CEFR. Reflection on learning styles and strategies and the cultural dimension of L2 learning and use complements the reflective practice of goal setting and self-assessment.

IILT's approach to assessment

Neither the DES nor IILT ever specified a maximum training entitlement for adult refugees. IILT's goal was always to bring learners to the point where they felt comfortable using English for their particular daily purposes. In practice most of them attended classes for between six and 12 months, after which they entered employment or mainstream vocational training. From time to time DES officials asked informally whether IILT's learners should take a standardised English language test as a way of demonstrating the effectiveness of our courses and confirming that the state was receiving value for money. We always replied in the negative for two reasons. Firstly, tests designed for more or less homogeneous populations of learners following internationally similar programmes of English language instruction are inappropriate for an infinitely diverse population of adult immigrants. Secondly, the need to prepare learners to take a test inevitably narrows the focus of teaching and learning towards the tasks and linguistic content of the test in question, and that would have been diametrically opposed to our pedagogical culture.

For several years we were satisfied that the ELP provided all the assessment and certification we needed. But then we began to ask ourselves whether we were doing the best for our students by sending them on their way with nothing more than an informal validation of their sustained learning effort. Also, some form of externally monitored assessment was an obvious way of confirming the quality of our courses. These considerations led us to explore the possibility of having the courses accredited by the Further Education and Training Awards Council (FETAC). FETAC assessment is based on student portfolios, which FETAC monitors regularly to ensure that stated standards are achieved. This system of assessment commended itself to IILT for three reasons. Firstly, our courses were already underpinned by the practice of portfolio learning and assessment, so that it was a relatively straightforward matter to accommodate FETAC modules within our existing framework: FETAC assessment was unlikely to impose inappropriate constraints on teaching and learning. Secondly, with the exception of ESOL modules, our students were taking the same

FETAC modules as Irish learners: English was the medium of their learning but not the primary focus of their assessment. And thirdly, our learners could leave us with their ELPs but also with FETAC certificates that have a value within the national system of further education and training and thus help to promote integration.

How things grew

For the first three or four years of its existence IILT was driven by the pioneer spirit. The organisation was small (there were fewer than twenty employees), administration was straightforward, and management was largely a matter of mediating our pedagogical principles to teachers who were eager to make innovations of their own. In other words, the management skills we needed were essentially those we already possessed as researchers and teacher trainers. We like to think that the ethos we created was similar to the team culture attributed to small enterprises by Southon and West (2002) (see Alderson, Chapter 1 of this volume). From time to time we ran into hostility from educational sectors that felt we had taken funding that should have been theirs by precedent or tradition, but this was never more than an irritant.

As we have seen, IILT was established by analogy with the private sector but funded from the public purse. This may have seemed a convenient solution to a small-scale problem at the end of the 1990s, but common sense suggests that it was unlikely to remain so for long. In the private sector companies rarely stand still; they either shrink or grow, and it was IILT's fate to grow. This quickly brought to an end the idyll of management by research and teacher training. Although latterly most of IILT's Dublin learners came to Ireland as asylum seekers rather than programme refugees, the Irish government continues to accept small numbers of programme refugees whose admission to Ireland and subsequent integration is managed by the Refugee Agency's successor, the Reception and Integration Agency (RIA). It remains government policy to disperse groups of programme refugees to different parts of the country, which meant that IILT was obliged to develop outreach courses. This introduced a whole new level of management and administration into our activities, since the establishment of each new outreach programme required us not only to recruit teachers locally and find accommodation in which to hold classes, but to establish record-keeping systems and reporting procedures. To begin with we also ran into serious funding problems because the DES paid for outreach courses in the same way and at the same rate as for the courses in Dublin, whereas the outreach courses involved us in additional costs. It took three years to begin to find a solution to this problem. Finally, IILT was caught between three government departments: it was funded by and reported to the DES; the RIA is part of the Department of Justice, Equality and Law Reform; and when the RIA informed IILT of the need to establish a new outreach programme, it could do so only when the DES had secured approval from the Department of Finance. Needless to say, the frustration and anger so easily generated by delay mostly fell directly on IILT.

Growth and the passage of time also brought us up against the harsh realities of industrial relations. We began by paying our teachers more than they could earn in the private language schools; with time we also introduced a number of basic benefits and created terms of employment that were as favourable as the funding available to us would allow. In addition we always paid national wage agreements on time and in full. But with unionisation the teachers began to focus on their long-term career prospects, and this led them to request terms and conditions that we could not meet, not least because those terms and conditions were based on public sector norms. Enter micropolitics. The RLSU was established in 1999 as part of the Irish government's National Development Plan, which officially came to an end on 31 December 2006. In the spring of 2007 the DES commissioned a policy study on the provision of English language courses for adult immigrants in general, which was bound to have significant implications for the future of IILT's English courses for adult refugees.

The limbo into which we were cast became an increasingly uncomfortable place. It was soon abundantly clear that countrywide provision of English language programmes for adults with refugee status could not survive for long on the basis of inadequate public funding channelled to the private sector. What is more, when an election fell due in the summer of 2007 Irish politicians at last came to the conclusion that they could make electoral capital out of the immigration issue. *The Sunday Independent* of 21 January 2007 reported that it was the intention of Fine Gael, the largest opposition party, to make immigration an election issue and that the party was formulating a comprehensive policy on immigration, including 'English-language training for migrants and their children'. This brought a riposte from the then Minister for Justice, Michael McDowell, who was reported in *The Sunday Times* of 28 January 2007 as promising the introduction of a citizenship test, including an English language component, for immigrants wishing to settle in Ireland. The test, he said, would be designed to establish that immigrants had 'knowledge of the country and a minimum standard of English' (*The Sunday Times*, 28 January 2007: 1). This seemed to mark the beginning of a process that would bring Ireland into line with the United Kingdom and other western European neighbours – something that in our view is both undesirable and inappropriate. In the event the governing coalition was returned to power, though the Minister for Justice lost his seat and promptly retired from politics. A Minister for Integration was appointed and in January 2008 the new Minister for Justice introduced an Immigration Bill that received a hostile response, especially from NGOs involved in immigrant affairs. By the summer of 2008 the long awaited policy study on the provision of English language courses for adult immigrants had still not appeared.

Example 2: ESL in Irish Schools

A new challenge for the Irish education system

Some of the refugees and asylum seekers who came to Ireland in the 1990s brought their families with them; others started families after their arrival in Ireland. It is a legal requirement that all children and adolescents between the ages of four and a half and 15 must attend school, regardless of the status of their parents. Thus from the mid-1990s primary schools began to receive pupils and post-primary (secondary) schools began to receive students whose first language was neither English nor Irish. In 1999 the DES determined that each non-English/Irish-speaking child or adolescent was entitled to two years of English language support and that such support should be provided on a withdrawal basis (in most cases this amounts to one special class each day). The DES also established funding mechanisms to meet the additional costs that schools would incur. At primary level there was no allowance for the first two non-English/Irish-speaking pupils, one tariff for between three and seven pupils and another for between eight and 13. Schools were awarded an additional full-time post if they had 14 or more pupils requiring English language support, and two additional posts if they had 28 or more such pupils; a third full-time post was sanctioned only in exceptional circumstances. At post-primary level additional teaching hours were funded from the first non-English/Irish-speaking student onwards. Funding for teaching hours also reached the level of a full-time post with 14 students, but full-time posts have rarely been created. Those charged with teaching English as a second language had the same qualifications as other teachers in their sector. A few of them, especially at post-primary level, had experience of teaching EFL in their summer holidays, but on the whole they were not specialist language teachers. It should be noted, however, that in Ireland primary teachers are mostly generalists and that one of the subjects they are required to teach is Irish. In 2000 we were asked to develop and deliver a programme of in-service support for primary and post-primary ESL teachers.

Early work with primary and post-primary ESL teachers

We had already undertaken some work relevant to the school sector in fulfilment of two of the terms of reference attached to the RLSU:

- to develop English Language Proficiency Benchmarks for use with refugees of all ages;
- to advise the DES on the language needs of pupils at first and second level who are not native speakers of English.

Specifically, working with two groups of teachers who were already delivering ESL classes, we had made some progress in the development of English Language Proficiency Benchmarks, adapting the first three proficiency levels of the CEFR (A1, A2, B1) to make them age-appropriate and domain-specific. We chose B1, or Threshold Level, as the exit point for English language support because it is the level at which the learner starts to become a wholly independent language user.

In the summer of 2000 we completed the first drafts of the primary and post-primary Benchmarks, expressed in the same 'Can do' terms as the scales of the CEFR. We also developed preliminary versions of European Language Portfolios, with checklists of 'I can' descriptors derived from the Benchmarks. And in the autumn of 2000 we launched a series of twice-yearly one-day in-service seminars. To begin with, primary and post-primary teachers attended the same seminars, but as the numbers of teachers grew and the materials we had to mediate became increasingly specific, it was necessary to organise separate seminars for the two sectors. We brought new materials of one kind or another to each seminar, but we also used these regular meetings with teachers to get them to contribute to the development of some of our products – for example, a handbook for mainstream teachers on how to cope with a variety of mother tongues and ethnicities in their classes, and a guide to the Irish school system for newcomer parents, which was translated into 10 of the most widespread immigrant languages.

Achievement and consolidation

Teachers were quick to accept the Benchmarks and the ELP; the former reflected their experience of learner progression in the classroom, while the latter provided a ready means of mediating the curriculum to their learners. In Ireland in-service teacher training is not normally provided on a continuous basis but in response to particular events, like the introduction of a new syllabus or a change in the form and content of public examinations. By contrast, we encouraged ESL teachers to attend all our in-service seminars. This had the important effect, especially at primary level, of enabling teachers to form their own regional and local networks; it also meant that we learnt a great deal from the teachers as they became more experienced and confident. In 2003 we revised the two sets of Benchmarks (IILT, 2003a, 2003b) and the two ELPs (IILT, 2004a, 2004b) and launched a project to develop simple communicative tests based on the Benchmarks (for further details, see Little, 2005; Little & Lazenby Simpson, 2004). In the school years 2003–2004 and 2004–2005 we presented draft tests at in-service seminars, recruited teachers to pilot them for us in their schools, revised the tests in light of the feedback we received, and prepared them for general use. Thus by 2006 we had a curriculum scaled according to the first three proficiency levels of the CEFR, primary and post-primary versions of the ELP that mediated the curriculum to learners and encouraged a reflective approach to teaching and learning, a suite of placement and achievement tests, guidelines for the development and management of ESL programmes in schools, a number of information booklets and guides, and a wide range of photocopiable learning materials and activities. We had also embarked on a partnership project with the Southern Education and Library Board in Armagh (Northern Ireland) to develop a toolkit of guidelines and activities to promote inclusiveness in primary schools on both sides of the border.

Growth and new challenges

When the DES first provided for ESL teaching at the end of the 1990s it was widely believed that the need for such provision would disappear with a downturn in the number of refugees and asylum seekers coming to Ireland. The downturn duly occurred, but it was more than compensated for by migrant workers from countries that became members of the European Union in 2004. As a result, the population of pupils and students requiring special ESL provision grew beyond all expectations. Our first in-service seminar, held in June 2000, was attended by 37 ESL teachers from primary and post-primary schools around Ireland. In the autumn term of 2005 seven primary in-service seminars held in different parts of the country were attended by a total of 548 ESL teachers from 411 schools; 305 of the teachers were newly appointed. The single post-primary in-service seminar was attended by 66 teachers from 60 schools; 48 of the teachers were new to ESL. At this point funding constraints obliged us to limit in-service seminars to newly appointed ESL teachers only. Nevertheless, in the autumn of 2006 more than 400 teachers attended the five in-service seminars organised for primary ESL teachers.

Some problems

Between 2000 and 2008 we made a significant contribution to the development of ESL teaching in Irish schools, especially at primary level. But we did so against all the odds; and those odds derived partly from the structures originally put in place by the DES and partly from an absence of proactive policy-making. The structures embodied two serious weaknesses. The first was the one-size-fits-all approach to ESL, which entitles all non-English/Irish-speaking pupils/students to a maximum of two years of ESL support irrespective of their age. The system works well for children beginning school at the age of four and a half: by the end of their second school year they are to all intents and purposes native speakers of English. But it works less well for children who come to Ireland towards the end of their primary schooling, and less well again for those who come when they are of post-primary age. Almost the first advice we gave the DES in this regard was that consideration should be given to developing an immersion programme for immigrant students at post-primary level. But despite the production of several discussion papers, no action was ever taken. The second systemic weakness concerns the post-primary sector. Not only is there no provision to fund dedicated ESL posts; principals are obliged to ensure that every teacher has a full timetable. This means that in many post-primary schools ESL support is delivered in the first instance by teachers who have hours to spare. We heard of one school where 11 different teachers were involved, which made continuity of focus and content quite impossible. To make matters worse, none of the teachers had any training to teach ESL beyond what they might have received by attending IILT's in-service seminars.

Perhaps believing that we had the 'problem' of ESL in some sense under control, the DES apparently did not feel it necessary to make policy that would consolidate the gains we had made. For example, there was no recognition of the need to revisit the once-fashionable theme of language across the curriculum in order to develop pedagogical approaches that would continue to provide at least implicit English language support for non-native-speaker pupils/students in mainstream classrooms after their two years of special provision. Also, no steps were taken to introduce extended training programmes and special qualifications for ESL teachers, and the providers of preservice teacher education mostly continued to ignore the ESL issue. Only very recently have primary degree and postgraduate diploma programmes begun to include (usually elective) modules on teaching ESL and on the challenges posed by linguistic and cultural diversity in the classroom. Revealingly, one such module is included in a postgraduate course in Special Education Needs that is not otherwise concerned with normally-endowed pupils; in other words, pupils whose home language is not that of the host community are assumed to be 'remedial'.

As early as 2004 it was clear to us that our work in this sector could not continue indefinitely on the basis of twice-yearly in-service seminars. Accordingly, we sought to discuss with the Teacher Education Section of the DES how best to move the work we had begun into the mainstream. For more than two years we made no progress. There seem to have been at least three reasons for this delay. Firstly, in 2003–2004 the DES underwent significant restructuring, which inevitably meant that officials could devote less time than otherwise to 'external' issues. Secondly, as late as 2004 there was still a sense in the DES that the 'migrant issue' would go away in a few years and thus did not need to be drawn into mainstream policy development. Thirdly, although the Teacher Education Section is responsible for many schemes designed to support the professional development of teachers, it has a 'hands-off' approach to such schemes, engaging with them only to elicit regular financial reports. IILT was thus by no means alone in its failure to draw the DES into forward-looking discussions.

A better future?

In 2006 the DES established an internal task force to address the ESL needs of migrants. One result of this was the decision, noted above, to commission a policy study on the provision of English language courses for adult immigrants. Another was a surge of new policy-making for the school sector. On 13 February 2007 the Minister for Education and Science announced that in future there would be no cap on the number of ESL teachers appointed at primary level (1450 were expected to be in post by the end of the school year 2006–2007) and the maximum of two years' English language support per pupil/student would be treated flexibly. Following this decision the DES agreed to deliver to all primary schools in the country a copy of IILT's newly produced handbook for ESL teachers (IILT, 2007). Early in 2008 the DES and the Northern Ireland

Department of Education sent to every primary school in either jurisdiction two copies of the toolkit for inclusivity that IILT had developed in collaboration with the Southern Education and Library Board (Armagh). And in the early summer of 2008 each primary school in the Republic received a copy of the English language tests we had developed between 2003 and 2006. For a short time IILT was working closely with the task force, and we had high hopes that policy would continue to develop to the advantage of non-English-speaking pupils/students. Certainly the potential existed for the kind of partnership that Figueras (this volume) advocates between language education professionals and the organs of government.

There were, of course, challenges that still had to be addressed. We remained deeply concerned about the situation of ESL in post-primary schools, which we believed was unlikely to improve without a policy decision to remove the constraints identified above. It was also necessary to take account of significant changes in the profile of the immigrant population. Prior to 2004 newcomer pupils and students were drawn from many different countries; no national, ethnic or linguistic group dominated the rest. But then, with the sudden but entirely predictable influx of migrant workers from new EU states, the nature of the ESL population underwent a radical change. We now had a very large number of children and adolescents from Poland and significant numbers from Latvia and Lithuania. This raised two closely-related policy issues, mother tongue maintenance and the provision of bilingual schooling. To date, the DES has excluded immigrant languages from the school curriculum but paid for mother tongue classes, provided they are organised by the immigrant community in question and take place outside normal school hours. This policy appears to have been dictated by considerations of feasibility and cost, but with the recent changes in scale it might be more cost-effective to provide for the maintenance of some mother tongues within the school system. The most superficial consideration of how this might be done would raise the question of bilingual education, delivered partly through the mother tongue and partly through English. It is too soon to predict with any certainly how many Poles, Latvians and Lithuanians will stay in Ireland long-term. Certainly the Polish government hopes that those of its citizens at present in Ireland will return to Poland, and to that end, according to a report in *The Sunday Times* of 1 October 2006, the Polish government has sought permission from the DES to open a Polish school in Dublin. The intention is to teach the Polish curriculum through Polish, so the school would do little or nothing for the English language proficiency, and thus integration, of its pupils/students. It remains to be seen whether the DES can work with the Polish government to identify and implement a more appropriate way of providing for the development of Polish learners' literacy in their mother tongue.

Conclusion

Our involvement in the provision of English language programmes for adult immigrants first came about by accident, and we were invited to set up the Refugee Language Support Unit more or less by default. The private language schools had shown themselves incapable of responding to the challenge posed by a relatively small number of adult refugees, and the DES's solution was effectively to establish its own private school, but at arm's length. As a result of our success in this domain we were invited to support the teaching of ESL in primary and post-primary schools. In either case we were required to report on our activities annually and to return audited accounts, but for the rest we were left to our own devices. This allowed us to apply key pedagogical principles, especially those that cluster around the construct of learner autonomy, with greater rigour and control than would have been possible in any other circumstances. We were also able to design and implement European Language Portfolio models that quickly became indispensable to the teaching/learning process. Self-assessment using 'I can' descriptors derived from the CEFR showed itself to be a powerful means of developing learners' language learning awareness and capacity for self-management. And in the school sector we developed communicative tests that support and complement a task-based pedagogy on the one hand and learner self-assessment on the other. All this brought us much professional fulfilment, for which we are duly grateful.

At the same time, our work always existed in a policy vacuum, and this was a source of great frustration. Too much of what we achieved remained largely cut off from the educational mainstream, and new challenges that have arisen in the last two or three years have still to be seriously examined. To begin with, immigration may have seemed to pose short-term problems that were best dealt with by short-term measures. But for several years it has been abundantly clear that immigration will be part of Ireland's reality for the foreseeable future. Recommendation 1625 (2003) of the Council of Europe's Parliamentary Assembly calls on member states to 'create interministerial task forces on integration to steer and monitor the integration of immigrants working in consultation with the voluntary sector, community organisations and immigrants' (Council of Europe,

2003: 2). No such task force exists in Ireland, far less a statutory body charged with responsibility for advising government departments on immigrant issues, including those that have to do with language and education. Recommendation 1625 also states:

> Integration policies should have the dual aim of providing immigrants with the means to function in the society where they live and develop their potential while preserving their cultural and ethnic identity, and familiarizing the non-immigrant population with the rights of immigrants, their culture, traditions and needs. (Council of Europe, 2003: 1–2)

Like other Council of Europe member states, Ireland has some distance to go before it can claim to have fulfilled this ideal. The Netherlands, a country with a long tradition of immigration, is currently experiencing serious problems of social cohesion. In 2006 Peter Mair summarised the situation thus:

> There are upwards of two million non-Western immigrants in the Netherlands, more than 10% of the population, and many of them struggle to come to terms with their host country. The children in this growing community will soon constitute a majority of schoolchildren in the four major cities – Amsterdam, The Hague, Rotterdam and Utrecht – and, following the example set by many of their American cousins, the white middle class often take flight from their old city centres. Relations between the native and immigrant communities have never been very good, but they have now sunk to a new and sometimes quite dangerous low. (Mair, 2006: 13)

Ireland is still a long way from this situation. But that will change if the government does not develop and implement policies that address the increasing linguistic complexity of Irish society in ways that explicitly promote social cohesion; and it can do that effectively only if it creates and exploits appropriate transversal structures within and between its departments.

Postscript

For a number of years we attempted to engage the DES in discussion of how best to mainstream IILT's activities, but without success. Letters and telephone calls went unanswered, sometimes for many months. We had long taken the view that English courses for adults with refugee status belonged most appropriately in the Vocational Education sector, which is the main provider of adult education; while in-service support for teachers of ESL in primary and post-primary schools could, we thought, most effectively be provided through the network of local Education Centres. At the same time, however, we believed that it was important to retain a specialist unit that could develop and disseminate curricula, teaching methods, learning materials and assessment instruments.

In June 2008 the DES responded to a proposal the directors of IILT had made three months earlier by informing them that it intended to transfer funding for all IILT's activities to other agencies, with more or less immediate effect. The directors had no alternative but to begin the process of putting IILT into voluntary liquidation. Forty-four members of staff lost their jobs and there was every prospect that the large amount of support materials IILT had developed and made available electronically and in print would disappear without trace.

The DES issued a press release that attributed its decision to IILT's 'withdrawal of services' – a grotesque distortion of the proposal submitted in February 2008. Predictably, no mention was made of IILT's contribution over the past decade or its very high international profile. We shall probably never know exactly what prompted the decision to close IILT at this precise moment, but three factors not mentioned in the press release almost certainly played a role. Firstly, the lease on IILT's premises was due to expire in August 2008. Already in 2007 the DES had identified alternative premises, and early in 2008 agreement was reached on a programme of refurbishment. Unfortunately, however, the DES failed to include provision for such refurbishment in its budget for 2008. Secondly, in early 2008 the Irish economy went into a decline that quickly threatened to become a recession. Cuts in public funding were widely expected, and IILT was not the only educational project to be terminated. Even though its activities were to be transferred to other agencies, there were likely to be at least short-term savings. Thirdly, many people in Ireland believed that the large-scale immigration of recent years would somehow go away, now that the economy was no longer booming.

The sudden demise of IILT is final confirmation that it is inappropriate to use a private company to deliver public services. But a partnership of trust between language professionals and the organs of government could surely have found a way of mainstreaming activities without losing the wealth of human and material resources that had been built up over a decade. We deeply regret that the DES could not bring itself to enter into such a partnership; and we deeply deplore the loss of jobs and the DES's waste of resources.

Note

1. On WWW at http://www.telegraph.co.uk/news/main.jhtml?xml=/news/2006/12/08/ublair208.xml (accessed 12 December 2006). We have tried but failed to trace a comparable public statement by the then Irish prime minister, Bertie Ahern.

References

Beacco, J-C., de Ferrari, M. and Lhote, G. (eds) (2006) *Niveau A1.1 pour le français (publics adultes peu francophones, scolarisés, peu ou non scolarisés). Référentiel et certification (DILF) pour les premiers acquis en français.* Paris: Didier.

Council of Europe (2001) *Common European Framework of Reference for Languages: Learning, Teaching, Assessment.* Cambridge: Cambridge University Press.

Council of Europe (2003) Recommendation 1625 of the Parliamentary Assembly. On WWW at http://assembly.coe.int/documents/adoptedtext/ta03/erec1625.htm. Accessed 20.2.07.

Council of Europe (2005) *Migration and Integration: A Challenge and an Opportunity for Europe.* Council of Europe Parliamentary Assembly, Doc. 10453, 7 February. On WWW at http://assembly.coe.int/main.asp?Link=/documents/workingdocs/doc05/edoc10453.htm. Accessed. 20.2.07.

Council of Europe (2006) *European Language Portfolio: Key Reference Documents.* Strasbourg: Council of Europe. On WWW at http://www.coe.int/T/DG4/Portfolio/documents/keyrefdocs.doc. Accessed 20.2.07.

Hawthorne, L. (1997) The political dimension of English language testing in Australia. *Language Testing* 14 (3), 248–260.

IILT (2003a) *English Language Proficiency Benchmarks for Non-English-Speaking Pupils at Primary Level (Version 2.0).* Dublin: Integrate Ireland Language and Training.

IILT (2003b) *English Language Proficiency Benchmarks for Non-English-Speaking Pupils at Post-primary Level (Version 2.0).* Dublin: Integrate Ireland Language and Training.

IILT (2003c) *Immersion Programme for Non-English-Speaking Students Entering Post-primary School.* Dublin: Integrate Ireland Language and Training.

IILT (2004a) *European Language Portfolio: Learning the Language of the Host Community (Primary).* Dublin: Integrate Ireland Language and Training.

IILT (2004b) *European Language Portfolio: Learning the Language of the Host Community (Post-primary).* Dublin: Integrate Ireland Language and Training.

IILT (2007) *Up and Away. A Resource Book for Primary Language Support Teachers.* Dublin: Integrate Ireland Language and Training.

Little, D. (2005) The Common European Framework and the European Language Portfolio: Involving learners and their judgements in the assessment process. *Language Testing* 22 (3), 321–336.

Little, D. and Lazenby Simpson, B. (1996) Meeting the language needs of refugees. Some general principles, a report on current practice in Ireland and elsewhere, and some recommendations. Unpublished report commissioned by the Irish Refugee Agency and the Department of Education and Science.

Little, D. and Lazenby Simpson, B. (2004) Using the CEF to develop an ESL curriculum for newcomer pupils in Irish primary schools. In K. Morrow (ed.) *Insights from the Common European Framework* (pp. 91–108). Oxford: Oxford University Press.

Mair, P. (2006) Review of Ian Buruma, *Murder in Amsterdam: The Death of Theo van Gogh and the Limits of Tolerance. London Review of Books* 28 (24), 11–13.

Southon, M. and West, C. (2002) *The Beermat Entrepreneur. Turn Your Good Idea into a Great Business.* London: Pearson Education.

Chapter 6
The Commercialisation of Language Provision at University

GLENN FULCHER

Introduction

In recent years there has been a significant change in the provision of language education in UK universities, largely driven by political and economic factors. This chapter argues that both modern foreign language teaching (MFL) and the teaching of English to speakers of other languages (TESOL) have been affected by the same trends, albeit in very different ways. However, both have suffered, and university organisational structures frequently bring MFL and TESOL into conflict. In order to understand recent developments in the provision of English for Academic Purposes (EAP) and academic literacy programmes we believe it is essential to be critically aware of the changing perception of TESOL and EAP from university senior management and international officers who are eager to recruit as many international students as possible in an unfavourable economic climate for UK HE.

These issues are clearly controversial, not least because commentators approach the topic from very different perspectives. The changes have also caused deep divisions and animosities that blight many departments in UK HE, where power, finance and resources are keenly fought over (see Alderson, Chapter 1). However, there is at least one commonality upon which most will agree: TESOL/EAP has been increasingly seen as a source of income primarily through providing international undergraduate and postgraduate students for academic departments. The income from foundation and presessional language programmes has also been welcome, especially when the income can be used to cross-subsidise activities that increasingly cannot raise enough to be self-funding.

This income generation has led to one of the strangest situations in higher education that is difficult, but not impossible, to understand. On the one hand, university managers continually push all academic units to bring in funding to cover their costs, contribute to overheads, and generate a profit. Arguably, TESOL/EAP units have been phenomenally successful in this respect; yet, once they are 'commercially successful' they are perceived as 'merely' a commercial activity rather than an academic one, and therefore may be vulnerable to privatisation. This has led directly to the outsourcing of TESOL/EAP and foundation programmes, where they exist, to commercial providers.

This chapter does two things. Firstly, it looks at the general emerging picture of language education in UK HE and places TESOL and EAP activities within this context. Secondly, it reports on survey research carried out in early 2007. In this research, questionnaires[1] were sent to 104 TESOL/EAP providers in UK universities. The purpose of the survey was to investigate (a) the current place of TESOL/EAP provision within UK HE in relation to related disciplines and the organisational structure of the institution, (b) the perception of the place of TESOL/EAP in these relationships by TESOL/EAP professionals, and (c) the institutional perception of TESOL/EAP as an academic and entrepreneurial activity. In order to triangulate on the data provided, a separate set of questions was sent to three of the larger organisations currently soliciting universities to outsource TESOL/EAP provision, or enter 'partnerships' (Appendix 1), and academic registrars at universities that had outsourced, or were reported to be on the verge of outsourcing, received a parallel set of questions (Appendix 2). We report on the responses to these questionnaires, which raise serious issues for TESOL/EAP providers. Information from the questionnaires is illustrated, where appropriate, with information from two universities where TESOL/EAP is in crisis. Throughout, all institutions and individuals concerned will remain anonymous.

This chapter concludes by summarising issues of immediate importance and concern for existing TESOL/EAP provision in UK HE.

Modern Languages vs English?

The modern foreign language department in a UK university suffers from two major problems that will not go away. All too frequently, activities related to TESOL that are connected to MFL operations suffer as a result.

The first is the fact that English is now the de facto lingua franca of the world. As Swales (1998) recounts, when Bismarck was asked in 1898 what the most important determining event of modern history was, he replied 'the fact that North America speaks English'. While some researchers may talk of English as a lingua franca 'uncoupled' from its native speakers (Seidlhofer *et al.*, 2006), both Bismarck and Swales saw clearly that it is the power and dominance of North American culture and the communication of scientific discovery in English that has contributed to its unchallenged dominance in international communication, including the internet. Or as Wright (2006: 36) correctly observes, it is the social, political and economic factors that have led to the near extinction of French as a lingua franca at the expense of English. With the one exception of Spanish, which is spoken much more widely than other European languages (Godenzzi, 2006), the study of modern foreign languages is decreasing in the United Kingdom (CILT, online; Kelly & Jones, 2003; Marshall, 2002; Robey, 2002; UCAS, online; Watts, 2003) and there appears to be little that can be done to stem this decline. At the same time, the demand for English around the world is growing at an ever-increasing pace as new groups of people wish to partake of the social, educational and economic opportunities that its acquisition brings.

The second problem is that we no longer think of a country being uniquely defined by its culture, and its culture being defined by its language and literature, in the same way that this was held to be the case by von Humboldt (Hacking, 1990: 187). He held that our very ability to think and reason was closely tied with our use of language, and in an early version of the Sapir-Whorf hypothesis, argued that cultural, scientific and national advancement was closely tied to our ability to master language:

> For the course of development of intellectual capability generally stands in natural harmony with the correct course of development of language. For since the need of thinking wakens language in man, in the same way that which flows purely from its conception also by necessity advances the successful advance of thinking. If however a nation equipped with such a language would sink into intellectual inertia and weakness for other reasons, it would be able to work itself out of this state more simply through its language. (von Humboldt, 1836)

It is rather ironic that our early 21st century view of a nation and its culture as the myriad of statistics related to births, deaths, marriage, illnesses, migrations, economic productivity and the activities of the 'average man', was first developed and promulgated in Germany (Hacking, 1990: 34), and later became the bedrock of Foucault's (1975) claim that the de-humanising of individuals is achieved through the classification and description that modern statistics and recording makes possible. Today, students do not believe that they must understand the language and literature of a country to understand its culture or do business with its people; rather, understanding arises through the statistics of economics and the language of commerce.

Today's teachers of German might even join with Nietzsche in his assessment of the impact of Bismarck's reliance on the Prussian Statistical Office to provide 'the truth' as a basis for political action:

> The Germans – they were once considered the people of thinkers: do they still think at all these days? – Germans have become bored with spirit, Germans have started to distrust spirit, politics absorbs all the seriousness from really spiritual matters – *'Deutschland, Deutschland über Alles'*, I am afraid that this was the end of German philosophy...' Are there any German philosophers? Are there any German poets? Are there any *good* German books? This is what I get asked by people abroad. I turn red, but with the courage that comes to me even in desperate situations I reply: 'Well, *Bismarck!*' – Should I also admit what people are reading these days? ... Damned instinct of mediocrity!.... (Nietzsche, 1888: 186–187; italics in the original)

These reasons for the decline in learning modern foreign languages also explain the growth in TESOL, and the radical expansion of English-medium higher education in Europe (Coleman, 2006: 8).

Decline and Conflict

Kelly and Jones (2003: 26) noted the growing trend for modern language departments to cease teaching language, and to concentrate on literature or cultural studies. This trend has continued, with academic departments branching out into media studies and film, culture and business, in an attempt to retain academic status. This has been achieved with varying degrees of success around the country, as some departments have been closed, or face the threat of closure, because of low recruitment. Language teaching has increasingly been placed within a language centre, where students can study a language as an elective module within another degree, or study it as an extra-curricular activity (Bickerton, 2003; Coleman, 2004). Kelly and Jones (2003: 26) also note that these arrangements frequently lead to conflict between the department and the language centre. Teaching the language is now seen as a 'lesser activity' that can be done by academic-related staff, and is frequently undertaken by hourly-paid staff hired on an as-needed basis from native speakers working in other jobs in the local community.

The conflicts between those who retain academic status and the new class of language *teachers* are small compared with the potential conflict between MFL provision in general and TESOL/EAP staff when they are placed within the same centre. Modern foreign language teaching does not generate income to cover its costs, and rather than provide adequate internal subsidies, institutions most frequently require the cross-subsidy of MFL from TESOL/EAP commercial activities. In addition, the new MFL teachers frequently see TESOL/EAP teaching as 'less academic' than teaching an MFL. MFL students, for example, are easily found roles as English teachers or assistants for overseas placements, whereas it would be unthinkable for an EAP student to be given French or German teaching in the language centre. The residue of von Humboldt's legacy still drives hierarchies and power structures today, as Example 1 clearly shows.

Example 1

MFL activity is subsidised by the university at over a quarter of a million pounds per annum. MFL staff believe strongly that ability to communicate in an MFL is the most important skill a student can acquire, without which they are culturally and intellectually inept, being unable to see the world through the eyes of other peoples. Over the years, therefore, expenditure has grown to almost double the subsidy, and is cross-funded by EAP activities. More recently, MFL staff have been encouraged to generate income to cover their additional expenses and reduce dependence on the centre and EAP by offering language and cultural services for business, full-cost language courses for the community, translation services, and other innovative programmes. This has been resisted by MFL staff. They have argued that no one would pay for such courses or services, because people do not understand or realise the dire cultural and intellectual state into which they have sunk; nor do businesses recognise their need for cultural and linguistic insights. Nevertheless, an extensive language teaching programme should be available for students free of charge, and for the community at a heavily subsidised rate, to encourage the regeneration of culture and learning. TESOL/EAP staff teach throughout the year on foundation and presessional programmes, and on summer schools, in order to generate income, none of which is reinvested in their activities. MFL staff teach fewer hours and have no responsibilities from May to October, other than visiting the countries of the language they teach to maintain their contact with the language. They view themselves as 'teachers' and do not wish to engage in research or scholarship. Within the last few years an MFL practitioner replaced an applied linguist as Head of centre and all attempts to introduce reform or encourage research ceased. The only research-active members of staff left because they were marginalised and alienated by MFL teachers. The remaining TESOL staff are engaged purely in income-generating teaching to support MFL. As a result of the growing deficit the university has decided to axe any MFL activity that cannot break even once the subsidy is removed. TESOL/EAP finds itself in an 'anomalous' situation and its future is unclear.

In Example 1 the MFL teachers do not have the status of academics. It would be impossible to recruit anyone with an interest in research even if the will to do so were present; indeed, existing staff are fearful and resentful of anyone who conducts research. It has become a teaching activity staffed by teachers with interests and qualifications more suited to secondary school learning, and this has happened because of the decline in demand for advanced MFL learning at university. While demand is extremely high for English language, it is precisely this very demand that has led to its loss of academic status; treated as an income-generating activity by MFL (for survival) and the university (for income), it has become a mass-teaching operation.

This is not an isolated case. However, we should stress that this does not characterise the situation in all universities, as we shall see when looking at the data from the survey presented below.

The Success of English and Its Commercialisation

The fact that English has become the world's lingua franca is a matter of great controversy, and a source of conflict within Europe, as we have already seen. European countries fight with great vigour to keep their language among the listed 'working languages' for many reasons, including the perceived advantages of encouraging international communication with their citizens, economic growth, spreading the national culture, teaching the national language both at home and abroad, and strengthening national identity and pride (Ammon, 2006: 333). Their arguments are supported by appeal to the official policy of the European Union to promote linguistic diversity. Nevertheless, English is becoming the language of instruction in HE across the European Union at a startling rate (Coleman, 2006).

The need to communicate in English for global business, access to information and learning has created a market for English-medium instruction around the world, leading to a situation in which there is more provision than demand. International students are more mobile, and pay higher fees than home or European students; this is a source of income that is greatly desired by all institutions of higher education (Coleman, 2004). In this environment language education, particularly TESOL/EAP, has become highly commercialised. Even within Europe where there is a policy of language diversification, Coleman (2006: 3–5) notes:

> National self-interest in attracting fee-paying international students seems likely...to overtake any altruistic implementation of the Bologna Process, leaving the way free for market forces.

In short, 'The phrase "international students" increasingly means not the "organised mobility" of mutual exchanges, but the "spontaneous mobility" of fee-paying individuals'.

Example 2

With MFL in radical decline, a professor of a modern European language was appointed Head of School with a brief to balance the books. Within the School was a TESOL/EAP department that offered a range of EAP programmes and an MA in applied linguistics. From years of independent activity as an autonomous department it had built up a clientele with excellent word-of-mouth return business, experience in where to market and when, and substantial financial reserves. After the professor's appointment, members of the TESOL/EAP department were summoned to a consultation meeting, and as they were to learn quickly, 'consultations are invariably full and wide-ranging. They come in two flavours. The first and more common is window-dressing that helps to validate a decision long since taken' (Webb, 2005: 38). It was announced that English and EAP teaching would be moved into the language centre with all MFL teaching, and applied linguistics would move into the newly constituted MFL department that would concentrate on culture, media and film studies. This happened with surprising speed. The reserves helped offset losses for one year, and the new applied linguistics grouping was required to generate enough money to pay most of the infrastructure charges for the new department. With lack of investment and inability to take decisions about marketing in either applied linguistics or EAP there was a quick decline in recruitment. Within three years the new department of culture, media and film studies was told that it must shed staff to achieve target savings; applied linguistics staff were given compulsory redundancy and a plan was devised to outsource EAP teaching to an organisation that claimed it had the marketing skills to do what the university could not. The commercial organisation now undercuts the activities of the EAP unit in the language centre, and can guarantee university entry without the need to take an internationally recognised language test.

In this second example, the university undermined its own capacity to operate in the international market by treating its EAP and applied linguistics activities as a purely commercial enterprise designed to generate funds for its School and the university. The story shows one way in which the value of the activity can lead to its over-exploitation and demise, but it is not the only way in which it can happen.

UK HE is currently the target of commercial organisations seeking the outsourcing of TESOL/EAP provision precisely because it is the most lucrative activity. This commercialisation emphasises and embeds the notion that these activities are not academic, but pre-university teaching. Interviewing an anonymous employee from Exeter University, Shepherd reports her as saying:

> 'I am no longer on the payroll of the university', Moore [not her own name] says. I am working entirely for a commercial organisation, and I really don't like it. Opportunities for research under this new 'joint venture' have been taken away from me. Added to that, and as a result of this venture, the university now seems to treat international students as cash cows. It seems that we might have to work for more hours for less money as well. (Shepherd, 2007)

Shepherd reports that the commercial operation in question admits that it will employ lesser qualified staff at lower rates as their business expands, and university authorities argue that in an increasingly competitive environment it is essential for universities to look for new ways to recruit international students. As the commercial operations require lower fees than the university, this is one way to attract them.

It is against this background that the current study was undertaken.

Methodology and Data Collection

In January 2007 the websites of all UK HE providers were identified and placed into an Excel spreadsheet. Each web site was visited and an attempt made to find the TESOL/EAP providing department or unit within each institution. The number of clicks required to find the providing department ranged from two to 15. In total, 106 providers were identified. One department did not have any contact details, and communication with the main university contact email did not result in a reply. One further university only gave the contact details of an individual who had left the university some months previously. This reduced the total to 104. Of these, only 49 departments provided any information on the staff or listed the Head.[2] The remainder only gave generic email and postal enquiry contact details. A questionnaire was prepared and sent to a named individual where available, or to the generic contact address. The return rate was 20%, the majority coming from named mailings. This return rate is not unusual for survey research and is sufficient to draw conclusions when results are interpreted in conjunction with information from web sites and other sources. After the results had been summarised a number of telephone interviews were conducted to clarify and expand on comments from selected questionnaires of interest. Based on reports of commercialisation and outsourcing from a number of institutions, two further questionnaires were prepared, one for commercial organisations (Appendix 1) and one for the academic registrars of universities who had entered outsourcing or 'joint venture' agreements (Appendix 2).

Findings

TESOL/EAP providers

The previous sections report in general terms the responses of TESOL/EAP practitioners to the questionnaire. Each heading reflects the content and purpose of the sections of the survey instrument.

Organisation and activity

Only three of the providers were departments in their own right, and most were a unit or section within an academic department. Perhaps not surprisingly the majority were placed with MFL, but this was not always the case. Being placed in a Business School was the second most likely structural location. A smaller number were placed in Central Services or the International Office. The range of locations within the structure of the institution indicates the uncertainty institutions face about the place and role of TESOL/EAP. This was made clear by a number of responses that referred to their 'anomalous position' within the institution.

Of the three departments which were providers in their own right, two offered MFL as well as English. Only four of the responding providers did not offer MFL, but were specialist TESOL/EAP providers either in central services or autonomous units within an academic department. One of these units had offered MFLs in the past, but these had been phased out.

The providers who offered MFLs reported a range of relationships between MFL and EAP. For the most part the pattern was for MFL provision to be subsidised to some extent, while EAP was seen as income generating and possibly used to cross-fund other activities. The extent of cooperation between the two was generally minimal, amounting to sharing facilities, space and support staff. At its worst, there was open hostility between the two activities because of unequal working practices, the perceived unfairness in income generation and expenditure, and greater likelihood that MFL staff will be supported in a promotion application.

However, there are a few exceptions to this generalisation. In one academic department that contains both MFL and TESOL/EAP activities they report a synergy of interests, drawing on the expertise of both groups of staff to deliver innovative postgraduate programmes in language teaching, and develop jointly taught undergraduate degrees. This can be exceptionally productive in intercultural communication studies across a range of programmes. Income generated from activities in which all participate are ploughed back into opportunities for staff to engage in research and scholarship geared toward personal and professional development, as well as conducting research for programmes related to academic literacy. However, in this particular case the department is autonomous and financially independent, even though it is self-financing. Where the EAP unit is not allied to MFL there is generally less conflict, but it is not clear that their academic status is held to be any higher.

Most respondents said that they offered teacher training programmes, whether these are introductions to teaching or Masters in TESOL/applied linguistics. Perhaps not surprisingly, the independent academic departments reported having a range of students from taught postgraduate programmes to supervised PhD students, and one department reported that staff taught across programmes, including EAP and supervising research. However, half of the respondents reported a trend for the unit to become more isolated from academic departments that house postgraduate programmes, with their own teaching becoming more related to EAP and opportunities to contribute to postgraduate teaching declining.

Only two respondents, both from academic departments, reported that research was of extremely high priority. In one case, members of staff are reported to be encouraged to generate their own research profiles and to help them do this they are provided with periodic sabbaticals and internal support mechanisms such as seminar series and the opportunity to contribute to research projects. Another respondent reported that research was encouraged and that research activity was linked to promotion. However, in most cases respondents indicated that research had no place in their unit. Most respondents spoke with a single voice, saying that there was no encouragement to do research and that staff were expected to teach as many hours as could be fitted into the working week. This was also true of most of the units that delivered postgraduate programmes, and even one of the departments that also supervised research students. Given this result, we went back to sample web sites in the database to search for evidence that research was being conducted in any of the 104 targeted providers in the UK. Similar proportions were discovered to those in the sample returns.

Academic activity and entrepreneurship

Respondents almost unanimously claimed that the institution saw their activities as primarily entrepreneurial, and that their primary functions were to generate income and increase the number of international students applying to the university. Only two respondents claimed that they were not viewed in this way, one because all of the income generating activities had already been outsourced to a commercial provider. The commercial provider did not want the less lucrative activities and left those within the TESOL/EAP unit.

Not surprisingly therefore, commercial income was of most importance to all respondents, although MFL providers usually received some central grant for teaching, and some in-sessional EAP is also funded by central grants. However, many institutions expect the unit to provide an in-sessional programme and cross-fund this from commercial activities. Academic departments and some evening language classes attract lower levels of teaching income. No department or unit reported receiving anything for its research activity, even if a large number of staff were research active and being returned in the UK's periodic Research Assessment Exercise. Two respondents reported other sources of income: top slicing of international student fees for in-sessional provision, and departmental transfers for in-sessional programmes. This shows a wide range of arrangements for funding in-sessional EAP activities across institutions, reflecting an institutional uncertainty with how to deal with this kind of international student support.

Activities which generated the most income were foundation programmes and presessional (primarily summer) TESOL/EAP programmes. Only one respondent claimed that the highest income generation came from undergraduate and postgraduate provision, but this was also the academic department that was the outlier in every way in this sample. One further respondent indicated that a postgraduate programme was the most profitable, but that was only because foundation and presessional programmes had already been outsourced to a commercial organisation by the institution, and the unit had been instructed not to enter into competition with the new 'partner'.

Finally, apart from the autonomous departments, only one respondent indicated that any surplus, after costs and infrastructure charges, was retained by the unit.

EAP staffing and provision

Staffing for EAP provision is primarily on academic-related contracts, with fluctuations in staff numbers during the summer when larger numbers of international students attend presessional programmes. Staff on academic contracts are employed across the sector, but most of these are concentrated in the academic departments. In this sample, half of the staff reported on academic contracts were in one institution, our outlier. What is most notable is the trend to employ hourly paid, seasonal staff. This is reported in both TESOL/EAP and MFL activities where language learning is provided for the community (evening classes), or in two-hour slots for students studying full time on other degree programmes. There is clear evidence of the slow but widespread de-professionalism in employment practices, unless staff are employed in academic departments that require (and encourage) staff to be research active. Outsourcing operations to commercial organisations will speed up this trend.

One of the criticisms of commercial operations that have moved into universities is that they will be unable to understand the institution or talk to academic colleagues in other departments to design EAP programmes geared to their needs. Academic literacy, the argument goes, can only be successfully developed by professionals who are academically capable of understanding the communication needs of the students in relation to the academic communities of which they wish to become members.

From the survey results it appears that the majority of university providers have ad hoc academic contact with other departments, relying for the most part on individual course tutors to establish whatever personal contact they feel appropriate. Among these ad hoc contacts, the most frequent appear to be with Business Schools, many of whom actively inform the EAP providers of their requirements. In institutions where receiving departments have tailor-made courses (and sometimes pay for them directly) there is more contact at the planning phase. A number of institutions prepare post-course reports for students and send these to the receiving department. Only three respondents reported any formal contact between the EAP unit and the receiving departments. In one case this was a loose liaison arrangement, but with staff sitting on the Programme Boards of other departments. In the other two cases there is a contact person in each department, and the use of a coordinator to ensure that feedback and information from departments is incorporated into programme design and delivery. Feedback on student performance is also provided to the contact person. In one case courses are even taught collaboratively, but this is certainly not the norm.

The range of contact between TESOL/EAP units and receiving departments therefore varies tremendously, from very little ad hoc personal contact, to highly structured systems for initial input to course design through to feedback on student performance. Less academically integrated programmes are much more easily outsourced.

Testing

When outsourcing contracts are signed it has been widely reported that the commercial operator insists on using its own tests or other assessment procedures for exit from its own programmes and entry to the university on a programme of the student's choice. This bypasses the normal requirement for an IELTS, TOEFL or equivalent score at a particular level. This virtually guarantees entry to the university, and is part of the recruitment strategy of the commercial organisation.

Currently, half of the institutions in the sample returning questionnaires offer their own tests or assessments as an alternative to internationally recognised tests, and one said that such a test was in preparation. However, of these, three reported that the test was only used 'as a last resort' where it was not feasible or practical for a student to take an internationally recognised test by the decision date. In such cases, the internal test or staff recommendations were accepted by the institution. In the remaining institutions, evidence for the validity of the local test rested for the most part on a correlational study, the results of which are not publicly available, and on the use of external consultants to work on the design of the test, or, in one case, to provide accreditation. Only one institution provides full information on the content, properties, claims and evidence to support test use, and places this in the public domain. None of the institutions use their test as a replacement for internationally recognised tests, and their web sites still state entry and exit criteria in terms of these tests. Nevertheless, failure to provide more information on test use and suitability for purpose weakens the case for resistance to the use of alternative tests or assessments.

Outsourcing

Two-thirds of respondents reported that their institution had been approached by a commercial organisation with a view to outsourcing activities with which they were primarily concerned. These organisations were only interested in the most lucrative parts of the operation, including foundation programmes and EAP provision. The approach was made to senior university management and all respondents reported that they were informed about the approach and initial presentations made by the commercial organisation only after the event. In three cases the university management rejected the proposals and the departments/units concerned only discovered this *post hoc*. In two cases where discussions on outsourcing are still underway, one unit has not been consulted at all, while the other has been invited to comment. What is clear from the evidence is that just because a TESOL/EAP department or unit does not know of an approach made to the institution, it cannot assume that such an approach has not been made or that discussions for outsourcing are not underway. In most of the cases where outsourcing has taken place, by the time the department/unit is consulted the decision has already been made.

Where approaches have been made, whether rejected or accepted, what is offered by the commercial organisation is identical. The first promise is to boost international student numbers entering undergraduate and graduate programmes at the university. The second is to invest in the university infrastructure with particular reference to buildings in which to house and teach the incoming international students. Entry requirements to foundation and/or EAP courses are usually lowered, as are prices, to achieve targets. Outputs to the university at the other end are usually determined by the organisation's internal assessment procedures. Examples of the kinds of claims made are illustrated by the following example: students are admitted with 'GCSE or equivalent' in their subject, and IELTS 3.0–3.5 or lower; the organisation claims that within two years these students will have achieved the equivalent of IELTS 6.5 on their own assessments, *and* be ready for direct entry into the *second* year of undergraduate study. While language professionals realise that the claims are bizarre, they appear to be accepted at face value by many senior university staff.

Discussion

The data collected and the analysis of information from web sites suggests that TESOL/EAP units are being pushed further and further into the role of income generation through teaching large numbers of international students. Staff are increasingly being treated as 'teachers' with no remit for scholarship or research. Programmes are commercially sensitive, and are frequently cut at very short notice if numbers fall to below financially viable levels. One respondent said that the staff in their unit had been driven to teach for so many hours that no other activities were possible, and it had become extremely difficult to manage links with receiving departments or spend time on designing programmes that prepared students for target academic literacies. It was admitted that what they were being required to do could easily be done by a commercial organisation with 'lesser-qualified teachers'.

Among the more optimistic respondents there was a sense that the existing knowledge and experience within the university unit would be enough to defend against any approach to the institution by a commercial organisation. Nevertheless, there was a recognition among some respondents that their unit and the commercial organisation were operating in the same market. This reflects one of the deepest crises of TESOL/EAP provision in UK HE: is it qualitatively different from what others can provide? If it is, what makes it different, and how can this be demonstrated? Presumably, the answer lies in what makes any university department different from a non-university teaching operation: its research, research-led teaching, an informed approach to course design and delivery, a scholarly and questioning environment, the study of assessment and language acquisition.[3] But these are precisely what is being denied to TESOL/EAP units as part of the commercialisation of language education.

Commercial organisations (see Appendix 1)

The questions in Appendix 1 were circulated to three of the main commercial organisations currently running outsourced operations in the UK, two owned by media groups and the third by a property developer. The questions were broadly designed to cover the key issues that have been raised with outsourcing, namely: testing and assessment, claims relating to the rate of student progress, the provision of academic literacy skills (including cooperation with receiving departments), quality control and staffing policy and qualifications.

Two responses were received, both of which declined to address any of the questions posed. One response claimed that the relevance of this research and the questions in Appendix 1 to their activities is marginal, in that their interest was in providing 'subdegree' programmes to a host university. While it is incumbent upon the reader to interpret a reluctance to respond to the questions in Appendix 1, it is clear that this particular organisation sees the foundation and TESOL/EAP programmes offered within universities as 'subdegree' or 'pre-university' teaching, and convincing some universities authorities of this does not appear to be unduly difficult. The analysis provided above gives some insight into why this is the case. The second response argued that the premises upon which the questions are based were false. The response claimed that all programmes and assessment were validated and controlled by the 'partner' university, delivered by professional staff, and subject to 'robust' assessment criteria. These, it is claimed, are no different to the arrangements that universities have had with private preparation colleges for many years. There is some evidence to suggest that such claims can be maintained. However, this argument also presupposes that TESOL/EAP is a pre-university teaching activity, rather than a university level education in academic literacies that are also the subject of educational and applied linguistic research. The argument is an attempt to destroy the justification for an academic discipline, thus creating a single non-academic market for a lucrative activity.

Academic registrars (see Appendix 2)

In order to triangulate on the findings, the questions in Appendix 2 were sent to the academic registrars of all universities that have outsourced TESOL/EAP activities (or entered into 'partnerships', but left their own unit in place), and to those of universities that are currently considering outsourcing. Four responses were received, three of which declined to address any of the questions posed. The three that declined were similar in claiming that no outsourcing of university provision had taken place; the respondents assume that their own positions are ones of 'partnership' or 'joint venture'.[4]

In the case of the one response to the questions, the university had decided to retain the use of international tests for decision-making. The academic managers reported the commercial provider had not made any claims regarding the progress rates of students, only that the overall student experience would be improved. It was also clear that the university had gone to considerable trouble to ensure that programme coordinators from the commercial operation met with relevant subject specialists, and that the academic activities were to be overseen by the university. The spokesperson did, however, make it clear that the main reason for the arrangements was the need to tap into the 'partner' organisation's international marketing expertise, and acquire the promised £35 million investment in infrastructure. These are very powerful reasons for outsourcing provision in the short term, where universities fear falling market share of the profitable international student market.

Information on this particular operation from two independent sources indicated that prior to the 'partnership', the university unit suffered from the kinds of problems described earlier in this chapter. The commercial arrangements do appear to have improved the situation, but have nevertheless introduced the 'language-school ethos' that sees the activity as pre-university teaching, and the resulting loss of status and de-professionalisation of staff transferred to the employment of the new provider.

Outsourcing has been termed a 'partnership', even though these agreements, under whatever name, have been responsible for the take-over of entire departments (Shepherd, 2007), the removal of the more profitable teaching operation from the department, or the slow demise of a unit that is left. Respondents to the questionnaire indicated unanimously that these agreements have led to takeovers, or the decline of a unit that cannot compete with the 'partner' that has lower operating costs and (sometimes) the right to guarantee university entry. It is clear that the university authorities that enter into such agreements do not feel the need to acknowledge that what they are doing is 'outsourcing' because they agree with the commercial 'partner' that this activity is 'subdegree' teaching, or a pre-university activity.

Conclusions

When discussing the article by Shepherd (2007) above, we noted the argument put forward that outsourcing of provision from universities to commercial operations resulted in lower fees, thus enabling the university to become competitive. Our first observation must be that this is true of any activity undertaken by a university that maintains a large infrastructure and encourages research-led teaching. The argument therefore applies to all teaching activities and services. The university administration could be outsourced to a professional management company, or teaching engineering to a major construction enterprise. If a university argues that it needs to outsource in order to operate more effectively in the international student marketplace, it is arguably the case that the International Office should be closed and its operation outsourced first. Computing services or human resources could also be outsourced to dedicated providers. However, no such considerations are being mooted. The argument only applies to the teaching of international students in institutions where senior management has become convinced that TESOL/EAP provision is a subdegree/pre-university activity.

We have argued that this has come about because of the commercialisation of language teaching and the de-professionalisation of the activity within universities. In some cases this erosion has taken place in spite of serious attempts to avoid the change, but increase in teaching loads and lack of encouragement for the discipline has led to an inability to engage with the research and scholarship that informs the teaching of academic literacies. In other cases language centres have created a teaching-only community that resists engagement with research and scholarship, and is seen as anomalous by research active departments. In other cases, the TESOL/EAP unit has never had the opportunity to become 'academically respectable' because it is a central service along with cleaning and catering, or a recruitment tool within the International Office.

This research has revealed that the most successful TESOL/EAP units are those that exist within independent academic departments, offering a broad range of qualifications, including pre-sessional and foundation programmes, undergraduate modules, taught postgraduate programmes, and the supervision of research students. Within this environment it is more likely that formal links will occur between EAP provision and the receiving departments, and that staff will have the time, opportunity and encouragement to engage with research and let this impact upon teaching at all levels. We have come across one example of such a department that includes MFL provision, but this is a highly unusual case. For the most part, these academic departments focus upon applied linguistics, TESOL and EAP; MFL provision is frequently within a different faculty.

This is not to say that TESOL/EAP units or sections within other structures do not wish to be seen as university level, academic activities. Some achieve a great deal; but their structural location makes it difficult to achieve academic standing within the institution, and if they are placed in central services or the International Office, the ambivalence of the institution regarding their academic status has already been implicitly stated. University administrators are also easily tempted to de-professionalise the discipline in the search for new sources of income.

TESOL/EAP units need to look at their position in the institution and evaluate how they rate in the various areas and activities discussed in this chapter. They need to look at their staffing policies, their academic profiles and practices. Uncomfortable as it may be, the further away they are from equivalence with other academic departments, the more vulnerable they will be to the claim that they are doing 'subdegree' or 'pre-university' work, and therefore more susceptible to outsourcing.

Acknowledgements

I would like to thank the many people who responded to the questionnaires in such a relatively short period of time. My thanks are also due to Charles Alderson (Lancaster University) and Mary Anne Ansell (Oxford Brookes University) for their comments on an earlier draft of this chapter.

Notes

1. The questionnaire is not reproduced in this chapter due to length restrictions. The format closely followed the structure of the report of the findings shown in this chapter.
2. This is highly unusual. University departments normally use staff details and activities to attract students. Many of the websites actually advertise 'highly qualified and experienced staff' as one advantage of studying at the institution but do not provide any further information.
3. EAP has a long and distinguished history as an academic discipline, the early period of which was exceptionally well documented in Swales (1985). More recent treatments of the academic literacies and EAP related research can be found in Johns *et al.* (1997), Swales (2001) and Hyland (2006).
4. The claim that these are 'joint ventures' rather than 'outsourcing' has suffered a setback since the Advertising Standards Authority has ordered INTO to remove references to the misleading phrase 'university-led initiative' from its advertising: see 'High Principals' in Private Eye No. 1180, 1–29 March 2007, p. 7.

References

Ammon, U. (2006) Language conflicts in the European Union: On finding a politically acceptable and practicable solution for EU institutions that satisfies diverging interests. *International Journal of Applied Linguistics* 16 (3), 319–338.

Bickerton, D. (2003) *Institution Wide Language Programmes.* London: LTSN Subject Centre for Languages, Linguistics and Area Studies. On WWW at: http://www.cilt.org.uk/infos/rtf/informationsheet85.rtf. Accessed 19.11.08.

CILT. *Statistics: Languages in Education.* On WWW at http://www.cilt.org.uk/research/statistics/education/index.htm. Accessed 19.11.08.

Coleman, J.A. (2004) Modern Languages in British universities: Past and present. *Arts and Humanities in Higher Education* 3 (2), 149–162.

Coleman, J.A. (2006) English-medium teaching in European higher education. *Language Teaching* 39, 1–14.

Foucault, M. (1975) *Surveiller et Punir.* Paris: Gallimard.

Godenzzi, J.C. (2006) Spanish as a lingua franca. *Annual Review of Applied Linguistics* 26, 100–124.

Hacking, I. (1990) *The Taming of Chance.* Cambridge: Cambridge University Press.

Hyland, K. (2006) *English for Academic Purposes: An Advanced Resource Book.* Oxford and New York: Routledge.

Johns, A.M., Long, M.H. and Richards, J.C. (1997) *Text, Role and Context: Developing Academic Literacies.* Cambridge: Cambridge University Press.

Kelly, M. and Jones, D. (2003) *A New Landscape for Languages.* London: Nuffield Foundation.

Marshall, K. (2002) *General Introduction to Modern Languages in Today's UK Universities.* London: LTSN Subject Centre for Languages, Linguistics and Area Studies. On WWW at http://www.lang.ltsn.ac.uk/resources/goodpractice.aspx?resourceid=1392. Accessed 19.11.08.

Nietzsche, F. (1888) *Twilight of the Idols.* Reprinted in A. Ridley and J. Norman (eds) (2005) *The Anti-Christ, Ecce Homo, Twilight of the Idols, and Other Writings.* Cambridge: Cambridge University Press.

Robey, D. (2002) *Annual Update on Statistics from UCAS on Modern Foreign Language Applications and Acceptances to UK Universities*. London: UCAS. On WWW at http://www.lang.ltsn.ac.uk/resourcedownloads.aspx?resourceid=610&filename=ucaslangs_stats_2002.rtf. Accessed 19.11.08.

Seidlhofer, B., Breiteneder, A. and Pitzl, M.L. (2006) English as a lingua franca in Europe: Challenges for applied linguists. *Annual Review of Applied Linguistics* 26, 3–34.

Shepherd, J. (2007) Foreign wars. *Guardian*, 20 February.

Swales, J. (1985) *Episodes in ESP*. London: Pergamon.

Swales, J. (1998) Language, science and scholarship. *Asian Journal of English Language Teaching* 8, 1–18.

Swales, J. (2001) EAP-related linguistic research: An intellectual history. In J. Flowerdew and M. Peacock (eds) *Research Perspectives on EAP*. Cambridge: Cambridge University Press.

UCAS. *Statistics Online*. On WWW at http://www.ucas.ac.uk/figures/archive/subject/index.html. Accessed 19.11.08.

von Humboldt, W. (1836) On the structural variety of human language and its influence on the intellectual development of mankind. From *Über die Verschiedenheit des menschlichen Sprachbaues und ihren Einfluss auf die geistige Entwickelung des Menschengeschlechts* (Chap. 19). Berlin: F. Dümmler.

Watts, C.J. (2003) *Decline in the Take-up of Modern Languages at Degree Level*. London: Anglo-German Foundation for the Study of Industrial Society.

Webb, N. (2005) *The Dictionary of Bullshit*. London: Robson Books.

Wright, S. (2006) French as a lingua franca. *Annual Review of Applied Linguistics* 26, 35–60.

Appendix 1: Questions for Commercial Providers

Your organisation claims that its own testing and assessment procedures are valid for the purposes of entry and exit from your programmes. Exit guarantees entrance to the University programme of their choice.

Why does your organisation insist that it should not use IELTS or equivalent internationally recognised tests?

What validity evidence do you have to support the claims you make for your own tests/assessment procedures?

It is generally accepted that such evidence be placed in the public domain. As such, I would be grateful if you could send any associated documentation for independent evaluation.

Entry criteria to your facilities appear to be set much lower than a University EAP department would normally set. The claimed rate of progress is also substantially higher.

What score gain studies have you conducted to establish the claimed rate of progress?

How are exit scores linked to statements of likely performance in an academic environment?

Once again, I would be grateful to see relevant research reports.

In the provision of academic literacy skills it is critical that the syllabus match the requirements of the academic research communities into which students are about to enter.

What strategies do you have in place to ensure that the syllabus in your institutions is closely geared to the needs of EAP students?

I would be particularly interested to know of specific areas of cooperation and projects between EAP staff and content experts in ensuring alignment of provision with need.

When delivering academic programmes in HE there is always the question of quality control.

How do you intend to monitor quality in your centres? Will you adopt the same procedures as the University itself?

It has been widely reported that your organisation is capable of delivering these services at a much reduced cost to the institution and fee to the student.

Is this achieved by utilising staff who would otherwise not be employable by a University on the grounds of lack of qualifications or skills?

Do you re-employ University staff at rates lower than they would receive on HE pay scales?

The web sites associated with centres that you have already set up in UK universities do not list staff, qualifications, research interests or areas of expertise. Would you make available your staffing policy and pay scales for comparison?

Appendix 2: Questions for Academic Registrars

(1) What evidence did you obtain from the commercial provider that their own assessment procedures (rather than the use of international

language tests) were reliable and valid for entry to your institution, and how was this evidence evaluated?
(2) Commercial providers typically claim that they can get learners from a very low language competence to a level suitable for University entry in a shorter period of time than that claimed by University EAP departments/units. What evidence did you obtain from the commercial provider to suggest that this was an accurate claim?
(3) What strategies have you put in place to ensure that the commercial provider works closely with academic departments and content experts to ensure the alignment of provision with the needs of academic communities of practice?
(4) Is teaching in this area something your institution feels is fundamentally a 'non-University activity' in the sense that it is somehow 'not academic', and can therefore be outsourced without any concern? If this is the case, would you consider outsourcing any other teaching/research activity?

Chapter 7
The Role of Micropolitics in Multinational, High-Stakes Language Assessment Systems

MARK CROSSEY

Introduction

This chapter looks at how micropolitics can become decisive in attempts to develop educational policy in an international context. I argue that the success of such initiatives is largely determined by an interplay between macro and micro politics, and that the force and nature of the latter is very much dependent on the former. I explore this phenomenon on several different levels and argue that educational policy formulation can, in certain contexts, become more politics than education.

I offer a case study, that of efforts of member states of the North Atlantic Treaty Organisation (NATO) to standardise language proficiency testing according to commonly agreed descriptors of language proficiency, and use the example to argue that a direct relationship between macro and micro politics is decisive in the shaping and success or otherwise of such initiatives. Furthermore, I show how 'reform according to international standards' can be explicitly used by groups and individuals for political or personal ends within their own contexts and also how the success of change in educational policy is sometimes determined solely by a propitious local political climate.

Background: Political Motivations for International Cooperation on Language Education and Evaluation

There is nothing new in the assertion that educational policy can often be a vehicle for overt or covert political intentions. To recognise educational assessment in particular as a powerful tool in national state governance is an increasingly common phenomena and point of debate in the academic world (Madaus, 1990, in Shohamy, 2001: 99), if not as yet consciously in wider society, and case studies (Shohamy, 2001: 43–85) illustrate how implementation of policy change in the field of educational assessment might be seen to be related to the desire to:

- Use testing mechanisms in the implementation of a 'gate-keeping' policy. This might be for purposes of controlling access to higher education, certain jobs or positions in society, or indeed access to a given society by means of immigration control.
- 'Improve' or alter educational standards, practices and/or philosophies; the nature of which is now to be decided by a centralised authority charged with testing reform.
- Threaten or judge individual educational institutions or methodologies within a system, namely those which do not (or are not anticipated to) 'come up to scratch' under the new assessment policy.
- Discriminate against certain groups on the basis of ethnicity or political beliefs or status.
- Use testing reform to increase the status and attraction of a given subject or language, thereby influencing enrolment.

However, I believe that the nature of such political dynamics can differ and be even more complex in the less usual instance of a multilateral policy-making context and in which, officially at least, no one player or group of players is in control of the process. Here we go beyond the above large-scale political issues as individuals, and their sometimes more everyday motives, assume a more prominent role. In this chapter I argue that a combination of factors in such a context can lead to an almost unparalleled educational and political situation. I demonstrate how a range of complex macropolitical issues, when dealing with 'commonly agreed international educational standards', can combine and reinforce themselves to the extent of causing flux in international policy. However, I also go on to illustrate how this flux, in turn, leads directly to local micropolitical phenomena and tensions. The field of English language testing is arguably almost uniquely sensitive in this respect, as it increasingly embodies a combination of powerful political elements in the 21st century human experience: 'objective' and high-stakes assessment, often directly managed or commissioned by the state; language, which is a powerful political weapon in all societies, and the particular contemporary political nature of the English language, with its associations with business and commerce, immigration and its role in many areas of 'international' culture (cinema, pop music, etc.). In this multilateral context, policy change on language assessment can be used (in terms of face validity) as an important political gesture related to integration to international organisations. Furthermore, the true nature of the validity and reliability of the officially reformed testing mechanism is also sometimes seen as indicative of wider preparations of a given candidate for integration to an international body. Language assessment, as an ostensibly 'noncontentious' field, can also serve the political goal of fostering cooperation between nations in a given region or with a similar foreign policy. This can also be because of historical hostility, where the field of cooperation on language testing is seen by stakeholders as a useful tool for encouraging dialogue between states and even, on occasion, (as I illustrate in this chapter) between those in a state of war. Another factor might be a conscious policy decision to use international directives as a vehicle to wrest control over an important area of national governance, namely assessment, from powerful foreign bodies; this having implications for linguistic and cultural validity, revenue, political control and the development of local testing expertise (Tsagari, 2004: 38). Related to this, the standardisation (or centralisation) of national assessment systems may be seen by government as a method of regaining the faith of key stakeholders in state sector testing. This can be seen with efforts to reform state school-leaving certification examinations in Central and Eastern Europe in the late-1990s and early 21st century (see Pižorn & Nagy, this volume). Again, reference to 'international standards', in this case the Council of Europe Framework, has been key to political acceptance.

But there are other considerations beyond the clear macropolitical issues of this chapter's multilateral case study. Where a given member of the multilateral community under focus is undergoing a degree of societal flux, educational policy can become purely a vehicle for the political agendas of powerful individuals and groups, and even become largely divorced from the authentic educational community. A context of large scale societal change can lead to the following discernible influences in the shaping of educational policy:

- A purely local or individual interpretation of 'international standards', with no validation, either internal or international, of the claimed implementation of such standards.
- The situation of flux apparently being seen (at least by some parties) to be used by foreign individuals and/or agencies keen to impose their own national or cultural agendas.
- An assertion of control by certain individuals or groups over high-profile and fashionable educational reform processes in order to, ironically, maintain a status quo.

It is obvious that, in the particular instance of attempting to develop a multilateral policy on educational assessment, the process will at some point become hindered or even arrested by the issue of ownership: there are currently no mechanisms of governance on the international political scene which are able to secure successful public ownership and administration of a multilateral assessment tool of any kind. In the case of testing, the phenomenon of political ownership is particularly potent, as it is the process of testing and subsequent certification which determines much in the modern human experience.

In the case study central to this discussion, I argue that 'overriding' and 'official' multilateral policies are often negated by differing local or individual political agendas. The input of projects sponsored by foreign governments is also studied against the background of these micropolitical influences. I argue that the success of such projects (at least against project baseline measures) is often determined by these influences, which are often not openly discussed, quantified or even studied during the project design stage. The case study used to support this argument is that of the attempts of militaries to come to an understanding on English language proficiency levels in order to delegate staff to peacekeeping missions in sensitive and/or dangerous contexts.

The Impact of Macropolitics on 'International Standards': The Example of Attempts to Standardise Language Testing According to NATO Language Testing Proficiency Descriptors

Background: NATO and language testing

The need for international recognition of national foreign language assessment within the North Atlantic Treaty Organisation relates to greatly increased cooperation in professional and political arenas such as international peacekeeping and disaster relief operations, along with postings to headquarter structures such as NATO HQ in Brussels and SHAPE (Supreme Headquarters of Allied Powers in Europe) at Mons. However, I believe that NATO is unable to meet its own stated linguistic goals due to constraints in fully implementing a language training and assessment policy. The provenance of all these constraints is fundamentally macropolitical. Unless these constraints are somehow removed, it is hard to see how NATO member states will be able to successfully resolve their collective difficulties with the evaluation of foreign languages. This is because, first and foremost, there is currently no one official body within these organisations which has the ability to design and fully implement workable and valid language testing guidelines and specifications. But the issue is also arguably compounded by a lack of comprehension of the nature of language proficiency assessment at military command level, and no consistent channels of communication between educators and those responsible for military education policy implementation. In turn, the lack of coordinated and consistently enforced language testing policy within the NATO organisation has led to a perceived dominance of English language native speakers in decision-making in its command structures and hence direction of its political policy (Crossey, 2005). Controversially, the 2002 Stanag 6001 ('BILC Amplification') document (essentially an updated and more detailed interpretation of the original 1976 'Stanag 6001' document; which sets out descriptors of proficiency levels on which national testing systems of NATO members are to be based) describes the optimum proficiency level (5) as 'Educated Native Speaker', and this reflects an apparent institutionalised discrimination in favour of English native-speaker NATO member delegations (Canada, UK and United States). International English is here understood according to a native-speaker model [often now seen as an anachronism (Graddol, 2006: 115)]. This is surely an irony, given the necessary prevalence of non-native speaker communication at most levels of the organisation.

My case study necessarily focuses more upon the newer testing boards of former Warsaw Pact states, of which I have several years' close working experience. Key to this particular context is the political backdrop to high stakes testing within militaries undergoing profound structural and psychological transformation. However, concomitant to this analysis must be a general overview of testing throughout NATO, as the issue is far wider than simply expecting new members to adapt to the rules of the club. Does the club communicate its rules clearly and can it ensure that existing members implement these effectively? Also salient to this case are the working relationships between foreign agencies involved in Stanag 6001 implementation and their host Ministries of Defence (MODs); relationships between member states and relationships between the foreign agencies; and how language testing has become a central area of conflict between forces of reform and status quo within those militaries acceding to NATO, and how this situation has come about. It is also necessary to consider the attitude to language training policy held to date by NATO as a body; have these attitudes led to the perceived dominance of English language native speakers in the command structures of these organisations?

It would be injudicious, when analysing cooperation between militaries, not to compare the historical background and national profile of forces involved. Even a superficial comparison of the history and current issues facing the forces of long-term, new and would-be NATO member states gives an idea of the diverse contexts involved. For example, since its declaration of independence in 1991, Ukraine has had to create a military force from the remnants of Soviet military regions (consciously created to avoid association with the USSR's republic boundaries, in order to discourage any fledgling national military consciousness). This meant creating a huge (by European standards) structure from regional power bases with their related political dissonances, and all this in the context of chronic underfunding. The military in Ukraine, then, has found itself very much at the forefront of societal flux. The UK military, conversely, has a deeply entrenched regimental tradition, empowering it with a deep sense of tradition and pride but also arguably lending it to be somewhat resistant to change.

The 'Old NATO' was primarily designed as a Cold War alliance to counter the perceived threat of Soviet expansionism. The organisation has without doubt faced an identity crisis over the last decade at least. While members such as France have long been seen as hesitant towards the organisation (arguably more so following the US initiation of the 'War on Terror' in late 2001), growing reticence on the part of some long-term European NATO members towards the perceived dominance of the United States in NATO began in the early 21st century to manifest itself in discussions on the formation of a separate EU force, leading to growing concerns on the part of the United States' key allies in Europe on the effect of this proposed force on transatlantic relationships. It is clearly in the realm of speculation as to what degree there is a conscious policy to establish NATO as a key tool in the 'War on Terror', although some point to signs that this is indeed what the United States in particular would like:

> We're deconstructing the old NATO to build a new one to meet the threat of terrorism and weapons of mass destruction. (Nicholas Burns, US ambassador to the alliance at the organisation's 2002 Reykjavik summit)

The belief of some is that the organisation has always primarily served to satisfy US interests, and that the current attempt to redefine its role is bringing this characteristic more sharply into focus. At the time of writing though, the organisation continues to provide peacekeeping forces to key trouble spots and still has the commitment of most members to provide forces for these. How then, if at all, does NATO's policy on language training and testing reflect overall strategic objectives?

The expansion of NATO and subsequent increase in importance of English

The role of English language training in the military received greatly increased attention following the applications of former soviet satellite states to join NATO in the early-1990s, along with the global growth in provision to peace support operations, which is seen by many participating nations as beneficial in terms of easing political tensions in key conflict zones, as good training ground for personnel and (particularly in the case of those of poorer nations) as potentially lucrative for personnel. Similarly, language testing (in particular of English) in the military sphere as a whole can be very high-stakes. Research carried out by the British Council's Peacekeeping English Project ('PEP') in Ukraine shows very clearly the impact of professional use of English in life-threatening peace support situations:

> In December last year, K. served as a UN observer of the recent cease-fire between government and rebel forces in the Dafur region of Sudan. Before departing, K. acknowledged that good English was one of the principal reasons he was chosen for the mission as all communication, both between the UN observers themselves and with the warring factions would invariably be in English. When I asked whether interpreters would be used, he laughed and replied that they (the observers) would be operating as small mobile multinational teams patrolling and monitoring highly volatile areas. The presence of interpreters would, if anything, be a hindrance and would place an extra strain on resources. 'And what happens', he says, 'if we are attacked or see refugees being attacked? In such situations there isn't time for somebody to be sitting down translating things, as lives, possibly our own, will be at stake'. (British Council News, summer 2006)

However, it is also the case that the few examples of methodical research into the use of English on peace support operations (arguably the most high-stakes use of English in militaries) have had little or no effect on language training policy (Crossey, 2005). Militaries generally have a poor track record of commissioning or acting upon such research, which is usually inspired by individual research interests or the needs of external agencies. In many militaries, this approach to educational management has meant that teaching and testing staff are left with neither significant guidance nor responsibility for development of tuition, curricula or testing. There is little distinction here between long-term and new NATO members. The UK, for example, only relatively recently took serious steps to 'standardise the Stanag', with the awarding of a UK MOD contract to the University of Westminster in 2003, leading to the 'MODLEB' English examination suite. However, even after this move private UK providers still felt free to offer Stanag certification to foreign officers studying on their English courses in the UK. This has led to considerable confusion and political embarrassment on the part of other NATO member states who, when presented with certificates by officers returning from UK courses which obviously displayed a mismatch with their own levels, have on occasion felt unable to recognise them for posting purposes.

What is perhaps most difficult for the testing profession to understand about NATO's assessment of foreign languages is that, despite the insistence of many NATO Ministries of Defence ('MOD's) that Stanag 6001 certification in English proficiency be compulsory for large numbers of staff and postings, many member states or organisational HQs are unable to evidence reliable testing mechanisms (Green &Wall, 2005: 384). In fact, partially due to intervention (in the form of ELT programmes) by foreign agencies such as the British Council Peacekeeping English Project ('PEP') and its US analogue organisation, the Defense Language Institute ('DLI'), but also perhaps due to misconceptions of the true nature of NATO's 'membership requirements' by prospective member states, it is clear that most efforts in recent years to reform testing have been on the part of the new and prospective member states of central and eastern Europe and central Asia (Green & Wall, 2005: 381). Given the unique environment of the military, with its very high-stakes target language use scenarios, along with a culture of ostensibly unquestioned order and the associated very high status of official documentation and numerical data [always a powerful tool in assessment (Shohamy, 2001: 21–22)] this overall failure to address the issue of foreign language assessment should be of particular concern to the testing community. Crossey (2003) cites the potential effects of lack of standardisation within national Stanag testing systems, against both national and international criteria, as firstly, constant flux in terms of impact upon course and curricula design by national military ELT providers, as each tries to interpret a 'moving target', not sufficiently rooted in the Stanag 6001 document or national specifications; secondly, a lack of consistency in standards of international appointment decisions based on Stanag 6001 certification; and thirdly, an inability to draw any meaningful conclusions concerning either reliability or validity of the tests, due to a lack of consistency from session to session, in test level, content and administration. The comparative lack of resources devoted to language test development in many NATO states (Boyle, 2001: 30; Green & Wall, 2005: 388–389) implies that poor standardisation within the Stanag 6001 assessment system is not simply a national issue, but one which must significantly impact upon the working of the organisation; that is, if one accepts that foreign language skills are indispensable to interoperability.

Stanag 6001 multilateral recognition: The current picture

The decision to introduce guidance on a standardised understanding of common language proficiency testing (Stanag 6001) was taken by NATO in 1976. There is little documented evidence on the original development of this policy. However, as momentum grew in the late 1990s to assist the acceding states in their efforts to increase English language proficiency levels, it became clear that standardisation had not in reality yet been achieved by the organisation.

Bilateral and multilateral recognition of STANAG certification within NATO is entirely dependent on local policy-makers. This is illustrated in the phenomenon of 'nostrification', or the practice of local conversion of certificates issued abroad following a reduced assessment (often an oral interview). The practice is used by several European MODs but appears (according to a study of the situation conducted by the British Council in early 2006) ad hoc and often based more upon political considerations (some states automatically recognise the certificates of partners without any further assessment because, for example, these others offer free ELT courses; and others because NATO HQ organs apparently 'favour' the tests of these nations). This survey also revealed a strong awareness that member states are testing at different levels. The conundrum is whether to automatically recognise such foreign certification in the spirit of partnership, or to rigorously adhere to local assessment procedures and standards. In fact, both have been the case, with resulting difficulties in terms of (a) feelings of resentment on the part of locally-tested staff who feel they have been tested at a higher level, and (b) political difficulties between partner nations, where one nation's certification has been effectively discredited, often by new or soon-to-be member states who have taken advantage of free or subsidised courses offered to senior staff. But what is the answer, given such lack of standardised testing across the organisation? Not to recognise Stanag certificates issued by a partner military is, in effect, to openly state that standardisation of assessment within the organisation is a fiction. The alternative is to accept responsibility for posting issues, or even accidents, which may follow should the foreign certification turn out to be a poor representation of true proficiency levels.

The decision by the governments of the United States, UK and several other NATO members states (including Canada, Denmark and The

Netherlands) to directly invest in the English language training programmes of central and eastern Europe in the late-1990s heightened attention to the problems these states faced in acquiring 'Interoperability English' in a comparatively short space of time. But this work also began to more openly reveal differing interpretations of Stanag 6001 proficiency levels throughout NATO; partially due to a perceived complacency on the part of some long-term NATO states who have also in fact experienced chronic difficulties in the field (Crossey, 2005; Green & Wall, 2005: 384) but also due to a near-total lack of official discussion and agreement on a whole range of issues, including test content, format, and duration of validity of certificates.

Overview of Standardisation Efforts to Date: The Role of Micropolitics

There have been several attempts to coordinate work on Stanag 6001 testing. However, these have very often not been initiated by NATO as an organisation, largely due to macropolitical factors, some of which have been described above. This means that the initiative has often been left to external bodies, individual member states and committed individuals.

NATO itself: The Bureau for International Language Coordination

At the Oslo (2002) conference of the Bureau for International Language Coordination ('BILC') this organisation stated its claim to be 'NATO's source of expertise on language training matters' (from BILC website). Many delegates are ministry officials or military officers with responsibility for language training policy. The body has also created special interest groups staffed by these same delegates, one of which is tasked with Stanag 6001 testing and, in 2002, this group produced amplifications of the 1976 Stanag document. This was widely welcomed as a significant development by many member and accession states. However, a survey conducted within the Peacekeeping English Project in February 2006 revealed that no NATO members or accession states had yet implemented changes to their testing according to the amplification, and that, when changes had taken place, they were apparently piecemeal or restricted to the testing of English and implemented not by force of national directives but rather by individuals with varying degrees of official authority. NATO directives on language testing cannot be consistently enforced nor punitive measures taken against members who visibly fail to comply. However, the profile of the BILC testing special interest group at this time (some members were civil servants with no professional background in language training or testing) probably did not prove much of an incentive for the by-now more experienced testers of several NATO boards. However, BILC has since appeared to have recognised this weakness and has been more recently attempting to use genuine testing expertise from throughout the organisation in the design of a new BILC Benchmark Test, or 'BAT' (Vasilj-Begovic, 2006).

Foreign agency contribution

While foreign agency initiatives have the undoubted advantage of being spearheaded by professional ELT staff, as opposed to NATO policy-makers, motives behind such work have occasionally been questioned (Green & Wall, 2005: 392). The two main players have been the United States and the UK. The US Defense Language Institute has been heavily involved in direct language teaching in militaries, particularly those of Central and Eastern Europe, since the mid-1990s. UK input has largely been represented in the form of the British Council Peacekeeping English Project ('PEP'), which was established in 1995 by the British Government originally in order to meet the perceived English language needs of NATO accession states (later expanding to Central Asia and the Southern Caucasus regions for English in reforming armed forces). However, both nations' inputs have had a political character, with PEP's managing body, the British Council, openly regarding the project (by means of its representation of values such as transparent governance) as a key aspect of UK defence diplomacy (Meixner, 2005).

The United States has been less involved in the reform of internal testing structures of host states than the British Council PEP. However, there have been high impact initiatives, including US assistance in the development of the testing board of the Slovene MOD in the late-1990s, as well as Defense Language Institute tester training courses, at which military testers (selected by partner ministries of defence) are trained to a good level of familiarisation in the principles and practice of testing. Language testing conducted by the US military is generally regarded as 'reliable' by many NATO member states. This view is perhaps due in part to the direct experience of many key ministry staff in the region, many of whom have been delegated to English language courses at the DLI centre at San Antonio, Texas, but it is also due to the fact that the DLI is well resourced and, presumably, able to demonstrate test validity and reliability empirically.

Early in the life of the British Council PEP it was clear that examination reform would become a key part of the project's work. It has been claimed that examination reform is seen as a necessary agent in any overall ELT reform project and that it is simultaneously 'the most powerful area of influence in educational reform', albeit 'probably the most difficult to penetrate and influence from an outside perspective' (Bolitho, 2005: 190). By agreement between the UK and host ministries of defence, many PEP country projects were directly tasked with such reform work as soon as they commenced activities; and such UK-sponsored assistance to local ministry testing then acquired local political prestige. However, the PEP model of locally agreed activities and goals geared toward building on local systems inevitably meant that individual country projects to some degree reflected the skills, interests and beliefs of individual UK project managers, as well as local or regional contexts and needs. In the particular case of examination reform, it is arguably the case that the powerful nature of this work made it an attractive (albeit politically risky) activity which might usefully raise the local profile of the UK input.

Therefore, the difference in style and character of PEP and DLI inputs (Woods, 2006) has been reflected in the field of military language testing. Coordinated project work by PEP on Stanag testing began in earnest in 1998, with the project's formation of a special interest group of project managers, 'TRUMP', or 'Testing Research Unit for Military Purposes'. This group was initially made up exclusively of five UK appointed PEP country managers who all had a strong interest in the field. The group lobbied for funding for development of testing units in host countries with the stated aim: 'to empower NATO & PfP nations in the production and development of valid and reliable language tests according to NATO Stanag 6001'. This aim was supported by the Project Vision, which highlighted 'Training & Sustainability; Developing an Environment for Expertise and Communicating Ideas' (from TRUMP Mission Statement, 2001). TRUMP directly led to a number of key successes in the field. Most notably, one of TRUMP's founder members successfully bid for government funding to train a pool of 28 MOD testers in the PEP Region on the Principles and Practice of Testing Postgraduate Diploma/MA courses at Lancaster University. This meant that over time some military testers even became leaders in the testing field in their country and felt confident to push for comprehensive reforms in their ministry assessment policies. The success of the group meant that other project managers expressed interest in joining; but this proved a drawn-out process as the original membership wished to maintain the status quo, feeling that the original group 'had gelled'.

The group (with a couple of changes to group membership) then decided that the development of an able pool of testers was not enough, and in early 2004, the project's UK Government sponsors agreed to the creation of a PEP Testing Activity Coordinator post to introduce project-wide cohesion to the training to date. There was a concern on the UK side that the costly development of testers should now lead to 'pay-back' for the project as a whole and, in particular, for new projects for which the training of staff in UK would no longer be affordable or feasible (Atkinson, 2006), due to rapidly decreasing UK government support for ELT for central and eastern European military and interior ministry forces from 2002 onwards. The Testing Activity Coordinator then unilaterally decided to create a new testing special interest group, the International Testers of English in the Military ('ITEM'). ITEM was intended to supersede TRUMP, with membership widened to include the Lancaster-trained military testers. Policy direction would be determined by this expanded group, with the British Council reducing its role to facilitator of meetings (which would still be funded by the UK).

The first ITEM meeting, held in Warsaw in June 2005, was facilitated by the PEP Testing Activity Coordinator who pressed for the formulation of a group mission statement and skeletal specifications rooted in the current testing practice of the boards present. These draft specifications were also clearly related to the BILC 2002 amplification of the Stanag 6001 document. This was generally regarded by participants as a real breakthrough. However, there were issues with the group dynamic, with some delegations (according to post-course written feedback) seen by others to be dominating proceedings. It was felt by some that representatives of states which were perhaps finding reform of their military language testing systems easier due to political, resource and scale issues, were pushing the agenda to the detriment of genuine teamwork. There was also still, at this point, no serious belief by participants in the possibility of partner MOD funding of these initiatives. A second meeting, or 'ITEM 2' held in Komorni Hradek (Czech Republic) in February 2006, revealed problems associated with a change of British Council facilitator (the Activity Coordinator had resigned). In post-course feedback many participants made clear their feeling that there had been a change in policy: now the new British Council facilitator felt his role to be that of imparting his expertise to the participants. This caused bad feeling, as by that point several of the participants had completed the Lancaster Postgraduate Diploma or MA in Testing and had years of experience in the field. Specifically, there was a consensus that the new facilitator had insisted on a tutor-led, tester training approach, which went against the basic justification of ITEM as a core cell of trained, experienced testers engaged in the creation of lasting and quality testing products. This clash was not reconciled during the workshop. The UK's seemingly dominant voice had not yet been removed from the group, as policy could still be directed by the British PEP manager, and (quite possibly related to this phenomenon), the UK was still covering most costs for the group's work in the hope that its products would enable new PEPs (primarily in Africa) to undertake any needed test development work with minimal additional investment. Where participating MODs did assist in resourcing the group's work ('ITEM 2' was held on Czech MOD premises) the group was forced to compromise policy by accepting much less experienced local testers to 'repay good will'. At the 'ITEM 3' event, held in Veliko Turnovo, Bulgaria in June 2006, this problem was to an extent redressed by once again using external facilities; costing the UK slightly more but meaning that ITEM could once again direct its own membership and 'ensure high quality input'. The group re-established its dynamic and consolidated work on specifications at Stanag Levels 2 and 3. ITEM took a group decision at this point to use electronic media to promote these documents and policy decisions globally. Vitally, the UK facilitator had again been switched due to the departure of the previous facilitator from the programme, and the new facilitator (now the group's third) adopted a policy of delegated, rotated group facilitation by all members, which was generally well received by group members. Issues related to group dominance by certain delegations also seemed to have subsided. A further meeting ('ITEM 4') took place in early 2007 in Tallinn. The work of retaining original group membership was now under pressure, with some MODs requesting unsuccessfully that this policy be revised to accept new testers; the decision to create a high-experience-based and product-oriented working group had proved controversial. By ITEM 4, delegates of several countries were able to demonstrate increased support from their management in terms of covering their costs for the initiative. Sustainability of the project without dependency on UK funding therefore seemed to have partially come to fruition.

Impact of UK input

While it can clearly be seen from the history of the TRUMP and ITEM special interest groups that individuals and micropolitics have been key to progress or otherwise, overall UK policy was still officially directed by the aim of achieving long-term impact: by the policy of developing local staff, structures and resources using UK expertise and funds. However, as PEP is a government-funded project, rapidly shifting post-2001 UK geopolitical priorities became apparent and began to greatly affect all areas of PEP's activity in Europe, including ITEM, leading to the possibility that pledges to encourage permanent sustainability of partnership projects might not be fully followed through. This risked a replication of an earlier speedy UK geopolitical shift (and subsequent disillusion on the part of partners) which Hunter outlines in this volume. Nevertheless there had been notable long-term successes of UK input to military testing. The pool of testers developed remained largely influential within their MODs and also effected impressive changes in generally low-resource testing environments. These reforms began to be noticed by the wider military language testing training field, provoking debate on overall commitment to valid and transparent testing within NATO. Moreover, a key political success for the UK government as sponsors of this work was the recognition of valid and transparent testing procedures as a positive product by many MODs, and therefore as a potent enabler of effective and potentially improved contribution to international peace support operation missions. There were also purely political effects; for example, testers from the militaries of the southern Caucasus states of Azerbaijan and Armenia were still working together at the time of writing, under the auspices of the British Council project, on reaching a common understanding on language testing (although officially still hostile following the war of the mid-1990s) by means of participation in a regional working group.

The efforts of individual member states

It is difficult to document precisely individual ministry moves to research and develop descriptors and specifications for Stanag 6001 in a bi/multilateral setting precisely because communications within the organisation on such matters have traditionally been poor. In August 2003 the Chief of Foreign Language Training of the Romanian MOD organised a conference at Brasov to which member states of NATO and its less formal sister organisation Partnership for Peace ('PfP') were invited. This event was designed to explore all areas of direct MOD to MOD cooperation on Stanag 6001. This was deservedly hailed at the time as a breakthrough (Green & Wall, 2005: 382) but in fact little has happened since, with no follow-up to this laudable effort from any partner MOD and little evidence of full implementation of or further discussion on the comprehensive code of practice developed at the event. The reasons for the failure to continue this valuable work cannot be precisely documented; however it could be argued that it is largely down to the will of individuals to embark on such initiatives, and that this has been sporadic at best due to the macropolitical issues characteristic of NATO which I have outlined above.

How Micropolitical Agendas Impact on Multilateral Educational Policy

The lack of support from NATO on educational policy has had a profound effect within the transforming militaries of democratising societies eager to join or cooperate with this powerful military-political pact. The continued lack of direction and expertise on the part of NATO HQ structures has hampered progress in language assessment throughout the organisation. It has also created bad feeling on the part of those new member states (mostly ex-Warsaw Pact members) who committed heavily to language testing prior to accession (often at the cost of significant political and personal trauma) only to find out that many long-term members had much less transparent assessment systems than their own. In the context of dramatically shifting political and psychological realities often found in the militaries of the former Soviet Bloc, any systemic change has tended to stem from chance: by 'lucky appointments' to influential posts. This in turn has often been backed by 'positive' political support. Such individuals are therefore often seen to be 'in the right place, at the right time'. Conversely, once this conducive political climate weakens, systematic flaws and/or lack of will of other influential individuals can result in upheaval and even collapse. There is also a strong case for claiming that systematic weaknesses in some democratising militaries have been seen as advantageous by individual politicians, MOD civil servants and language training managers and teachers. This can be in order to secure personal influence: for example by means of an informal system of patronage or by gaining control of or influencing a high-prestige language training and certification process. It can also be in order to maintain or assert the authority of a particular group of individuals closely identified with the agent (in terms of background, politics or regional and ethnic origins) within the wider military.

An example: The interplay of macropolitics and individuals in the Polish Stanag 6001 project

The progress of Stanag 6001 implementation in Poland (with which the author was closely associated) should be placed in the context of wider ministerial policy on language training and, in turn, how these decisions relate to the overall political realities of the Polish military at the time. In autumn 2002, the Polish Ministry of Defence announced its new training development plan for the period 2003–2008, which included increased funding for ELT, along with more specific and far-reaching language requirements for national and international posts. All English language-trained staff were to be tested by the Stanag system and ministry personnel, for the first time, publicly admitted that a continued shortfall was likely in those trained to 'minimum professional' levels of English (especially for the land forces) and this was a cause for concern. However, difficulties in changing testing policy were compounded by the historical and political landscape in which the STANAG implementation (initiated in stages from 1998) took place in Poland. The Polish armed forces of the 1990s were heavily influenced by the political compromises of Poland's 'Round Table Agreement' of 1990, which meant that, as late as the early 21st century, the Polish military was still managed to a significant degree by those senior staff directly involved in the imposition of Martial Law in the country from 1981–1983. While the country made good progress in talks for NATO accession, it is arguably the case that this had little to do with actual reforms in military training policy, which in practice remained largely Soviet Bloc in style. What is more, this success in negotiation and eventual accession in 1999 actually hid significant problems in enacting reforms encountered by successive Polish governments. Ministers of Defence and MOD Training and Personnel Department chiefs apparently lacked the will to address the weakness of a system which allowed for the continued undue influence of individuals on the fairness and transparency of language training and testing practices. This is likely due to the political situation within the Polish MOD, which was still largely managed by senior officers trained in the Soviet Union [with generally low levels of English, even in positions which in many countries would be occupied by junior staff or civil servants; in 2006, these Moscow-trained officers were starting to be systemically excluded from posts such as Defence Attaché (*Newsweek Polska*, 2006b)]. Conversely, in the view of some ministry officials, tremendous strides had been made: an officially centralised language testing system had been put in place and ahead of planned reforms in the school leaving testing system (the latter had been deferred until 2005 due to political controversy: Poland, it should be noted, has a similar historical experience of school-leaving examinations to that of Slovenia and Hungary, as described by Pižorn & Nagy, this volume).

The context changed somewhat following a change of government in late 2005 to a largely right wing coalition. The simultaneous appointment of Radek Sikorski as Defence Minister brought great speculation as to the future form of the military as a whole (*Newsweek Polska*, 2006a: 34) along with considerable focus on the field of language testing. Sikorski, an Oxford University graduate, began to visit STANAG 6001 examination sessions and introduced the practice of personally interviewing officers delegated to senior postings requiring English. This led, in June 2006, to his immediately removing a general from a post requiring significant multilateral cooperation following his 'examining' him in English (*Dziennik*, 2006: 25). The Minister did not refer back to the testing board or order the general to be retested. There are clear professional and political implications. (Sikorski, who resigned in February 2007, was known for his uncompromising views on the role of former communist officers in the Polish military.)

The Polish Stanag testing system, then, still fell well short of being a transparent and effective instrument for the Polish MOD a full eight years after its official introduction; with no legally backed code of practice and whose centralised system was yet to be fully put in place (*Dziennik*, 2006: 24). However, the experience is far from unique in NATO, with many long-term member states still unable to demonstrate a transparent and reliable language testing system. In the absence of systemic safeguards, the success of these testing systems will still be dependent on the will and input of individuals with political influence: from individual examiners and invigilators right up to the Minister of Defence. Such systems will always be seen as primarily political rather than meritocratic.

Conclusions: Relevance of the NATO Experience to International Educational Policymaking

In this chapter I have used the example of the attempts of NATO and its member states to reach an international understanding on language proficiency levels to demonstrate how micropolitics, in the context of an unfavourable macropolitical climate, can become the determining factor in educational policy implementation. In cases of seismic societal change, 'educational' policy can even become divorced from educationalists and left in the hands of politicians and civil servants; many with their own overt and covert individual intentions. Alderson (2004: 5) claims that the testing profession often appears heavily engaged with the technical aspects of test validation, whereas practitioners often appear to have much more everyday and nonspecialist daily concerns. The NATO scenario appears to bear out the claim well. Furthermore, individuals or groupings can sometimes freely exploit the transformation of educational policy to the advantage of their own agendas. Such motives must be borne in mind by all stakeholders prior to interventions and should be considered for overt incorporation as key risk (or opportunity) factors in project baseline studies.

References

Alderson, J.C. (2004) The shape of things to come: Will it be the normal distribution? In M. Milanovic and C. Weir (eds) *Studies in Language Testing* (Vol. 18) (pp. 1–26). Cambridge: Cambridge University Press.

Atkinson, E. (2006) Special Interest Groups in testing – What are they doing? *PEP Newsletter* 22, 5. Published by British Council. On WWW at http://www.britishcouncil.org/pep22.pdf. Accessed 19.11.08.

Bolitho, R. (2005) British ELT and the mainstream. *IATEFL Liverpool 2004 Conference Selections* (pp. 182–192). IATEFL Publications. *IATEFL 2005: Cardiff Conference Selections*. In B. Beaven (ed.) Canterbury. On WWW at http://www.hltmag.co.uk/jan06/mart03.htm. Accessed 26.11.08.

Boyle, C. (2001) Language testing for NATO. *Language Testing Update* 29, 30–32.

British Council (2006) *British Council News*. Summer 2006.

Crossey, M. (2003) An exploration of bias in Polish STANAG examinations: Comparing course graduates and non-course graduates. Unpublished MA thesis, Lancaster University.

Crossey, M. (2005) Improving linguistic interoperability. *NATO Review*. On WWW at www.nato.int/docu/review/2005/issue2/english/art4_pr.html. Accessed 19.11.08.

Dziennik (2006) Generalicja nie zna jezykow. 06/06, pp. 24–25.

Graddol, D. (2006) *English Next: Why Global English may Mean the End of English as a Foreign Language*. London: British Council.

Green, R. and Wall, D. (2005) Language testing in the military: Problems, politics and progress. *Language Testing* 22 (3), 379–398.

Madaus, G. (1990) Testing as a social technology. *The Inaugural Annual Boise Lecture on Education and Public Policy*. Boston, MA: Boston College.

Meixner, H. (2005) Gentle warriors: Britain's defence diplomacy in Romania since 1990. In D. Deletant (ed.) *In and Out of Focus: Romania and Britain. Relations and Perspectives from 1930 to the Present*. Bucharest: Cavallioti.

Newsweek Polska (2006a) Prezydent ma ostatnie słowo. 23/07: pp. 32–34.

Newsweek Polska (2006b) Miotła zmian. 30/07: 5.

Shohamy, E. (2001) *The Power of Tests: A Critical Perspective on the Uses of Language Tests*. Harlow: Longman.

Tsagari, C. (2004) The Greek State Certificate of Language Proficiency (KPG): Some preliminary considerations. *Language Testing Update* 35, 29–40.

Vasilj-Begovic, J. (2006) Benchmark Test (BAT). Presentation at BILC seminar Tallinn, October 2006 (unpublished).

Woods, P. (2006) The hedgehog and the fox: Two approaches to English for the military. In J. Edge (ed.) *Re-locating TESOL in an Age of Empire* (pp. 208–227). London: Palgrave Macmillan.

Chapter 8
Challenges and Constraints in Language Test Development

GARY BUCK

Introduction

In this chapter, first I will explore the challenges and constraints that test developers face in real world test development situations, with particular emphasis on those that require the test developer to deviate from preferred professional practice. Second, I will explore how these constraints arise. I shall argue that constraints arise from three main sources: project givens, conflicting values, and micropolitics. Finally, I will discuss the ethical implications for professional practice.

The professional work of the test developer

It is possible to divide the work of language testing specialists into two main types: research and theoretical work on the one hand, and test design, development and programme management on the other. Theorists or researchers usually have considerable control over their work environment, including what work they do, how they do it, and who they work with. Test developers or testing programme managers, on the other hand, usually work in a complex context, with a variety of constraints, and need to interact with a variety of other stakeholders who often have very different interests, and who may control important aspects of the testing specialist's work. In other words, the real world of building and running testing programmes can be very messy, and test developers not only need the professional skills to produce good measurement instruments, but also need to be able to apply these skills in creative ways, to novel situations, where they will often lack the authority, the budget, the time, or the staff to do the job how they would like. Thus, negotiation, compromise and concession are a major part of every test development project. Furthermore, this often takes place in a complex organisational structure, with others operating under their own particular imperatives – sometimes legitimate and sometimes personal and idiosyncratic – who will often have a completely erroneous or simplistic idea of what is involved in making good tests.

There is no doubt that making fair and accurate instruments to measure educational achievement is a complex undertaking that requires a wide range of professional skills and extensive resources. Briefly, after the purpose of the test has been clarified, it is necessary to define a construct and then write design specifications that will measure that construct; then items need to be written, reviewed and revised, and finally piloted to ensure that they work as intended; the resulting data needs to be analysed, and a number of test forms created. These test forms are essentially a collection of items, and the next step of the process is to turn these into measurement instruments: we have to equate the various forms, such that we know what the equivalent scores are across each form of the test; we have to scale the tests, that is, define a measurement scale (which may be an established scale, or may be a new scale we create) and then link performance on each test form to that scale. Then we need to set performance standards, to determine what scores are appropriate for what levels of performance, or to produce other information, such as normative data that will allow users to interpret the test scores in terms of meaningful real-world performance. The assessment will then need to be supported by validation studies to ensure that it works according to plan, by technical documentation, by large-scale trialling, and so on. And this only represents the start of the process, because once a testing system has been designed and built, it needs to be continually supported by recycling through the above processes, as new items are written, new forms are produced and new parallel measures are created. Finally, all this needs to be supported by an ongoing programme of quality control, technical support, research studies, and so on.

Most of these tasks require higher-order professional skills. The main professionals required are:

- Language testing staff who understand the decisions the test needs to make and who can design a construct, and write specifications to operationalise that construct: This work is usually carried out by staff with a doctoral degree in language testing.
- Staff who can write good items: Writing items is a complex skill and is generally carried out by professional item writers who have a master's degree in applied linguistics, ESL or a related field, plus

significant experience writing items, since it generally takes a number of years to become skilled at writing good items, especially multiple-choice items.
- Staff with technical assessment skills, often called psychometricians: To carry out the statistical work, including item analysis, scaling, standard setting and validation. This work is generally carried out by staff with a doctoral degree in psychometrics or educational measurement.
- Staff for production of the actual tests: For paper and pencil tests this requires basic graphic design, page layout and print management skills, but for computer or internet-based tests, digital designers, programmers and advanced IT specialists are required.
- Staff to deliver and administer the tests: which is often a complex logistic operation, whether in paper and pencil or digital format.
- Trained raters to score samples of language performance on speaking and writing tests. These are usually ESL professionals who have undertaken a number of hours intensive training in using the scoring rubrics.

Most of these professionals are highly trained, and often in short supply.

Building and running testing programmes is a far more complex and resource intensive enterprise than it seems, since much of this work is not obvious to the nonprofessional. Many people seem to think that all one needs is to write a few items, give them to test-takers, and report the number of items correct. And this perception is often shared by those who control the budget and most of the other important stakeholders on the project. Thus, assessment professionals often find it difficult to convince senior managers, or budget planners, to provide the necessary resources.

Major Constraints on Test Development

The main focus of this chapter is how the context in which test developers work leads to constraints on what they can and cannot do. But first we should explore what the most important constraints are. We can divide these into system constraints and resource constraints.

System constraints

The first set of constraints that the test developer must take into account is how the test should be delivered. In the case of an established testing programme, these are often important characteristics of the programme, and are not open to change. In the case of developing a new testing system, these may be policy decisions made by the client, and as such will be outside the control of the test developer, or they may be decisions which the test developer, or others in the organisation, are free to make. The important issue, of course, is who makes the decisions.

Platform

It is increasingly common to have a choice of three different delivery platforms for language tests: paper and pencil, computer and internet-based. Each of these platforms has its own characteristics, and some are better for one purpose and some for another. Ideally, decisions regarding which is most appropriate would take into account the measurement implications of using each platform, but decisions about the platform are rarely based on measurement needs.

The computer screen, especially since the development of the world-wide web, is a graphically rich environment, and the decision to go with a computer-based or internet-based test has implications beyond matters such as the look and feel of the test. Test items are complex, and with traditional multiple-choice comprehension items the interaction between the text, the question, the correct response and the distractors is often complex and relatively unpredictable. Managing this complexity is a skill that good item writers possess. However, once we add to this the additional complexity of how the visual information interacts with the other parts of the item, the task of the item developer becomes significantly different. The visual information can have many different functions: to facilitate and aid comprehension, to show paralinguistic features such as facial expressions, to create context, or to illustrate possible interpretations. The visual information can also have many levels of realism: it can be purely symbolic or it can be realistic; it can be presented as drawings, cartoons or photographs. Each of these has advantages and disadvantages. Integrating this into traditional multiple-choice items requires complex new skills on the part of item writers; skills that we are only now beginning to explore. Not only does the move to computer-based or internet-based delivery require a new set of item-writing skills, but computer programmers and other technical computer experts have to be brought onto the team, and a new set of project management skills are needed, because this has become a software development project as much as a test development project.

Consider an extreme example of how decisions about the platform can affect the test development process. Recently, on a project to revise a large-scale, high-stakes, pencil and paper test, after a year of work, the project team were informed by a senior manager that this was now to be a computer-based test. As a result, almost all the work that had been done in the previous year was no longer relevant, and the project team had to start again, more or less from the beginning. Such is the power of senior management to overrule and interfere.

Testing time

Another common constraint is the time available for delivery. It is a fact that, all other things being equal, the longer the test the more accurately it will measure the construct, and the more thoroughly it can cover a broad range of content. Hence, there is always a tension between the test developers' desire to make the test as long as possible, and the practical constraints of how much time the test-takers can be reasonably expected to spend taking the test.

But this decision is often out of the hands of the test developer. For example, schools have their days divided into class periods that are of a specified length, and obviously school administrators would like to maintain that. Recently, on a project to develop a K-12 test of ESL in response to the US *No Child Left Behind* legislation, an administrator decided that the test had to be administered during a 50-minute class period. While this seems like an obvious decision for an administrator to make, the test really needed to be longer, and the test developer was left with the difficult problem of not having enough time to administer a sufficiently reliable test.

In some situations, testing time can have considerable cost implications, especially in the case of computer-based or internet-based tests. Administration requires computer time, often referred to as *seat time*, and large numbers of computers require considerable capital investment. Seat time is a significant cost, and the test developer can often come under pressure to reduce seat time; that is, to make the test shorter, and the length of the test may be determined by an accountant, rather than by an assessment specialist. A similar situation can arise in schools, which often do not have enough computers available, and testers can find themselves in vigorous competition with teachers for lab time. Given that most educators see teaching as more beneficial to students than testing, the tester often has to compromise.

Pressure on test length is probably greatest in the case of speaking tests. Most speaking tests are administered in one-on-one situations; that is, one test administrator interviewing one test taker, which is expensive. At such times, assessment specialists often come under pressure to reduce the testing time, and this has obvious quality implications for the test. On one large-scale, international testing programme, the length of the speaking test was kept to the very minimum by the test developers, 15 minutes, which allowed 13 minutes for testing time, one minute for the test-taker to enter the room and get seated, and one minute for the examiner to determine the score and enter it into the score sheet. But local administrators, who had to deal with the complex logistic problem of processing hundreds of test-takers, and also covering the considerable costs of room hire, pressurised examiners to complete the whole interview in 12 minutes. This left only about 10 minutes for the actual interview, and the test no longer produced an adequate speech sample for a reliable test.

Item format

There are many different item types, or test tasks, for the test developer to choose from, and each one has advantages and disadvantages; some are more appropriate for one purpose and some for another. Ideally, the competent test developer will choose whichever is most appropriate for the task in hand. However, in many cases, the item format is not the choice of the test developer.

One powerful influence that test developers are often unable to ignore is popular notions about tests and how they should appear. For example, in the United States the multiple-choice format is very common in high-stakes testing systems, and both test takers and test users expect them, which puts considerable pressure on the test developer to use the multiple-choice format. But some cultures do not use the multiple-choice format at all, and consider it an oddity. In the Soviet Union, performance assessments were very common, whereas in the United States, performance assessments are often considered expensive and wasteful. In Japan, English has traditionally been taught using the Grammar-Translation method, and tests have tended to follow suit. While developing college admissions tests in Japan, I was expected to follow culturally-based expectations about what tests should look like. Language testing research, or the experience of test developers with PhDs in language testing, were considered irrelevant, since they did not apply to the Japanese context. Test developers ignore such cultural attitudes at their peril.

Facilities

Many tests require specialised equipment, and its availability needs to be taken into account. Perhaps the most common form of equipment is the audio system needed to deliver listening tests. A small tape recorder at the front of a room with 50 test takers is unlikely to provide fair assessment to those sitting at the back. As an extreme example, consider the case of a national testing system developed for a third-world country, where audio players were not available throughout the country, and hence the test developers had no option but to deliver the listening tests by having them read aloud by the test administrator. For a standardised test, this is a problem: even with the best training in the world, different speakers present the material at different speeds with different emphasis, and so the test delivery was no longer standardised. Furthermore, the speakers needed to see the material in advance in order to practice reciting it, and in a poor country where corruption is endemic, that raises security concerns. Problems with audio equipment are common in many situations, as many local administrators have limited experience with audio equipment, and they often do not realise what sort of equipment is needed to deliver clear sound to a large room of test takers.

Another problem with large-scale tests is how they will be scored. If scanned sheet readers are available, it is much cheaper to use those rather than have the scoring done by hand, and so the test developer will be under considerable pressure to use multiple-choice items that can be read using these machines. Such decisions have considerable cost implications and are often forced upon the project manager, even though they may not be the best option from an assessment perspective.

Resource constraints

As noted earlier, making good tests is very resource intensive, yet sufficient resources may not always be available. When they are not, the test developer will face a considerable challenge making tests of the necessary quality.

Budget

The basic resource for any project is the budget available. Given that non-professionals often have an oversimplified idea of what is required in test development, this often leads to a gap between the budget made available and the test developer's professional judgment of what financial resources are necessary to do a professional job. Indeed, insufficient budget is probably the norm. In the many years I have been designing and developing tests, I have never had sufficient budget to do the job to the standards I wished.

Lack of budget impacts virtually every aspect of any project, since almost all resources have to be paid for. But there are other resources, apart from budget, the lack of which can have a serious negative impact on any test development project.

Professional expertise

One of the biggest challenges the test developer faces is to find the necessary professional specialists to do the job. Such specialists are often in short supply. There are probably no more than a handful of language testers who enter the profession in any one year. Completing a PhD takes many years, and hence the supply is very inelastic. The same applies to psychometricians. Good item writers usually take two to four years to develop their skills after they finish their master's degree. Programmers are in constant demand, and finding ESL professionals to score tests can be a considerable challenge.

Finding qualified staff has become particularly difficult of late. There is a general increase in language testing worldwide, due to the expansion of the European Union and increased globalisation, as governments, organisations and companies are requiring proof of language competence. In the United States, the 2001 *No Child Left Behind* education act is an attempt to enforce accountability by a considerably increased burden of testing in schools, with the result that psychometricians and educational measurement specialists are in very short supply in the United States.

Many test developers cannot afford the staff they need to complete their project and have to make do with whatever they can find. Item are written by untrained or inexperienced item writers, and language testers have do the psychometric analyses themselves. For example, one well-established, high stakes language testing programme I know has traditionally paid quite low salaries, and as the demand for assessment professionals has risen, the programme has had increasing difficulty finding suitable staff. As a result, qualified staff were grossly overworked, many items had to be written by inexperienced item writers, and the complex psychometric work was done by less qualified staff. Under such circumstances, it was virtually impossible for staff to maintain the high standards required, and quality dropped noticeably.

Pilot test-takers

All test items need to be piloted. In order to pilot items, it is necessary to find a sufficient number of test-takers, and ideally, they should have similar characteristics to the target test-takers, so that results from the piloting will generalise to the operational use of the test. Finding such test takers is often a problem.

Piloting may take different forms. For small scale piloting, for example to see whether items engage test-takers in the manner intended, or to see whether the instructions and the task are clear, a small sample of between about five to thirty might be enough. But for other purposes, much larger numbers will be required. Calibrating items on a Rasch scale usually requires a minimum of about 100 test takers, although psychometricians will often ask for many times that. Three-parameter IRT models may require a sample up to 2000 test-takers.

Some norm-referenced testing programmes require the provision of normative data. In the US educational system, for example, test developers are required to show the performance of different target groups on the test. This information may be provided for different states, different genders, different racial groups, and so forth. Providing this information can require field testing on a carefully designed sample of tens of thousands of test takers.

Obviously, a huge budget helps. In the case of small-scale piloting, a few hundred dollars added onto a large project to secure the services of a few dozen test-takers may not be a significant expense. But paying for ten thousand test-takers is a substantial expense, as well as a considerable logistic exercise, and it is often difficult to get the budget for that. But even then, it is not always easy to secure the numbers by offering payment. Large numbers usually require working through schools, or other educational institutions, where educators are generally trying hard to keep the amount of testing to a minimum.

But there is no alternative to piloting tests. Unless that is done, and done properly with a sufficient number of test takers similar to those for whom the test is intended, we have no idea whether the items are working properly, or whether the test is any good at all. Most lay people can understand the need for piloting, but what they often have difficulty understanding is why the sample of test takers needs to be so large, and why the pilot sample needs to have the same characteristics – age, ability level, education, and so on – as the prospective test takers.

There are ways around this, but not many. In the case of an existing testing system, the ideal situation is to embed pilot items in the operational administrations, and then omit those pilot items when calculating the test-takers' score. But for a new testing system, this is simply not possible. In such a case, the best strategy is to cooperate with a potential user of the test, and offer them use of the finished instrument for free, or at a reduced price, in return for help during test development. For example, one project to develop a placement test for language schools offered two years' free use of the test in return for piloting it.

Development time

It takes time to build an assessment system. Most high-stakes test-development projects take two years or more from conception to completion, depending on a variety of factors. Projects can be completed in less than that, but this is rare and some projects take much longer. The project that resulted in the iBT TOEFL in 2005 started in the early-1990s.

Time is money, and we have already discussed how many projects are under-funded. There is often considerable pressure for test developers to complete a test as quickly as possible simply to make the project cheaper. But there are many other reasons why time could be short. School years have a fixed cycle, and test administration often occurs at some fixed point in that cycle. If tests are not ready in time, they may not be implemented for another year. As an example, on a project to develop an ESL test for use in the US K-12 educational system, a senor educational administrator decided that the piloting of items would take place in April and May, which were the only dates when schools would have enough time. Yet the test needed to be ready for use by September the same year, which required an enormous amount of work to be completed in the four or five intervening months. If either the piloting date, or the delivery date had been missed, the introduction of the test would have been delayed for one whole year – something quite unacceptable to the schools that needed the test.

Understanding How Constraints Arise

These constraints arise due to a variety of reasons, which fall into three main categories: those that are given, as part of the project, those that arise due to conflicting values and responsibilities within an organisation, and those that arise through micropolitics.

Project givens

Every test development project has a purpose, and takes place in a context, and these define many of the constraints of the project. For example, the delivery platform – paper and pencil, computer delivered or internet delivered – is usually something that is given, just as the time available for administration may be a given, especially in a school situation. The types of tasks used on the test are often given, or at least customs and local attitudes need to be taken into account. And the availability of special equipment, such as audio players, computers, or scan-sheet readers is often known in advance. The budget available may also be known in advance: it is always prudent to enquire about the budget before undertaking any project. Certain types of expertise may not be available, such as professional item writers, psychometricians or graphic artists. Many projects suffer from a shortage of test-takers on whom the test can be piloted. And finally, some projects are just short of time – the tests need to be ready by a certain date, which is not negotiable.

Such constraints are part of every test development project. The test developer will often know what these are before the project starts, and be able to take these into account when developing project plans. However, things do not always work out as planned, and it is quite common for promised resources not to materialise. The reasons that happen are the subject of the next two sections.

Values and conflicting priorities

Organisations tend to be areas of struggle in the sense that different people, with different values and different responsibilities, cooperate and compete to attain the organisation's goals. It is important to realise that the values and goals that testing professionals share among themselves are often not shared by other members of the organisation.

In science, all measurement is accompanied by some degree of error, and it is considered a basic requirement of good science to attempt to estimate the extent of that error. Educational measurement is no different in principle, but because we are attempting to measure something in the learners' mind, something we cannot observe directly, it is very difficult to identify what we are measuring. Furthermore, the amount of error tends to be very large compared to many other measurement activities, and it is very difficult to estimate the error accurately. As a result, assessment specialists continually struggle to improve the reliability and validity of their assessments. We never get it right, but this imperative drives us all, and this is the unspoken subtext of all our professional work. It is our underlying ethic, and the foundation of our professional integrity. Most nonprofessionals do not understand this important fact.

Accountants and budget directors, on the other hand, are responsible for the financial well-being of the organisation, and have a responsibility to use funds prudently and efficiently. Given that test development is resource-intensive, and given that most nonprofessionals often do not understand why those resources are needed, it is easy to see how a responsible budget director would be very reluctant to give the project leader what s/he requests. Project managers who approach the business manager with requests for four qualified and expensive professionals full-time for a year and a half, tens of thousands of dollars for item writers, payments to pilot test-takers, money for travel, administrative support, and so forth, are often greeted with shock. This frequently leads to a demand for compromise. Arguments that this will result in a poorer quality instrument are often treated with suspicion.

Of course, sometimes one wins the argument, but in my experience, after the budget has been promised, and as the project progresses, such promises may not be kept. The problem is that lay people often think that a test is a test, and as long as it looks like a test and produces scores, then everything is fine. Notions of reliability and validity are subtle and abstract, and the evidence can be arcane and probabilistic, and hence difficult to interpret.

Disputes between the assessment professionals and the business office are ongoing on almost every large-scale testing programme I have known. In essence, assessment professionals are driven by the need to improve their assessments, and that usually means continually fine-tuning the tests, whereas those responsible for the administration have to run a complex logistic operation and need long-term stability to do that efficiently. Fine-tuning is the last thing they want. The marketing and sales department usually see themselves as being in a service industry, where they need to build a strong client base and satisfy client needs. Their aim is satisfied clients, which can easily translate into demands for easier tests, and higher pass rates. Assessment goals are often incompatible with the goals of the business office, and disagreements can erupt into very passionate arguments, because both sides are right according to their own values, and both sides have much at stake.

Another common area of conflict between the assessment professionals and the business office arises because of the use tests are put to. Assessment professionals tend to be very fastidious about what is, and what is not, an appropriate use of their tests. Many are shocked when a test such as IELTS, designed as a test of academic English, is used to test the English ability of foreign doctors applying for the right to work in an English-speaking country, or as a test of the general English ability of those applying for citizenship in an English-speaking country. They consider such uses to be unethical. Business people often do not understand this. They feel that since the test required substantial financial investment, they have a strong duty to maximise revenue. They do not understand why assessment professionals believe it is wrong to use a test for a different purpose from which it was made. After all, 'an English test is an English test, right?' But even if one wins this argument, there is one argument one cannot win: there is no suitable test available anyway. Business managers will argue that those certifying the doctors, or those immigration officials, have to choose between 'our' test, another unsuitable test developed by a rival, or use nothing at all. Most business people have no difficulty deciding which they prefer. Again, in this dispute, both sides are right according to their own values.

I have come to believe that, in the last analysis, there is a fundamental conflict between the needs of good assessment practice on the one hand, and sound financial management and good business practice on the other.

Micropolitics

The discussion in the section above deals with conflict situations in which all the participants are acting in the best interests of their organisation, to the best of their knowledge and ability, according to their own values and responsibilities. Of course, not everyone does act in that manner. That is when micropolitics comes into play. By micropolitics, I mean the actions of individual members of the organisation, based on their preferences, attitudes and personal agendas, rather than the needs of the organisation. Of course, the motives and actions of people and the micropolitics of organisations are complex, multifaceted and usually open to a variety of interpretations. Micropolitics are a continuum, at one end of which we find responsible management practice, somewhere in the middle we find management decisions influenced by personal motives, and at the other end we have management actions determined entirely by self-interested manipulation. When we judge human actions, especially those that affect our projects, we may differ regarding where on that continuum we place particular actions – what may appear to be self-interested manipulation to one may seem like responsible management to another.

It is easy to understand why micropolitics are so important in test development. Creating new tests and new testing systems is, by definition, change, and organisational change is a political process, and is often threatening to individuals and departments in an organisation. Furthermore, individuals have a complex hierarchy of needs, and when these are not met, that can lead to behaviours in the workplace that are less than optimal – at least from the perspective of the project. It is often difficult to know precisely what the motives are for decisions handed down to the project. No one explains, 'I am feeling insecure and I have a need to force my decisions on you guys in order to make me feel better' or 'I need to make sure that my rival for promotion is not as successful as I am.' There is always some rationale, some 'good' reason given for the decision. Usually the real reasons are unspoken, and project staff are left with their suspicions, and their frustrations.

In the case mentioned earlier of the decision to replace the paper and pencil test with a computer-based test midway through the project, that could have been a high-level executive decision passed onto the team by the senior manager, a simple desire of the manager to impress his superiors by modernizing the test, or the manager attempting to assert his authority for personal reasons. The decision clearly had nothing to do with making a better measurement instrument, since the relevant measurement experts were not consulted. The project team never knew the real motive, although they had their suspicions.

The more authority and power the individual has, the more they can influence a project. For example, on one testing programme that based its reading and listening tests on the US government's ILR scale, one of the senior officials in the funding agency felt that the ILR scale had been getting easier over the years, and s/he was determined to put that right. As a result, the assessment experts on the test development project, who had considerable experience in using the ILR scales, were under continual pressure to make test items harder and harder. The project leader was quite aware of what was happening, and did his best to prevent it, but with only partial success. We may speculate regarding the personal motives of this senior official – was this a genuine mistake, did the official have a personal need to assert some authority, or was this interagency power politics? – but the point is that her/his personal view took precedence over that of the testing professionals. Powerful people usually get their way, right or wrong, and the rest of us have to live with the result.

On another project I am aware of, rivalry between two senior executives of the company, the vice president and the director of the testing division, was the unspoken subtext underlying almost all high-level discussion of the ongoing test development project and the future plans of the testing division. If the test development project went forward successfully, this would have bolstered the status of the director of the testing programme, probably to the detriment of the vice president. The result was continual and 'aggressive' oversight by the vice president which had a considerable negative impact on the project. The vice president would no doubt argue that the oversight was necessary and part of her/his responsibility. In these cases, there is often no clear basis for proving what you believe – personal motives are complex, and most people have multiple responsibilities, and so interpretations of such situations can vary.

Sometimes an individual's fears determine how things will be done. In another case I am aware of, a large test development organisation had been conducting oral proficiency interviews for many years. Then a new head of the organisation was appointed, and decided to revise the interview procedure. The revised procedure had some problems – which were obvious to any testing professional – but suggestions that reliability studies were needed always fell on deaf ears. No reason was given, but it seemed clear to those involved that the new head was afraid of submitting her/his new ideas to rigorous validation. Even when the system had been in place for 10 years, making high-stakes decisions for tens of thousands of military personnel, no one knew the reliability of the procedure.

However, the effect of personalities and power politics are not always based on direct pressure. Many project staff know what the boss would like, and set out to provide that. For example, on one testing programme I am aware of, the department head was very interested in English grammar. Grammar is obviously important in language testing, but whether it should be tested in context, or whether it should be explicitly tested has been a topic of considerable debate among language testers. However, in this particular situation, the test development staff felt that they had to include a test of explicit grammar, regardless of their own personal professional views. So the test had an explicit grammar section. The director did not insist on this – my own view is that s/he would not have done so in the face of sound professional reasons to do otherwise – but the decision was based on a desire to please the director, or a desire to avoid possible censure, not on an objective evaluation of the needs of the assessment.

Micropolitics occur within the project team, too. On another large scale testing project, most of the team had PhDs in language testing, but three members from one large and powerful department did not have research training, but were in fact very experienced item writers with Master's degrees in applied linguistics. After one of these three took offence at some (perhaps imagined) reference to their lack of training in language testing research, the project leader clearly felt that it was important to the project to make sure that did not happen again. The result was that the project design and research effort became dominated by the need to take account of the feelings of these three members, and to make sure they were not offended. Their suggestions were almost always accepted, their interests and their ideas became the driving force behind the research design and their personal preferences determined decisions about which outside consultants were used and which were not. Yet these staff members did not have formal training in research methodology, and were not qualified to make these decisions. This had a very disastrous effect on the project, which did not proceed in the most rational and effective manner.

To make matters worse, organisations often do not keep adequate records, and decisions driven by inappropriate micropolitical motives often cannot be reversed. As an example, the programme manager running a large-scale international testing programme decided to expand the programme, and a project had been in place for over two years to develop additional modules and enhanced score reports. All the stakeholders in the testing system had been consulted, a number of research studies had been carried out, and a business plan, complete with long-term financial projections, had been approved. Then, about one year before the enhanced system was to be introduced, the organisation spun off a subsidiary company, and the testing programme was transferred to the new subsidiary. There was bad feeling between the programme manager and the directors of the new company and so the project was cancelled: no announcement was made, but resources dried up and the project just died. The hard work of the project team, carried out over a number of years, was wasted. The irony of this particular case is that after a few years, the new managers of the programme, who had no access to historical records, decided that they needed to modernise the test, and they set about developing additional modules; in effect repeating much of the work that had been done before. With no institutional knowledge of the work that had been done previously, they started again from scratch. A few years later, long after the original projected completion date, the programme came out with a watered-down version of the original project.

Conflicting values or micropolitics?

It is normal to wish to arrive at some understanding of the complex professional situations in which we find ourselves, since the more we understand, the better we can function. Yet differentiating between reasonable disagreements that are based on conflicting values and different responsibilities, on the one hand, and micropolitical acts motivated by personal goals on the other, is difficult. One never knows exactly what legitimate imperatives are driving the other people who interact with one's work, and hence one can never determine what personal motives are at work. Is that parsimonious accountant actually being responsible in a difficult financial situation, or is he simply throwing his weight around; or perhaps something between the two? Just because someone is being awkward and uncooperative does not necessarily mean they are acting from personal motives, or that they are wrong according to their own values or responsibilities. It is difficult to claim that something is happening because of micropolitical motives.

And indeed, in many cases, it makes no difference what the motives of the other people are. One makes one's case, the argument is won or lost, and then acceptable solutions are sought in order to complete the project as best one can. Agonising excessively over the motives of others is generally a waste of time and energy.

Ethical issues

Ethics is an important issue for assessment professionals. Most testers have a feeling that their tests are not sufficiently accurate, and tend to be acutely aware of the impact that tests can have on the lives of test takers. In such circumstances, a strong concern with professional standards and ethics is healthy, and only to be expected. So what are the ethical implications of all this? What follows are my own beliefs, and I fully expect that many assessment professionals will have quite different opinions. But the point about professional ethical standards, as with all moral standards, is that if they are easy to attain, we have set our sights too low. I believe we should set our sights high, which means we will always fall short and always be struggling to do better – rather like the continual struggle to increase the reliability and validity of our tests.

I believe we are all responsible for our own work, and to the extent that we make decisions that affect the lives of test-takers, we have an ethical imperative to ensure that those decisions are made to the best professional standards we are capable of attaining. However, I also believe it is unreasonable to hold a test developer responsible for decisions that they are not free to make. I worked as a fairly junior assessment professional on the TOEFL programme. Should I have been held ethically responsible for all the decisions made by the TOEFL programme? I do not believe that would have been reasonable.

However, the question arises who is responsible? Even the managers of the TOEFL programme are not free to make whatever decision they want, and probably neither is the president of the organisation. So where does ethical responsibility lie? Large-scale, high-stakes testing is generally a corporate endeavor, and to (mis)quote Dr Johnson, 'the problem with corporations is that they have neither a shin to be kicked, nor a soul to be damned'. In other words, they are impersonal, and it is often unclear who should take responsibility. In such a case, all one can really do is to take a hard look at the organisation, and ask whether one is comfortable with what one sees. Many assessment organisations take their ethical responsibility very seriously. But not all organisations do. Sometimes a test developer will take a look at the overall performance of the organisation they work for, and decide that perhaps ethical standards are not as high as they ought to be and they should start looking for employment elsewhere. Such decisions are often very difficult, especially for those with family responsibilities. But at times, many who work in the assessment industry will have to make such hard decisions.

However, although we cannot control all the decisions that affect our projects, we can inform the decision-makers of the implications of their decisions. If the accountant does not want to pay for professional item writers, we can explain the cost of using poor items, both in dollar terms and in measurement terms. If the pilot sample is not appropriate, we can explain what the possible results will be. We can quote professional standards, and we can explain to the decision-makers, or indeed to any other stakeholders who will listen, just what their responsibility is, and what the implications of their decisions are. And it is important to put this in writing, and that decision-makers know why it is in writing; namely, if things go wrong, they will bear the responsibility.

Such explanations are never popular, and they have soured a number of my work relations, but they do two important things. First, even though we cannot always insist on ethical decisions, by making sure that decision-makers know the implications of their decisions (which may be explained in terms such as wasted investment, or bad publicity, rather than in terms of ethical imperatives) we pass the ethical responsibility onto others and we can thereby clear our own conscience. Second, it is surprising how often this strategy results in a change of mind. Most business people do not want to be told that the rival test will be obviously better, or that the possible scandal will land on their desk. It is important to stick to the facts and be honest, sometimes brutally honest, to everyone involved with the test, in order to preserve one's self-respect. Everyone wants to hear good things about their test, and those with a financial stake in a test may encourage the assessment professional to lie. Assessment professionals must resist this, and if the pressure becomes too strong, it may be time to look for other employment.

In a complex and difficult world, we all have to set our own standards. I find that as I spend more time in this field, I see less black and white, and more shades of grey. I am certainly much less ready to rush to ethical judgment than I used to be. Maybe this is only to be expected, given that I am often the one presented with the ethical dilemmas. Over the years, I have come to feel that it is easier for those with secure university positions to take a strong stand than it is for those who work in practical test development organisations, simply because their livelihood is not at stake.

Conclusion

In this chapter, I have deliberately refrained from offering solutions or advice on how to deal with the situations I describe. Each situation is unique and too complex to offer general advice. The main point is that real world test development takes place in a complex context, and that context has considerable influence on all aspects of the test developers' work. There is no such thing as a project that runs according to text-book rules. Each project is different, and the good test developer is the one who can adapt to the requirements of each project, and still produce a good product despite the constraints.

Language testing is a challenging field. Research and theory development require rigorous thinking and intellectual creativity, and are crucial for the long-term development of our field. But the more difficult and more interesting challenge is creating real assessments. The practical test designer and developer must not only find immediate answers to the researcher's questions, but must apply those to a very complex, constrained situation and produce quality assessments, often without having all the 'right' resources. This requires rigorous thinking, intellectual creativity, complex problem-solving, considerable empathy, high-levels of dip-lomacy, a good business sense and sound project management skills. A challenge indeed.

Chapter 9
The Politics of Examination Reform in Central Europe

KARMEN PIŽORN and EDIT NAGY

Introduction

This chapter addresses the complex issue of establishing external school examination models in two post-communist countries (Slovenia and Hungary) with virtually no tradition of external assessment, democratic education, relevant quality control procedures, or expertise in external testing. We will show that, however perfect a system one might wish to establish, it is always possible for individuals to undermine the innovation. We describe events, who was responsible for developments, and try to uncover hidden agendas. We are convinced that the most important element of any reform project are the individuals and their ambitions, personal agendas, openness to change and attitudes to professionalism: in short, micropolitics.

In both contexts, documents dealing with the proposed educational outcomes and desirable changes in the educational system were drawn up according to the latest international recommendations on educational policies. However, it was the implementation process of the 'nicely worded' goals that was either problematic or was not achieved at all. Blame for failure of the good intentions of the innovative national examination projects in the two countries does not lie so much with institutions as it does with individual decision-makers. These individuals, including politicians, ministers, directors of educational institutions, heads of examination boards, testing team leaders, and so on, who had the power either to encourage good testing practices leading to valid and reliable test results or to allow invalid examinations and worthless certificates, exercised their arbitrary power in different ways. Some were determined to fulfil their mission and put their energy and effort into improving testing systems. Others invested time and energy in hindering developments.

The chapter contains two case studies, preceded by a common introduction in which we first briefly describe the background of the political and educational systems of the two countries since the 1980s and then discuss why international (educational) standards were suddenly perceived as important. The first case study gives a detailed first-hand account of Slovenia, the reasons for political and educational changes since its independence in 1991, the impact of an influential educational leader, a rationale for the implementation of external assessment, the implementation process of the examination reform in languages in primary and secondary schools and the impact of decision-makers' decrees on the quality of tests, teacher training and other aspects of life.

The second case study focuses on a major educational reform project in Hungary, the implementation of a school-leaving examination model. A description is first presented of what language examinations were like before Hungarian independence, the need for change, which institutions were involved in the reform project, and what the project's aims, objectives and achievements were. The implementation phase is then discussed, providing a detailed account of activities and events and finally summarising the problems that occurred due to inappropriate staffing within teams and institutions.

Background

In order to understand the events and reactions of decision-makers it is important briefly to describe the background to the political and educational systems of the two countries. In the early-1990s Slovenia successfully seceded from the Yugoslav Federation and Hungary finally escaped Russian domination. It is hardly surprising that after more than 40 years in largely centralised and ideologically controlled political and educational systems, the need for reform was urgent. In order to join the European Union and to improve standards of living, political leaders realised that international standards in industry, the economy and in education would have to be met. Moreover, educational standards were necessary to enable the comparison of programmes and institutions. Crucially, the philosophy of the EU that every citizen has the right to live and work in any other member state made imperative the development of transparent learning outcomes and quality control procedures.

Before 1990, all school curricula were centrally prescribed and all instruction had to follow a common ideology. In addition, textbooks were heavily censored for any deviation from agreed political values and beliefs. From 1990, far-reaching changes in Hungary and Slovenia – especially the implementation of multiparty systems and the adoption of new constitutions – meant that the educational systems also had to change. In both countries, new laws and regulations established new aims and values, such as accessibility and transparency of public education, democracy, autonomy, equal opportunities and quality learning and teaching.

Until the mid-1980s regional school inspectors were responsible for the quality control of each school subject. However, with the political changes, this system of supervision was abolished as decentralisation was felt to be urgently needed. The so-called 'advisory' system that replaced this institutionalised quality control system unfortunately lacked clear guidance, and regional 'advisors' were not allowed to evaluate teachers' work. They could only give advice as and when requested by the school authorities or the teachers themselves. The new systems, where students were using a range of different textbooks and teachers could apply any teaching method, lacked quality control.

School-leaving examinations before the 1990s were only taken by upper-secondary school pupils (aged 18–19) and there was no external assessment in primary or lower-secondary education. In lower-secondary, standards were measured by teachers alone and the achievements of students from individual schools varied enormously. In contrast, the secondary school-leaving examinations in both countries date back to the Habsburg monarchy and have always constituted an important event in young people's lives. Unfortunately, form took precedence over content and the school-leaving examination amounted to little more than a rite of passage, whose results could not be trusted. During the communist regimes, examination papers were prepared by the teachers themselves and there was no external quality control. Test specifications were nonexistent, marking criteria were unknown, there was no set examination format, sample tasks were not available to students and teachers, no rating scales existed for open-ended questions, scripts were not double-marked, and so on. Inevitably, the difficulty of tests varied from school to school and even from teacher to teacher (see also Crossey, this volume).

However, new legislation brought about a change in quality control, namely the right of the public to oversee the quality of some aspects of education. For the first time, the issue of quality in education was raised and it was not welcomed with enthusiasm, especially among teachers.

In the mid-1990s the education authorities decided to implement and/or reform existing school-leaving examinations in all school subjects.

Although this was no doubt well-intentioned, implementing good testing practice is very difficult, especially if decision-makers have their own agendas, if the format of the exam has to change with every change of government, if the authorities are not willing to resource the exam reform adequately and if they do not see the need to educate the public in the importance of having valid and reliable examination results.

Slovenia

Political change leads to educational change

After seceding from the Yugoslav federation in 1991, Slovenia's main goal was to move towards the West as quickly as possible, and this was achieved when Slovenia joined the European Union in 2005, and adopted the Euro in 2007. Currently its economy is flourishing and standards of living have risen tremendously.

In April 1992, when Slovenia celebrated the first anniversary of its independence, the Liberal Democrat Party (LDS) won the elections. Its programme stressed the importance of a well-financed, fairly autonomous and diverse educational system. Fortunately, the new Minister of Education was a sociologist who had researched sociological aspects of education. Ambitious, hard-working, and open to change, he ran the Ministry of Education for over eight years and introduced new school curricula, the extension of primary education by one year, a new external secondary school-leaving examination, and external assessment in primary education (age group 6–14). However, although reforms may be introduced by determined individuals, they are implemented by people who have their own opinions and biases, and so micropolitics may frustrate innovation and change.

Rationale for the implementation of external assessment

The new legislation intended education to be more transparent to the general public, internationally comparable and accountable for its actions and outcomes to the taxpayer. The White Book on Education (Krek, 1996) introduced principles of equal opportunity and respect for individual differences which underpinned the change of the political system from a single-party to a multiparty society. The implementation of external national assessment was, therefore, supposed to assist the realisation of these principles. Before 1994, secondary-school grades were not comparable since each school had different ways of measuring knowledge and skills, and so nearly all faculties (at that time there were only two universities) were forced to introduce entrance examinations. These were usually designed by a single university professor and students had little or no information on how to prepare for the examinations.

The implementation of the examination reform in languages in secondary schools

As part of the reform, teams of teachers, assisted by national and international experts, defined the subject matter, teaching principles and standards that should be achieved by students at the end of primary and secondary education. Unfortunately, politicians and the advocates of reform did not take into account that such innovations take time, resources and training. As a result, subject curricula were developed with inappropriate standards because they had been established by merely speculating what a child should be able to do or know instead of researching children's actual abilities. Sometimes the standards were set too low or too high because influential team members assumed children's abilities should match their own children, the students they were teaching, or those of the school district where they lived. Thus individual experience and prejudice was an important factor in deciding on standards.

Test specifications for the external school-leaving examination were designed according to the new curricula and they were discussed with teachers but they were rarely supported by research data. Although subject testing teams were appointed, very little training in testing was offered to item writers, with the exception of the English team. Even today, more than 10 years after the first 'Matura' (secondary school-leaving examination), many teachers write examination tasks with little or no testing expertise. The belief that a good teacher automatically makes a good tester is still widely accepted.

In 1994, a trial Matura was administered in 10% of schools and in the following year, in all secondary schools. The trial passed without any questioning of results, despite the fact that in some subjects these were very low and the pass mark had to be adjusted. Clearly this was because the tasks had not been pretested. However, in the early-1990s, anything that was believed to promote Europeanisation quickly gained support. Despite the problems, the Matura was, in general terms, a success but its implementation met opposition from vested interests and entrenched values. Universities felt they would lose control over who could be admitted and who could not. (The old enrolment system had not been very transparent.) In addition, right-wing politicians felt that external assessment was alien to the traditional, Austro-Hungarian system. Adherents of 'permissive' and 'stress-free' schooling claimed that external assessment generated stress among teachers and students, undermined teachers' autonomy, was incapable of adequately assessing all curriculum goals, and might cause long-term damage to the health of students and their family. Because of such opposition, the authorities proceeded cautiously.

'The implementation of any reform involves compromise', as a Minister of Education said. In the case of external secondary school leaving exams undesirable compromises included an oral examination in which two tasks were prepared centrally and yet one was prepared by the language teachers themselves, although the marking criteria, the same for all three tasks, were designed centrally. Unfortunately the examiners were not standardised. In the early stages of the development of the exam, when a British Council-supported external consultant was still in Slovenia, a number of video-taped performances on the oral test were discussed with teachers and the marks awarded for each candidate were justified. However, these standardisation seminars were not compulsory and were ultimately abandoned, and so the reliability of the oral exam is in question. Yet the designers of the oral tasks may feel threatened by a model of assessment which pays attention to reliability of marking and which has no tradition in Slovene culture.

In 2004, with a change of government, the right-wing party began to reform grammar schools and the Matura exam. Influential opponents of the external secondary school leaving exams argued (without empirical evidence) that the washback effect of the Matura was negative and teachers could not be creative because they spent too much time preparing for the Matura. Some headteachers and educationalists also claimed that the Matura exam had narrowed the curricula to what is actually tested on the exam. No evidence was offered, and opponents were unable to answer the question 'What would students learn if there was no Matura exam?' The hidden agendas of the opponents of the Matura examination are unknown, but the opposition was not based on professional arguments or expertise in testing and assessment.

Another issue that most Matura subject committees (with the exception of English) failed to resolve is the need for pretesting. This was discussed in the very early stages of the implementation of exam reform but discussion was cut short by arguments to do with confidentiality, the 'difficulty' of finding appropriate test samples and cost. Interestingly, none of the decision-makers ever worried about the quality of individual tasks. It was thus not surprising that many tasks had no correct answer, or were answered correctly by all or, in some cases, by none of the students. This issue has never been openly discussed; indeed one of the present authors was severely criticised by an official for having built a bank of pretested tasks.

The implementation of the examination reform in languages in primary schools

In 1996, it was decided (and in 1999 it was implemented for the first time) to have a *nine-year primary school* (instead of the previous eight-year primary school) at the end of which a nationwide evaluation of achievement was to take place. The new primary school is divided in three three-year cycles, and it was planned that national tests at the end of the first and second cycles would simply be used for monitoring purposes, while external assessment at the end of primary school would constitute 50% of the measure of achievement (the other half was to be awarded internally).

The Liberal Democratic government encouraged the implementation of national assessment throughout its term of office. However, in 2000 the right-wing party came to power for about six months and assessment became a political football. It was decided not to implement the national exams in primary school and so, by the time the Liberal Democratic Party won the elections again and promoted national assessment once more, the subject testing teams' work had been greatly delayed. The first team meeting was held in spring 2001 and in February 2002 the first mock examinations were supposed to be administered. Given such pressures, the English testing team experienced a number of problems: the nominated team leader did not accept the position; in June 2001 the next nominee had no experience or training in testing and was very reluctant to accept the position. (Both nominees were university teachers with no experience in national assessment.) Two months later the team resigned because it was not possible to pilot and analyse the tasks in such a short time. In addition, there was very little financial support and virtually no administrative support.

The National Testing Committee, which made both technical and professional decisions about the exams, required each subject team to produce one paper which would be suitable for all levels and which most students (95%) must pass. However, they failed to provide guidance as to whether the test was supposed to check only minimal standards of knowledge, or minimal knowledge at each of the three levels set out in the syllabus. Another decision handed down by the National Testing Committee was that no exam could exceed 60 minutes in length and the oral part should not count for more than 30% of the final grade. By law, there had to be a written exam, and an oral exam was also possible but was cancelled in 2005 by the new government for unknown reasons, in spite of vociferous protests by teachers and educationalists.

The testing team for English were very aware of their lack of professional and human resources. Most team members had been chosen because of their experience of teaching in primary schools; only one person had taken a (short) course in testing. Yet the authorities claimed that the team's worries were exaggerated since classroom teachers write tests on a daily basis and should be capable of doing this kind of work. The decision-makers pointed out that the test designers could use the intervening four-year period to learn on the job and improve the tests. Of course, many decision-makers did not have expertise in testing, or even hands-on experience in item writing. According to the decision-makers other subject teams had managed to design test specifications and even final papers in a few months, and so they could not accept the team's concerns.

The testing team for English even suggested postponing the exam for a year, especially in light of the fact that these exams were officially seen as experimental and were being offered on a trial basis until the first full cohort came through the system in 2008. Fortunately, the authorities agreed to extend deadlines and to consider compromise, but it was clear that postponement by one year would only have been a last resort, as it could have had enormous political consequences for the government of the day. In effect, the team was indirectly accused of casting doubt on the whole concept of the nine-year primary school and national assessment.

In short, although the idea of implementing national external assessment was positive, it was not considered carefully enough. The decision-makers did not accept that national tests cannot be designed by classroom teachers who had no experience or expertise in testing. Even many of the team leaders were not specialists in testing. When the testing team for English expressed doubts in their language testing abilities they were considered odd by decision-makers and other subject test designers. In fact, without the support of the British Council, the Hungarian Examination Project team, and international testing experts, it would have been impossible to design tests of relatively good quality.

A further issue of dispute between the English testing team and the decision-makers was related to the oral part of the exam. The authorities decided that the oral examination for 14-year-olds should be performed during regular English lessons, that the teacher should perform the role of interlocutor and assessor at the same time, and that the other, non-assessed students should be present during the exam performance. They argued that assessing students in their own classroom in front of their classmates lent familiarity to the situation. They also pointed out that by assessing students during regular lessons there would be no timetable problems and the normal working day would not be disturbed. It was even argued that students would benefit from observing the 'new way' of assessing speaking skills.

The English testing team argued that an oral test would be easier to administer and fairer if conducted outside regular lessons. Nevertheless, the decision-makers insisted, and unfortunately, the oral exam story did not have a happy ending. In 2005 the oral exam was cancelled, supposedly saving money, reducing stress among students and freeing teachers from teaching to the exams.

Conclusion

To date, such governmental decisions appear to have had no positive results. First, the exams in Year 9 do not count for even half the final grade and cannot be used as criteria for secondary school enrolment, and therefore students have nothing to lose. Teachers complain that students are no longer motivated to take these exams and consequently, the results are not likely to show students' achievements. Another unreasonable decision by the government was that the testing teams should be changed, and the newly established testing teams then had only one month to write two live papers. The item writers were also changed and new, in many cases inexperienced, teachers were required to write a test for the whole population. In such circumstances, it is hardly surprising that one of the tests was so problematic that the tasks were openly criticised in the newspapers (Žibret, 2006).

Testing is, of course, a matter with considerable social, educational and ultimately political consequences. It is therefore perhaps not surprising that politicians, especially when feeling vulnerable to public opinion at election time, should ignore professional and informed advice and insist on particular courses of action for reasons of expediency. Reasoned argument often fails to prevail and recourse to a professional approach behind the politicians' backs is rarely possible. In such cases, compromise between an individual's defence of quality and political agendas often results in the latter overcoming the former.

Hungary

In this case study, an account of a major educational reform project in Hungary is presented, together with its objectives, the implementation process and the results: how the Project developed a new English school-leaving examination model in accordance with current good practice, including training, piloting, analysis, reflection and striving for evidence of validity and reliability. Project achievements and failures are described, and micropolitics is invoked to explain why things went astray: why the Project was opposed and ultimately ignored by the body officially tasked to develop exams, and how the proposed English exam model was rejected, without reference to professional standards or to evidence for the validity of alternative proposals.

Background

For many years, the school-leaving examination in foreign languages in Hungary was problematic: results were not comparable locally, regionally or nationally, the exam was oriented to grammar and translation, it did not reflect good practice in language teaching and it was thought to have negative washback. Teachers were not trained how to mark performances or how to conduct oral exams. There was no external monitoring, results were not analysed and students received no feedback on their achievement. The examination was much more of a social event, a rite of passage for students moving from adolescence to adulthood, than an exam where the students' knowledge and skills were tested (Alderson & Szollás, 2000).

Reform and institutions

In the mid-1990s the educational authorities decided to reform the school-leaving examination in all school subjects. The task to reform the Year 12 exam at two distinct levels (Advanced and Intermediate) in 10 subjects was given to a department of one institution commissioned by the Ministry of Education. The ongoing school-leaving examination papers were produced and the exams administered by a second ministerial institute, which was commissioned by the Ministry of Education, probably in a 'divide and rule' tactic, to develop school-leaving examinations in other foreign languages (these languages were, for unknown and doubtless micropolitical reasons, not part of the agreement with the first institution). Another set of school-leaving and university entrance examinations were the responsibility of a third institution, which commissioned a university department to produce the test papers. Thus three separate institutions were involved in Year 12 exam reform, with only minimal communication between them.

Reform of the English school-leaving examination: Aims and objectives

The British Council in Hungary aimed at the time to strengthen English teaching, and to enhance Hungarians' English language competence, and so in 1998 the Council agreed to support the Ministry in developing a new English examination model and implementing it. The Hungarian Examinations Reform Project was set up between two institutional partners, the British Council Hungary (BC) and one of the institutions involved in examinations.

The new school-leaving examination in English was originally intended by ministry officials to serve as a model for the other foreign languages and was planned to be up-to-date (communicative, skills-based, testing all four skills), reliable, standardised and compatible with European standards. It was envisaged that the new exam would have positive washback by spreading best practice in language teaching and testing.

To achieve this, the Project set the following objectives: (1) to identify and train teams of test developers so that they could develop the examination model, the test specifications and guidelines for item writers, (2) to establish an item production system, by recruiting and training item writers from all over the country and all types of schools, (3) to develop an item bank for the institution for all levels, and (4) to develop in-service training courses to help teachers prepare for the new English school-leaving examination. To achieve these objectives, the Council invited experts from the UK to develop local expertise in testing in Hungary. These objectives were all met, but, because of micropolitics, the system eventually failed to implement the Project's achievements.

Achievements of the exams reform project

The major achievement of the Project was a pool of experts in language testing and evaluation in Hungary, who are fully familiar with all aspects of testing. Language testing is now acknowledged in Hungary to be a specialist field and it is generally accepted that teachers need to be trained to be able to assess performances reliably, to conduct oral exams, to write tasks and to prepare their students for English examinations. There is now a much better understanding, especially among private examination bodies, of the need for pre-testing. The new school-leaving exam is skills-based and – as a result of a long campaign of professional argument – translation was removed from the examination model of other foreign languages and cultural background knowledge is no longer tested, despite resistance from some quarters.

Implementation

The development phase of the examination took three years, ending in 2001 when the Project handed over the new two-level School-leaving Examination Model, test specifications and calibrated sample tasks to the partner institution and the Ministry. Unfortunately, these documents then underwent various changes without consultation with the English team, because of micropolitics. The rationale behind the changes was supposedly to harmonise the specifications of the two major foreign languages, English and German. Although the English model had benefited from massive input from experts for several years, the German model was taken by certain ministry officials as the model to be followed. Despite a painful process of negotiation between the two test development teams, the agreed adjustments were not implemented and as a result the English and the German examinations were quite different.

As a result of the harmonisation process led by a ministry official in charge of all school-leaving examinations at the time, the following major changes were made to the original English model: (1) a new paper – Use of English – was introduced at Intermediate level (Use of Language was only tested in the original English model at Advanced level), (2) the paired oral examination model, which had been carefully researched and successfully developed over time, was changed overnight to an individual mode oral examination, following the German model (which had not been piloted), (3) the use of dictionaries in the Writing paper was introduced at both levels, and (4) double marking of the Writing and Speaking papers was reduced to single marking.

During the public consultation process that followed the publication of the revised proposals, several prominent figures in applied linguistics in Hungary failed to rally to the defence of the original English proposals and in one case, one eminent applied linguist declared, in reaction to the proposal that there be a paired element in the oral exams, that this was a nonsense since students would 'of course' be disadvantaged and 'it did not matter what research said: (s/he) knew that paired oral exams were unfair'.

Problems

Staffing

Staffing in the partner institution was always a problem: the first BC-supported team quit in the very early stages of the Project for financial reasons. The first team leader was not interested in test development and was unable to fulfill her role as team leader, so she left the institution. The second team leader only lasted for a short time, and after she left on maternity leave, there was no full-time team leader for English in the institution. The new team, which worked on the Project for four years, eventually resigned because they could not accept the radical changes made to the English model by the Ministry official. The current team – largely consisting of those original members who had resigned from the first team – came on board when the developmental work was over, and so lacked Project training and invaluable experience.

This third team sought to make their mark on the Project documents and introduce more changes without any piloting. They replaced the Project's rating scales with their own scales for Writing and Speaking, again without piloting, and consequently these turned out to be unusable. This team is currently in charge of producing tasks for the new school-leaving examination in English and the tasks and scales are still not piloted or analysed.

Once the Examination Model had been developed and handed over to the Ministry, the Project decided to distance itself from the official English exam in order not to be associated with its final form. Instead, the Project decided to change direction and focus on the teacher-training aspect of the reform. This involved the production of exam preparation materials for students and teachers, as well as teacher-training courses to help teachers prepare their students for modern English examinations. Six separate courses were developed (and accredited by the authorities) to train teachers for different components of modern English exams. Those tasks which had been produced by item writers during the Project were published in a series of test preparation books, after due piloting and revision (see http://www.lancs.ac.uk/fass/projects/examreform).

Features of the 'reformed' school-leaving examination

The most significant change to the Examination Model developed by the Project was that almost all quality control procedures were removed. Exam marking is neither standardised nor monitored, and so is unlikely to be reliable (the students' own teachers mark the papers). The Intermediate-level exam is widely regarded as worthless, as not only is marking unmonitored, but pass rates are very high, with a low pass mark established by law rather than empirically. The new exam, therefore, does not follow European standards of good testing practice: tasks are not piloted, test results are not analysed, there is no feedback to students and there is no benchmarking and level-setting.

This is exactly the same situation as existed for many years in Hungary before examination reform was launched and so nothing has changed to create a school-leaving examination of value for the majority of school-leavers.

Institutions in charge of reform and delivering the new exam

Traditionally there was no language testing expertise in Hungary: no formal training in language testing existed either at undergraduate or postgraduate level. The expertise of people working for the Ministry and its institutions simply amounted to having written school-leaving exams or university entrance exams for many years (as we have seen, without piloting or any empirical analysis). The department in charge of the development of the new exams had no experience in developing public examinations and it resisted, probably for financial reasons, the idea that special training was needed for test construction, pilot design and analysis of pilot results.

Institutions of the Ministry, each with a different role in the reform movement, were in competition and did not communicate to each other. Institutional rivalry – or rivalry between certain individuals – was damaging and was not professionally motivated.

The partner institution refused to discuss professional issues, not wanting to expose their views on different aspects of test development. The Project was never officially informed about the institution's plans for development, and had to rely on word-of-mouth reports from people outside the institution who heard things at second-hand from inside.

Whoever had a different view from that of the institution was soon labelled an 'interferer'. The BC's Project Adviser, a well-known testing expert, spent two years in the institution to support staff in the development of the new examination models, but was never invited to attend meetings with colleagues where professional issues were to be discussed.

The idea of partnership, with equal partners putting something into a joint venture and bearing responsibility for their own commitments, was foreign to the institution, which was resolutely suspicious of 'outsiders' (the Project team, all of them Hungarians) and 'foreigners' (the British Council). Their commitment to and involvement in the joint Project, the subject of the official agreement signed in 1998, was minimal.

The institution took virtually no part in any English piloting. The BC paid for all administration costs, incentives to teachers and analyses of the data but the partner institution failed to deliver its agreed commitments. They took no interest in the pilot results, and failed to discuss any relevant issues with the Project or the Adviser. In effect, the institution failed to keep its agreement with the BC and failed to pay for their share of the work: the funding allocated by the Ministry for the English piloting was put to other uses.

Individuals in institutions

The partner institution: As mentioned above, the institutional team leader, who worked only two days a week, had no experience or expertise in language testing. She managed to avoid taking any responsibility for two years. Whatever was agreed at meetings, she simply ignored and made no effort to take action. For example, it was agreed between the partners that there would be a nationwide pilot of tasks in all four skills, for which the BC commissioned some 40 item writers to produce items. She refused to contact schools and organize the pilot, and by so doing managed to delay the piloting of the first new experimental tests by six months. She argued that a private company should administer the pilots.

When the Project complained that she failed to deliver whatever had been agreed on, she accused the Project and the Project Adviser of having too high expectations. She failed to liaise between the institution and the Project and the lack of communication with her managers led to serious conflicts which could have been avoided if the Project had been aware that messages almost never got through to the authorities. Eventually she was persuaded to leave the institution.

Since the first team leader knew nothing about testing, an academic team leader had been appointed by the first Year 12 team to be in charge of the professional side of the work. As university teachers these team members were accustomed to receiving money from foreign projects. This first team was keen to receive benefits (UK study trips and fees for item writing) and the most important and frequent topic of discussion was how to calculate their fees. Because they saw themselves as professional test developers already, they were reluctant to accept that they also needed training in item writing. Other item writers accepted the financial conditions the BC offered, but the Year 12 team refused to produce tasks for every skill for a national pilot, refused the agreed financial conditions and quit the Project (see Alderson *et al.*, 2000).

The person responsible for test development within the institution does not speak a foreign language and was not trained in testing and assessment. Her main belief (also expressed by others in her institute) was that a good school teacher can write good test items without any training. No effort was made to influence the Ministry to make sensible decisions. Instead, as described above, her department decided on professional issues behind closed doors, partly to avoid clashes and partly to retain their image as 'professionals'. Such were the institutional politics within the partner institution.

Another individual within the institution was in fact the most influential person in the reform of foreign languages. She objected to many of the innovations being introduced by the English team and sought to block these. Because she was regarded as The Expert, her opinions were accepted by the Ministry unchallenged by decision-makers who knew nothing about testing. Needless to say, perhaps, she had not been trained in testing and clearly felt her position as Expert threatened by the Project. She played on xenophobic fears in Ministry circles by claiming that the BC was interfering with exam reform, and that the English team was developing something alien to the Hungarian system, which therefore could not possibly be implemented (despite the fact that all Project members were Hungarian secondary school and university teachers).

The Ministry of Education: The official in charge of the school-leaving examination reform (who also had not been trained in testing) was eventually involved in discussions within the partner institution. Despite her lack of background in testing, she made the decisions regarding the proposed school-leaving exam. She deleted paragraphs from the English Test Specifications document without consultation, refusing to acknowledge that this document was the result of 40 people collaborating, discussing for more than three years and then reaching complete agreement.

She attempted to get agreement over test specifications by selective revelation of governmental intentions. Where the English team were unable to accept her suggestions, she simply imposed her will, often claiming that it was the Deputy State Secretary who insisted on the changes. Unsurprisingly, it turned out on numerous occasions that this was untrue: senior ministry officials did not interfere with test specifications. She used 'the law' and ministerial decrees as excuses, claiming that 'legal conditions in Hungary did not allow what the English team was proposing'.

She ignored professional issues, including doctoral-level research, and refused to discuss the level of the exams, despite the Project's concern that it was crucial to define what was meant by Intermediate or Advanced tasks. In a letter to Project members in response to an invitation to a standard-setting workshop, she denied the relevance of standard setting, and regarded benchmarking activities as irrelevant to exam development. Instead she made a top-down decision about cut-off scores.

These examples show that one person in a powerful position, even without professional credibility, and especially if such people are determined to influence matters, is sufficient to override and undermine the work of those who are endeavouring to implement professional standards and procedures. Once more, this emphasises the role of individuals and their agendas – micropolitics – within institutions.

The Development Team and the Project Members: The majority of people in the Project – secondary-school and university teachers – believed strongly that what the Project was doing was relevant for students in Hungary, that the work was of high quality and that the Project was contributing to the professionalisation of language testing in Hungary. They sacrificed weekends and full weeks every summer for several years to contribute to the reform. Unfortunately, the 'harmonisation' process divided the core team and very few people managed to fight for professional values against the opposition of the partner institution. Fortunately, among the core members of the Project, two secondary vocational school teachers had the courage to stand up and fight in public and private fora for professional values. Others were more willing to compromise and sacrifice professional values ('we can't have everything'), either because they wanted to be on the right side of the Ministry and its official or did not want to spend energy fighting for the positive features of the English model. Even when warned that they were being manipulated, they agreed to accept modifications to the Test Specifications that were unacceptable to the Project as a whole. When the ministry official asked the core team not to show the BC and the Project Adviser what changes they had agreed to, they obeyed without question.

Conclusion

Any testing project involving a major change on a national level is very complex. When such projects are set up, the people involved often concentrate on the technical side of the matter: how to train people to develop good measuring instruments, design good test specifications, how to train item writers to write good tasks and how to train teachers to mark performances. This is clearly very important, but the social and political aspects are equally important. Politics had a considerable impact on the development of national assessment in both Slovenia and Hungary. The consequences of the decisions taken by particular people in powerful positions sometimes supported and sometimes undermined the quality of the tests.

It is crucially important that professional standards be maintained, and that test designers should make every effort to persuade those in power to take professional decisions. Decision-makers frequently lack relevant expertise and are able to frustrate professional test development, to impose their own agendas (hidden or otherwise), and to implement inappropriate tests. However, dialogue may not always be fruitful, even where it is possible, as the aims of some individuals may be other than to develop the best possible assessment system. Without taking political and personality factors into account, any major innovation is at risk and may even be doomed to fail.

References

Alderson, J.C. and Szollás, K. (2000) The context: The current school-leaving examination. In J.C. Alderson, E. Nagy and E. Öveges (eds) *English Language Education in Hungary. Examining Hungarian Learners' Achievements in English* (pp. 9–21). Budapest: British Council Hungary.

Alderson, J.C., Nagy, E. and Öveges, E. (eds) (2000) *English Language Education in Hungary. Examining Hungarian Learners' Achievements in English*. Budapest: British Council Hungary.

Krek, J. (1996) *Bela Knjiga o Vzgoji in Izobraževanju v Republiki Sloveniji*. Ljubljana: Ministrstvo za šolstvo in šport.

Žibret, A. (2006) Zataknilo se je pri biologiji. *DELO*, 30th May 2006. On WWW at http://www.delo.si/index.php?sv_path=43,49&so=Delo&ar=16e15473b334bcdf5fd269836a6e7d1204. Accessed 19.11.08.

Chapter 10
Language Educational Policies Within a European Framework

NEUS FIGUERAS

Introduction

Europe has changed a great deal since the end of World War II in such tangible aspects as geopolitics and the economy. Many European citizens circulate freely across borders and use the euro in their day-to-day transactions. However, this freedom of circulation does not readily apply in the field of education. Even today, most European citizens still need to go through numerous bureaucratic procedures in order to have their academic records recognised and accepted. Indeed, in the field of languages, citizens are often obliged to pay a fee to take a commercial language exam to attest their language proficiency before being accepted in another member state's educational institution or gaining employment abroad.

This chapter discusses why it is still impossible to discover the nature and quality of language education in different European countries and what levels of proficiency are achieved, despite the huge sums spent on a myriad projects, activities, agreements, documents and reports. I argue that European educational macropolitics, with their excessive ambition, inadequate planning and lack of focus, actually foster micropolitics – actions taken either by individuals or by institutions. Micropolitics need not always be negative – in some cases they are the main driving force that can help achieve a goal – but they can also lead to inaction or inadequate behaviour and undermine development, making European language education policies rather unsuccessful.

I begin by providing some background and outlining what has been going on in Europe over the past 10 years and I then proceed to analyse concrete situations where micropolitics have played an important part, due precisely to the nature of European macropolitics. I take examples from different areas in which I have been involved professionally and conclude that micropolitics should not be ignored or downplayed. Education authorities, both at European and at national levels, should plan ahead to promote positive micropolitics, limiting, in so far as it is possible, their negative effects.

Europe from 1996 to 2006: Networks, Actions, Programmes and Publications

The 1996–2006 decade in Europe has seen frenetic activity in the domain of education. Activity has been most hectic in the area of languages, and language learning has been labelled a priority in order to fulfil the strategic goal of becoming 'the most competitive and dynamic knowledge-based economy in the world capable of sustainable economic growth with more and better jobs and greater social cohesion' (European Council, 2000: para. 5). Communication in the mother tongue, and communication in two foreign languages were listed as the first two basic skills within the eight principal domains of key competencies (European Commission, 2002).

There have been enormous numbers of actions, programmes and networks, which have used up large amounts of European funds to analyse, discuss, compare and make proposals in relation to diverse pan-European language educational endeavours, with the intention of improving existing practice in member states. Many European institutions and individuals have benefited from such funds. Thanks to networks such as Eurydice, Europeans can access statistics about education in Europe, and thanks to the Socrates Programme and its many different actions (Gruntvig, Comenius, Arion, Erasmus, Minerva, Lingua), many professionals have enjoyed the possibility of visiting a foreign country and of working with European colleagues, thus gaining new perspectives on the nature of education in countries other than their own.

European funding has also gone to the Council of Europe: to its Language Policy Division in Strasbourg and to its European Centre for Modern Languages (ECML) in Graz, Austria. The Council of Europe has promoted not only the development of the *Common European Framework of Reference for Languages* (Council of Europe, 2001) and many related documents, but has developed a *Guide for the Development of Language Education Policies in Europe* (Beacco & Byram, 2003), and has also undertaken a number of studies of language policy in Europe. The ECML funds training and dissemination activities that relate directly or indirectly to Council of Europe policies and activities.

International organisations such as the IEA (the International Association for the Evaluation of Educational Achievement), the OECD (the Organisation for Economic Co-operation and Development) and UNESCO (the United Nations Educational, Scientific and Cultural Organisation) have also been active in Europe, and their work has provided theoretical underpinnings on numerous issues. The IEA has made important contributions on writing (Purves, 1992) and conducted the only available large-scale comparative assessment of foreign language attainment, and the OECD has published widely on the definition of competencies (Rychen & Salganik, 2001). These organisations have also provided facts and figures on various aspects of world education, ranging from how much mathematics or geography children in different countries know, to how many books or computers an average European household owns, or how many hours per week are allotted to different subjects in the curriculum.

Such an impressive array of activities, albeit described very briefly in the above paragraphs, should be enough to make the reader aware of the efforts of the European Union to contribute to the competence building of European education professionals and to the improvement of language policies across Europe.

Despite these efforts, however, very little seems to have changed in education since 1996, apart from the fact that terms such as 'European', 'transparency', 'comparability' and 'accountability' have become buzz words for government officials and language education professionals alike. When asked about the activities of European institutions and the objectives of European policy the reactions of language education professionals are contradictory. While they say that they support and endorse what they believe are 'European' policies and objectives, and despite the fact that some may have participated in projects or study visits, or claim to have read European directives, they will readily confess to ignorance and confusion as to what exactly these are, what they mean and what their impact may be in their own field of action, and in their own context.

Why is this so? On the one hand, the truth is that only a few thousand European professionals have in fact been involved directly in the activities described above. Although there are many opportunities to obtain funding for projects, information is not easy to find, and eligibility is not straightforward, as very strict requirements need to be met. Moreover, one has to be willing to put up with the great amount of paperwork and documentation which needs to be assembled before, during and after the activity being funded. The whole process of application and selection is long and cumbersome, and, to make things worse, the names and functions of the programmes change every few years. Many education professionals cannot afford to spend the necessary time and energy to put together a project proposal and usually lack the necessary administrative and managerial expertise to be able to complete a project successfully. This is partly why the names of the same individuals and institutions appear over and over again in European projects – the names of those who have not only the relevant information but also can count on the infrastructure necessary to be involved successfully in such projects. To make matters even worse, the majority of these professionals either have little contact with those occupying the posts which will have an influence on policy development, or they are more interested in issues other than language policy per se.

Moreover, the outcomes of the projects, activities and research studies carried out by the active individuals and institutions described above are not disseminated properly. They are published in highly technical documents and project reports, which are either kept in offices in Brussels or are sent to national government officials who may or may not browse through them and then put them away to gather dust. When the information contained in such documents is relevant, those who need it do not even know it is available, and those who received the documents have forgotten they ever saw them. Many institutions, such as the OECD or the Council of Europe, have now developed web pages that list the documents and reports they publish, but it is still difficult to find what one is looking for or to gain a coherent overview of the huge amount of documentation. Such documents ought to be sent to university libraries, where they would be indexed and catalogued and where researchers could access them, use them and disseminate them. One example of such inadequate circulation is the series 'Studies on Language Policies', from the Language Policy Division of the Council of Europe. This series contains over 20 titles by well-known authors, in both English and French, addressing topics as diverse as training for language planning, language repertoires, developing the intercultural dimension in language teaching or the concept of international English. Copies can be obtained on request – but only provided one has heard about them by word of mouth or seen them quoted.

Europe is drowning in studies, publications and information which consume large amounts of money, and yet those who should have a clear global, coherent and unified picture of European objectives in order to develop national language policies do not seem to be able to use them. This is especially worrying if one considers that most governments have a European office or a Socrates Agency, with staff who are charged with the coordination and dissemination of European activities. These professionals are the ones with first-hand information about European policies, the ones who know the differences between the various activities and networks outlined above, who have valuable information on how to apply for and obtain European funding, who attend meetings in Europe, who channel funds and who receive policy documentation. But it is doubtful whether these professionals themselves have a global, coherent picture of what is going on and are in a position to disseminate it both upwards to their superiors and sideways and downwards to their colleagues and fellow government officers. In many cases, these officials have been chosen for the post because they speak foreign languages, and because they are willing to travel, not because they are key players or have political clout in their respective Ministries. European offices in most member states play administrative and managerial roles, are often understaffed and their officers have little time left to process the paperwork after much travelling and many meetings abroad. Thus, although these posts are perceived as influential, I would argue that those holding them have little time to lobby for European policy and the micropolitics they generate are in fact rather limited and related to providing useful information to friends and colleagues who can then obtain European funding more easily.

European institutions do not appear to have managed to create networks that can act as levers for change in the member states, and therefore the funding allocated to European activities and projects is not used to its full potential.

This extremely complex situation raises the issue of sustainability, an important concept which has emerged lately in assessing the impact of programmes and which needs to be given some serious thought. Sustainability is related to clarity of objectives, detailed planning and clear leadership, necessary ingredients for successful implementation of any new development, and these ingredients have too often been absent in European education endeavours. Their absence has facilitated what Black and Gregersen (2002) describe as a 'failure to see', which causes a 'failure to move' and, as a consequence, a 'failure to finish'. No wonder the efforts made have yielded so little.

Hargreaves and Fink (2003: 3) have described and researched the concept of sustainability in different domains of education. They have studied the importance of leadership in schools and how leadership – or lack of it – can affect the outcomes of any project or plan for change. Their definition of sustainable leadership is relevant to European macropolitics, and the lack of sustainable leadership lies at the heart of many of the problems created by micropolitics.

Sustainable leadership matters, spreads and lasts. It is a shared responsibility, that does not unduly deplete human or financial resources, and that cares for and avoids exerting negative damage on the surrounding educational and community environment. Sustainable leadership has an activist engagement with the forces that affect it, and builds an educational environment of organisational diversity that promotes cross-fertilisation of good ideas and successful practices in communities of shared learning and development (Hargreaves & Fink, 2003).

European Projects, a Sustainable Endeavour?

If one examines European projects for the three clear ingredients mentioned above, namely clarity of objectives, detailed planning and clear leadership, one comes to understand why initiatives that meet with widespread acceptance, support and enthusiasm, nevertheless do not always result in success. In this section I describe my experience in three very different European projects in which I was involved: DIALANG, CEFTRAIN and Speakeasy, and I will show why they were unsustainable.

The projects were different in funding, duration and deliverables, but in all three micropolitics played an important role and were instrumental in the final outcomes, mainly due to the absence of Black and Gregersen's (2002) three main ingredients for successful implementation.

DIALANG

DIALANG secured in 1996 the largest amount of money ever granted to an education project in the EU. The project had extremely ambitious objectives, namely that of developing tests linked to the CEFR levels in all the official languages in the Union. The project, initially supposedly to take only one year, was extended over nearly 10 years in three different phases, due to its complexity. It struggled through severe difficulties: managerial, organisational and logistical. These difficulties had to do with the innovative nature of the project as well as with its ambitious objectives, both in terms of time and amount of deliverables, which worked against one another. Eventually DIALANG resulted in very useful outcomes: a fully operational on-line diagnostic testing system in 14 languages, including a self-assessment module and explanatory feedback, and the necessary tools to maintain the system. DIALANG was also the source of significant research studies (Alderson, 2005). In fact, the online version of the diagnostic tests (www.dialang.org) regularly receives up to four thousand hits per day.

DIALANG was for many – insiders and outsiders alike – chaotic and frustrating. Many individuals worked very hard, on their own and in small teams, often part-time or overtime. All partners had to overcome cultural and personal differences, and those with managerial responsibilities were at a loss to reconcile what the contract said, what Brussels understood it said, what project members said they could do, what they said they would do and what was actually done. In many respects, micropolitics were positive in DIALANG, much was achieved with a lot of enthusiasm, for little money and for little glory.

Unfortunately, after so much work, effort and money, the project – now used widely across the world – may be discontinued because the European Union was not willing to invest further in the (successful) system and no educational institution could afford the financial burden and risk of maintaining and updating it. In short, the European Union invested considerable sums of money without thinking about sustainability beyond the period of public funding, and without checking that the project could have a life of its own as a working system. In that respect, DIALANG can be seen as a project of doubtful sustainability.

CEFTRAIN

CEFTRAIN was a two-year project with rather modest funding which aimed at providing online training materials to familiarise teachers in all educational contexts with the contents and descriptive levels of the Common European Framework of Reference. The project brought together partners with different backgrounds and different interests, differences which emerged at painful meetings and which resulted in all the partners agreeing not to ask for a two-year continuation of the project, despite its very useful deliverables, both in the form of a CD and Webpages (www.ceftrain.net). There is no empirical evidence of the impact of the project beyond the dissemination activities carried out by the various members, and the materials are not used systematically for the training of teachers across Europe, not even in the context of the partners' own countries. Moreover, the WebPages will most probably cease to be maintained and operational when the subscription period paid for by project money expires.

Speakeasy

The Speakeasy project aimed at helping those involved in secondary school modern foreign languages teaching and assessment to devise reliable tests and tasks that would give a clear indication of pupil performance and capabilities in speaking. This objective was to be achieved by producing packs of practical teaching materials (including a CD-ROM) as an exemplification of good practice. I have no information about the outcomes of this project, since my institution (and myself) abandoned it because of the perceived inability of the coordinating institution to properly lead and manage the project. Within the first year of the project, three different coordinators had been appointed yet they did not seem to have been briefed in any way by their institution and they had difficulties in leading the project.

Lessons learned

In theory, these three projects contained Black and Gregersen's (2002) three ingredients, because they are a compulsory requirement in order to obtain European money. The partner members agreed to draw up objectives and a detailed action plan and there was also agreement on who would lead the project. Unfortunately, drawing up objectives and an action plan in order to obtain funding is only a declaration of intent, and intentions often constitute the main reason for discussion, disagreement and disappointment at project meetings. In all three projects, the objectives and action plan were far too demanding, and did not take into account the added difficulties of the different working cultures, or the different background and expertise of the partners. Micropolitics were also at play because, although coordinators were appointed, that did not necessarily mean clear professional leadership and it did not mean immediate respect from the partners. Exerting clear, sustainable leadership requires experienced professionals, and too many institutions assign this work to junior members who do not receive proper guidance from their superiors and who lack the expertise to manage projects efficiently. In cases such as CEFTRAIN and Speakeasy, insufficient awareness of the strict demands of European regulations, especially in financial matters and eligibility of expenditure, were a major stumbling block for coordinators, using up a lot of their time and that of the partners, time which should have been used to discuss content issues thoroughly or to assign workloads. This seriously harmed the projects' working atmosphere and caused many complaints and much frustration.

Figure 10.1 summarises the main stages of a project and includes in brackets the issues that are a threat to many European projects and often result in failure. The importance of leadership cannot be overstated, and it is important to note that, unfortunately, activity often stops with the end of the project. Ideally, the end should be a lead, either into another project, or onto regular activities in the same field to which the project is related. Not planning this last stage makes the project unsustainable, and

LEADERSHIP
- **Project proposal:** (what could be done)
- **Funding allocated:** (interpretation of what could be done)
- **Project starts:** (what should be done is assigned amongst partners)
- **Work starts:** (what should be done meets what can be done)
- **Mid-project:** (what could be done reinterpreted)
- **Results:** (what could be done is packed together and submitted)
- **End of project:** (end of activity)
- ▼ **No concrete plan:** (no further activity or development)

Figure 10.1 Project stages and leadership

this was the case for DIALANG and CEFTRAIN. The case of Speakeasy is somewhat different, as lack of organised sustained leadership hampered normal development.

Putting together and finalising a European project is inherently difficult and demanding, despite the fact that initial targets can be modified. However, authorities in the position of allotting funding should require proposals to be presented together with a feasibility plan that guarantees that the outcomes of the project will be used properly after the 'end' of the project – and this should be factored into the budget. The importance of responsibility and accountability should be taken more seriously by both sides: European institutions and the partner institutions. Institutions and individuals embarking on European projects should be made fully aware of the two main facets in any project, management and content, throughout its duration.

Unfortunately, once funding has been allocated, the way European projects are run from Brussels does not emphasise sufficiently the importance of content and deliverables. Rather, emphasis is placed on managing financial accounts and identifying the eligibility of expenditure. Thus, the priorities of the funder change during the development of the project, from objectives and content in the initial stages, to mere financial probity and careful accounting towards the end, such that the aims and achievements of the project are never properly monitored, and the gap between intentions and reality often causes disappointment in partners.

This gap between intentions and reality is all too common a feature of European initiatives and lies at the heart of negative micropolitics, as will be seen once again in the following section.

European Language Policy: A Contradiction in Terms?

Developing national education policies which incorporate sound theoretical principles and which are well suited to the needs of any given country is a very difficult task. However, the task becomes far more complex when the aims of the European Union have also to be met, and especially when the aims of the European Union can be perceived to be different from those of the Council of Europe. In this section I discuss the challenges that the interaction between national and European language policies presents for decision-makers. I point out the contradictions between the European Union and the Council of Europe documents and argue that the micropolitics affecting the implementation of language policy are all too often a result of insufficiently clear policies and macropolitics.

Recent developments in the European context can be regarded as positive for language policy planning. On the one hand, the Council of Europe has published a clear descriptive framework (the *Guide for the Development of Language Education Policies in Europe, from Language Diversity to Plurilingual Education*, Beacco & Byram, 2003). On the other hand, the European Union has issued a clear directive for action (the results of annual meetings since 2000, which established the goal of citizens learning at least two foreign languages and the need to set up systems of validation of competence based on the CEFR levels).

The *Guide* deals with the main issues at stake in language policy in Europe: the approach (the Council of Europe clearly advocates plurilingualism), the ideologies – linguistic and political – behind language policy, and the 'problem' of English – a language which in reality dominates language policy agendas in European member states. The *Guide* also provides terminological definitions, suggestions and recommendations for implementation of language policies and references to important texts in the field of European language policy. However, the *Guide* states that it does not 'advocate any particular language education policy measure' (Beacco & Byram, 2003: 7) and the main aim of the document is to present a point of reference for the shaping of policies for language education, establishing goals and identifying the technical means of implementing them.

The caution of the Council of Europe and the multi-faceted perspectives of the proposals in the *Guide* stand in stark contrast to the main results of the May 2006 Council of the European Union, as reported in the Press Release, which 'invites Member States to take all necessary steps to carry forward the process of establishing the EILC (European Indicator of Language Competence)',[1] a rather tall order for member states. The European Union thus takes a very different stance from the Council of Europe, most probably because of the nature of the institution itself, which is accountable to the agreements of its summits and the mandates of its ministers for action.

European proposals have very important implications at the national level. Each country in Europe has to integrate them into their own national policies, shifting from a traditional compartmentalisation of subjects towards the transversality of key competencies[2] where languages play a major role. This means in reality a huge overhaul of educational policy at a time when most countries are fighting underachievement, managing integration in the primary and secondary sectors and changing their university systems to meet the Bologna declaration, which has clearly stated aims for 2010. Those in power in European countries are therefore facing challenges of a very different nature in the European context and at home, challenges which are not only very demanding but also somewhat contradictory.

European policies request member states to:

- respect diversity, look at linguistic varieties, create a culture of multilingualism, all of which requires long-term planning, many resources and much innovation in existing systems (along the lines of the advice of the Council of Europe), and at the same time be ready to implement the proposals of the European Union which have a more mandatory nature;
- prioritise the teaching of at least two foreign languages from a very early age;
- accept the periodic monitoring of the foreign language abilities of its citizens by means of a European indicator, which is to be put in place as soon as possible.

Member states need to be able to reconcile long-term planning (change cycles are thought to cover a minimum of 10 years) with their period in office (usually four or five years), combining serious policy-based reorganisation with society's demand for immediate results. And it is important to bear in mind that those in power today want to be re-elected tomorrow.

The advantages for member states of being forced to take action by external, European authorities are obvious. With pressure from a European institution in the form of directives, parliaments do not question government plans, and funding and action follow very quickly, especially if there are plans for a comparative European study and there is some risk of being compared with other countries. The disadvantages, however, are also numerous. If there is no national debate on language policy, top-down approaches are favoured which do not always consider the real needs of stakeholders (in this case students, their parents and teachers), and no distinction is made between perceived needs and real needs, or immediate needs and medium-term needs. What happens very often is that macropolitics and micropolitics interact in a rather strange manner that aims at suiting both European and national or regional objectives.

An example of such a situation can be found in Catalonia. Due to a perceived social need to improve language competence in English, and in order to meet European directives (or a rather narrow understanding of them), a huge amount of resources was allocated in 2007 to qualify 15,000 teachers to speak sufficient English to be able to participate in European projects and to engage in CLIL (Content and Language Integrated Learning) in English in primary and secondary classrooms. Politicians, media and society alike are happy about the measures, which guarantee the teaching of English from the tender age of four. Unfortunately, the measures have not been decided upon on the basis of empirical evidence, on comparable experiences in other European countries, on consultation with experts, nor have they been clearly planned. Macropolitics meet micropolitics. Having made the announcement, the government is now at pains to find primary school teachers who speak English, and to find ways to qualify more teachers within a three-year period without releasing them from their teaching duties and without damaging already existing English language programmes that cater for other constituencies. Moreover, there has been no discussion about how to reconcile this English roll-out with the improvement of the poor results of school children in reading and writing in their first language, or in mathematics and problem-solving.

It is unfortunate that Catalonia has not looked at other European countries where the learning of English has been successful without having to extend the teaching of it to 12 years. It is also unfortunate that the teaching of French, a language spoken across a border which is only kilometres away, has been discontinued despite the demands of companies and chambers of commerce who complain of the difficulties of finding professionals who can speak French. The government has taken the easy route to please voters, and not made the effort to plan medium-term. It would be very useful if a monitoring study could be carried in order to document the implementation of this plan and to see what micropolitics it generates, how teachers of English react, how teachers of other subjects react, and how teachers-to-be react, whether there are ways of checking that the parties involved perform as expected and whether the language competence of students improves.

Such a study would contribute to filling one of the most worrying gaps in the literature and documentation of the Council of Europe and the European Union: the lack of evidence of research into the implementation of language policies in Europe. Although there is a lot of talk about beginning the teaching of foreign languages at an early age, and about teaching different subjects in a foreign language, there is no reference to previous research into such policy decisions. Nor is there any clear awareness that such research exists, much less what resources are required for successful implementation, or the need to conduct longitudinal research, or to pay attention to what teachers say. Policies are constantly revised but their impacts are seldom properly assessed.

It is of crucial importance to understand that change happens when it is maintained over time, and not only as the result of one-off actions, no matter how much funding is allocated. Fullan (1998) has followed the evolution of educational change since the 1970s, and sums up the meaning of change into two main components:

What is being changed and its meaning, and
How that is being implemented.

These two very simple straightforward statements echo the issues outlined in this chapter, and point at leadership and micropolitics. The way events are managed is as important as the meaning of the change as perceived by those affected. The way change is mediated to those involved, the way it is monitored and the way continuation is secured, checking that feedback on procedures is incorporated – all these affect the quality of the outcomes planned and are important factors to generate positive or negative micropolitics.

If change is not carefully planned and resourced, language policy will continue to be the victim of the immediate needs of politicians who want immediate results and who change policies as often as they deem necessary to fulfil their objectives: often simply to grab headlines and win the next election. The immediate reaction of officers and civil servants to these actions, for which they perceive no real objective, is, unsurprisingly, inaction while waiting for the government to change.

Foreign Language Competence: Policy in Practice

I have alluded above to European policies aimed to promote plurilingualism and multilingualism. I have also mentioned the curious situation where European citizens often have to pay to obtain certificates that attest to their foreign language competence, from commercial or quasi-commercial examination bodies, rather than acquiring believable and accepted evidence of their competence from state authorities (as Crossey, and Pižorn & Nagy point out, often school-leaving examinations are treated as worthless by employers and authorities in other member states). I have also pointed out that attempts are currently underway to develop a European Indicator of Language Competence, to be administerd in each member state of the European Union. In this section, I exemplify the problems of the implementation of policy and the ensuing micropolitics, by examining the case of foreign language certificates.

The success of the Common European Framework of Reference and its adoption in the private and the public sector in language education in Europe is unprecedented, and has been addressed in other publications which the reader is encouraged to consult for a full account of the uses of the document and the problems encountered in its application (Alderson, 2002; Alderson *et al.*, 2006; Figueras *et al.*, 2005; Morrow, 2004). Here I concentrate on the impact of the publication of guidance to examining bodies on how to relate their exams to the CEFR (Council of Europe, 2003). The piloting of a preliminary Manual by some testing institutions and exam boards has brought to the fore many issues which had gone unnoticed in the reported uses of the CEFR for learning and teaching purposes, in particular, only superficial understanding of the CEFR and a misunderstanding of its purpose. As far as language testing is concerned, the piloting of the Manual has also unearthed dubious practices in foreign language exams (lack of piloting, unreliable marking, culture bias, different levels of difficulties in different years, etc.) which lead one to suspect that many foreign language certificates are of very dubious quality.

Many institutions have published claims about their supposed links to the CEFR, by using a catchphrase which has become rather popular: *'according to the principles and philosophy of the CEFR'*, long before embarking on any serious work to relate their programmes, materials or exams to the CEFR according to the procedures listed in the Manual. Many of the institutions in the Council of Europe list of contributors to the piloting of the Manual had been making unsupported claims of their linkage to the CEFR well before the Manual saw the light of day. However, to date, three years after the start of the piloting phase, no examining institution in Europe has yet published a report with satisfactory evidence of the linkage of their examination to the CEFR levels.

Again, the ambitious ideal behind the European policy of having a transparent, comparable system of foreign language certificates, has triggered micropolitics, which in this context has unfortunately meant unjustified claims of quality and linkage with CEFR levels and resulted in confusion for stakeholders. For many private and non-governmental organisations and institutions, being able to claim linkage to or a relationship with a European standard is crucial for their survival, but such claims are rarely supported by published results of validation studies. In many cases claims are merely justified by using the European logo on a glossy brochure including the number of candidates who took the test the year before. Neither foreign language learners, nor employers or University admissions officers have a clear idea of what the levels on the certificates mean, how they compare with the CEFR levels, and how they compare with one another. But decisions are still made – in the same way as 10 years ago – on the basis of the reputation of the institution awarding the certificate, rather than on a careful reading of the details of the exam.

The problem of comparability of language certificates has been widely discussed by testing professionals across Europe in the past few years, and the Council of Europe has been repeatedly requested to set up a validation committee that would check on the quality of the exams available and on the validity of their claims of linkage to the CEFR levels (much as it has done for the monitoring of the European Language Portfolio, Council of Europe, 2006). Despite heated discussions on the feasibility of such a system of quality control and accreditation, no action has been taken so far, and international and European exam boards and member states alike continue to claim quality in their foreign language certification systems, without any external monitoring or checking of claims.

The absence of reliable instruments to measure language proficiency levels in terms of the CEFR has forced the European Union to devise a system whereby the level will be assessed of students of the most widely taught languages as they leave compulsory studies at the age of 16 or over: the European Indicator of Language Competence. If things go as planned, the European Indicator will coexist with the thriving industry of foreign language certification in Europe and with university entrance examinations, but it is not clear whether the information obtained thanks to the Indicator will be of any use beyond further language policy planning. It is also unclear how the information obtained thanks to the Indicator will affect the claims of existing commercial and quasi-commercial examination boards, which currently monopolise foreign language certification in Europe.

It would appear that the huge amount of activities over the past decade has not had much success in improving foreign language learning and assessment for the European citizen. The money spent has favoured – in a more or less direct way – the existence of a system outside mainstream public education that is available for a fee and which is in the hands of institutions which are not publicly accountable for their quality control procedures. The CEFR levels have provided an overarching structure to a wealth of already existing certificates, which is a positive achievement, but it is to be hoped that the effect will permeate deeper and allow for the establishment of a much simpler system of foreign language teaching, learning and certification which is part and parcel of each country's language policy and is therefore available to all European citizens at an affordable cost, if not free altogether.

In order to be able to do that and achieve a truly free European system of foreign language certification, there is an obvious need to reconcile the micropolitics of the private sector versus the public sector. This is a very difficult issue and much money is at stake. The public sector in the different member states needs to put in place a quality system of assessment of foreign languages in mainstream education, which is neither easy nor cheap (Pižorn & Nagy, this volume, discuss the situation in their countries, which are unfortunately not very different from the issues to be found in other countries in Europe). Unfortunately in most cases there is little or no expertise and private institutions (both profit and non-profit making) now dominate the language assessment market, and cost governments nothing. National governments need to develop very clear policies to meet the need to provide those graduating from free public education with free, valid and reliable foreign language certificates and the need to provide suitable foreign language certificates to those already in the labour market.

Is There a Way Forward?

So far, I have argued that European politics and policies go together and that the context where individuals work sometimes blocks actions which should take place and sometimes conceals actions which should NOT take place. An analysis of the various endeavours and contexts in Europe reveals the need to look carefully at organisational and managerial aspects in order to ensure that activities and efforts have more impact and are unaffected by four-year election cycles.

Those in posts of responsibility should take leadership and objectives seriously and monitor what goes on by checking carefully that macropolitics do not foster micropolitics. This will not be an easy task, because in fact the hierarchy of responsibilities is complex and is mediated both by contextual difficulties, by terms of office and by individual personal commitment. Most institutions and organisations in the public sector in Europe have many agents in their hierarchies, which are usually divided between those who are politically appointed and those who hold a permanent post.

The steps in the ladder of power are often subdivided, which makes the situation more complex. And indeed in some cases there are no permanent posts at all. In many respects the situation resembles the situation depicted in the popular 1980s BBC series *Yes, Minister*, where the politically-appointed coexist uneasily with permanent civil servants, and different characters with different objectives and very different agendas clash with one another.

What has been said so far may lead us to conclude this chapter on a negative or cynical note. There seems to be little reason for positive thinking. But whereas unclear European directives, top-down approaches and ambitious and insufficiently planned national ministerial endeavours have so far been unsuccessful and have been severely criticised by professionals, it may not always be so. Efforts have not been all in vain. Many individuals have learnt about European institutions, their potential and their shortcomings thanks to the activities described in the first section; they have attended meetings at the Council of Europe, have been to the ECML in Graz, have been involved in Lingua projects, and have come to the conclusion that they would like things to be done differently. This is a turning point. Seeing the need to change is the first step to make things change in reality. Many professionals have learnt that international or European comparative studies of educational achievement need not be the only driving force of national or local policies, and they have also learnt that, although doing things professionally costs money, doing things unprofessionally also costs money, and – in the field of education – endangers the future well-being of citizens. Some of these critical professionals may become government officials in the future, some who are now research students in universities may become senior department members, and hence their influence and leadership capabilities will gradually grow. What has taken place in Europe so far has had less influence than expected, but has not necessarily been wasted. It may well be that we all expected too much. The fact that this volume on politics in language education is being published, and the fact that it contains various chapters on European politics should encourage the belief that the situation will change for the better.

Notes

1. The European Indicator of Language Competence has a value of its own. It will tell us more about the multilingual capacities of young Europeans than we know at present, or than we can find out in any other way. But it is, at the same time, a symbol of more. When the Barcelona European Council called for the establishment of the indicator, it also observed that the teaching of at least

two foreign languages from a very early age was also an important part of the basic skills – part of the birthright of all European citizens' (Communication from the Commission to the European Parliament and the Council, Brussels, 1.8.05, p. 9). The indicator should record the proficiency of the sample at each of the six levels of the scales of the Common European Framework of Reference for Languages (p. 7). The European Indicator of Language Competence is being developed by the Surveylang Consortium. Information on timeline and characteristics can be found at www.surveylang.org.
2. Various approaches and definitions of this term have circulated in the recent past. Eurydice published a survey (Survey 5, 2002) which is very useful to clarify which terms are used in which countries. The publication is available at http://194.78.211.243/Documents/survey5/en/FrameSet.htm. Another useful document is the DeSeCo document, available from the OECD web (www.oecd.org).

References

Alderson, J.C. (ed.) (2002) *Common European Framework of Reference for Languages: Learning, Teaching, Assessment. Case Studies*. Strasbourg: Council of Europe.

Alderson, J.C. (2005) *Diagnosing Foreign Language Proficiency: The Interface between Learning and Assessment*. London: Continuum International Publishing.

Alderson, J.C., Figueras, N., Nold, G., North, B., Takala, S. and Tardieu, C. (2006) Analysing tests of reading and listening in relation to the Common European Framework of Reference: The experience of The Dutch CEFR Construct Project. *Language Assessment Quarterly* 3 (1), 3–30.

Beacco, J.C. and Byram, M. (2003) *Guide for the Development of Language Education Policies in Europe. From Linguistic Diversity to Plurilingual Education*. Main version. Strasbourg: Council of Europe.

Black, J.S. and Gregersen, H.B. (2002) *Leading Strategic Change*. Upper Saddle River, New Jersey: Prentice Hall.

Council of Europe (2001) *Common European Framework of Reference for Languages: Learning, Teaching, Assessment*. Cambridge: Cambridge University Press.

Council of Europe (2003) *Relating Language Examinations to the Common European Framework of Reference for Languages: Learning, Teaching, Assessment (CEFR). Preliminary Pilot Version of The Manual*. Strasbourg: The Council of Europe.

Council of Europe (2006) *European Language Portfolio: Key Reference Documents*. Strasbourg: Council of Europe. On WWW at http://www.coe.int/T/DG4/Portfolio/documents/keyrefdocs.doc. Accessed 20.2.07.

European Commission (2002) *Key Competencies: A Developing Concept in General Compulsory Education*. Brussels: Eurydice.

European Council/Lisbon (2000) *Presidency Conclusions*. On WWW at htttp:www.europar/.europa.eu/summits/lis1_en.htm. Accessed 25.11.08.

Figueras, N., North, B., Takala, S., Van Avermaet, P. and Verhelst, N. (2005) Relating examinations to the Common European Framework: A manual. *Language Testing* 22 (3), 261–279.

Fullan, M. (1998) The meaning of educational change: A quarter of a century of learning. In A. Hargreaves, A. Lieberman, M. Fullan and D. Hopkins (eds) *International Handbook of Educational Change. Part I and Part II* (pp. 214–228). Dordrecht: Kluwer Academic Publishers.

Hargreaves, A. and Fink, D. (2003) The seven principles of sustainable leadership. *Educational Leadership*. On WWW at http://www.ascd.org/publications/ed_lead/200404/scherer.html. Accessed 28.3.07.
Morrow, K. (ed.) (2004) *Insights from the Common European Framework*. Oxford: Oxford University Press.
Purves, A.C. (ed.) (1992) *The IEA Study of Written Composition I: The International Writing Tasks and Scoring Scales*. Oxford: Pergamon Press.
Rychen D.S. and Salganik L.H. (eds) (2001) *Defining and Selecting Key Competencies*. Göttingen: Hogrefe & Huber Publishers.

Chapter 11
The Micropolitics of Research and Publication

J. CHARLES ALDERSON

Introduction

In this chapter I discuss the difficulties that authors face in describing, discussing, understanding and publishing accounts of the role of the micropolitics of individuals and their agendas within organisations and language education projects. I address this by presenting a case study of an attempt to publish four case studies of the politics of language testing in which I was personally involved, and the problems, both practical and theoretical, which I faced in trying to get the case studies into print. I discuss the issues involved in documenting and discussing such case studies, as well as the ethics of publication. I argue that language education as a discipline needs to engage in critical self-reflection to see whether published accounts of language education, including development projects, textbook writing, test development and more, can tell the whole story, or whether there is more to tell than gets published. I argue that unless we are able to publish accounts of the 'true' state of affairs, we will not understand the dynamics, processes and outcomes of innovation, change and resistance to change.

From 35 years of experience as an applied linguist, language tester and language educator, I have met many different situations in language education within the compulsory and post-compulsory systems as well as in projects specially set up to tackle a specific issue or problem. I have also read much of the professional literature in my field and in related disciplines, as applied linguists are supposed to.

However, over time I gradually came to feel that much that I was experiencing did not match what the books and articles portrayed and theorised. Much of the literature is about rational solutions to language issues, informed by relevant theory. Authors argue about different approaches and theories to explain or cast light on issues, but on the whole the impression is given that if only we followed X method, used Y techniques, accepted Z approach, or applied a particular theory, we would make progress. In contrast, my experience convinced me that what seems to make the biggest difference to successes and failures in language education is not the theory or the policy, but the people who implement the policies, the teachers and trainers who have to interpret and operationalise the theory, and the organisations and institutions within which those individuals work.

Yet I could not find in the language education or applied linguistics literature anything that helped me understand the role of those individuals and institutions in shaping events. As I read further, I became convinced that there was a need for studies of the micropolitics of language education, preferably written in a style and language that would be relevant and accessible. Much of the literature I found within the political sciences, sociology, educational management, the management sciences and the study of behaviour in organisations was either heavily theorised and abstract or remote in context from applied linguistics. I felt that applied linguistics in general and language education in particular could benefit from descriptions and discussion of cases where individuals and institutions sought power to influence decisions, to protect themselves and their interests, to promote their own agendas, hidden or otherwise, and to bring about or to resist change. And so I decided to produce a book that would begin to address the issues I thought might be involved, to document some of the problems, and perhaps begin a debate in applied linguistics and language education of the role of individuals and institutions in change, or the lack of change.

It was in the early-1990s that I first began to draft a book about the politics of language education. At that time I was doing a number of consultancies in Africa and Asia, most of them funded by the British Overseas Development Agency (ODA – now renamed DFID – Department for International Development) and it became increasingly clear to me that much aid was political in the sense that it was intended not simply to alleviate poverty (since then an international byword) but to benefit Britain, the British taxpayer, British companies and institutions and incidentally British individuals like me, as well as those who lived overseas as Education Development Officers, as Key English Language teachers and more. But rather than dwell on the macropolitics of the situation, I was drawn to understand the motives of those individuals who were on the ground running, directing or acting as chalk-face workers on projects, for those were the heady days of ELT projects, aimed at producing new textbooks, new syllabuses and curricula, new examinations and more modern teacher training systems (for more on ELT projects, see the chapters by Hunter and Kerr, this volume).

I noted the exotic and almost colonial lifestyles of the expatriates, ODA officers as much as ELT teachers: large villas, servants, Land Rovers to travel around the rugged countryside, and I wondered at the motives of those working in aid. When one project was finished, they made sure either that they got another post in an equally exotic country, or that they extended their contract in the country where they were so well settled. Even when the original project was over they managed to persuade aid agencies to set up other projects that enabled them to continue living a life of neo-colonial luxury. I began informally to study and to write about the individuals, both expatriates and local figures who were influential in the setting up and running of projects, and from my experiences in Sri Lanka, Thailand, Tanzania, the Ivory Coast, Brazil, Mexico, Algeria, India and elsewhere, I wrote up vignettes of the characteristics, ambitions, careers, personalities (as far as I could perceive them) of many I had worked with. It seemed to me then as it does now that those individuals were crucial in the setting-up, designing, implementing, evaluating and wrapping-up of projects. Individuals could (and did) make or break projects – yet this was never acknowledged, publicly or privately. Evaluation reports written by insiders were almost invariably positive about the achievements of their projects, often without much empirical evidence, and certainly ignoring the negative elements that were often evident. Many individuals were more concerned, it seemed to me, to protect their own reputation, to further their careers, to get another attractive posting, than to conduct an honest, open and critical evaluation of their work. There were, of course, honourable exceptions, many of whom were not appointed to further projects, and who had to seek work back in the UK or in Eastern and Central Europe, for it was around this time that the Berlin Wall fell and major changes came about in Europe.

At the same time as I was drafting these anecdotes and notes about individuals for a possible book entitled 'Individuals in Projects', completely unbeknownst to me Robert Phillipson (1992) was completing his book *Linguistic Imperialism*, based on his experiences working for the British Council in Africa. Two years later Alastair Pennycook (1994) published his volume on similar lines, *The Cultural Politics of English as an International Language*, and this in turn was followed the next year by the edited volume by Tollefson (1995) *Power and Inequality in Language Education*. Clearly there was a growing awareness in language education of the need to reflect on the global role of English and the nature of the politics of that role, but although these books dealt with politics, they were concerned with national and international politics, rather than the role of individuals and institutions. I therefore felt encouraged that there was a place for a treatment of the role of the individuals involved.

I submitted a detailed proposal and four draft chapters to a publisher, but the proposal was turned down on the grounds, firstly, that I had not theorised adequately the behaviours I described, and, secondly, that I was presenting a one-sided view of events and actions based on little evidence, and with no consultation with the actors involved.

I shelved the proposal and instead went on to other things, editing a series of books on language assessment, working on a major project in Europe (DIALANG), taking two years' leave of absence from Lancaster University to work on a school-leaving examination reform project in Central Europe, and carrying out a number of consultancies in the region. It was the experience of working again on language education projects that rekindled my interest in the role of individuals in language education.

Language testing in particular has in the late 20th and early 21st centuries become increasingly concerned about the consequences that tests have for candidates and users and about the development of codes of professional ethics [see special issues of the journal *Language Testing* 13 (3) (1996) and 14 (3) (1997)]. Such discussions are welcome since if language testing, like language education, is to claim to be a profession, it must develop and follow professional standards, identify professional ethics, and acknowledge the importance of principles that should govern both thinking and practice.

However, what concerned me more than the detail of any code of professional practice was the nature of, and reasons for, unprofessional behaviour, and the lack of attention to this in language testing and in language education more generally. I argued that if we are to develop standards for professional practice, then we must be able to identify, describe, expose and explain the opposite – unprofessional behaviour. Yet it is extremely rare to come across accounts of such behaviour.

In summary, I believe, based on my experience of language education over four decades, that we must examine the motives, the incentives, the hopes and fears, the agendas, hidden and not so hidden – of *institutions* and of *individuals* within institutions. I claim that we can *only* explain unprofessional practice, by describing actors and practice in detail. It is because we have largely neglected matters of individual and institutional motivation that unprofessional practices exist and power and influence are wielded to individual and institutional advantage, rather than according to the dictates of a code of practice.

Whereas Shohamy (2001) uses the term 'agendas' to relate to the desire to bring about curricular innovation, to control access to opportunities, to impose particular sorts of knowledge, I see agendas as including the desire to influence events, to impede others from influencing events, to exclude competing agencies or to promote a particular product for commercial reasons, rather than only relating to particular educational benefits or policies. I argue that such agendas do not necessarily stem from the power of language in society, but from the ambitions and goals of particular institutions and individuals.

A Case Study

I presented a paper along the above lines at a conference in 1999, entitled 'The politics of testing' and similar papers elsewhere in 1999, 2000, 2001, 2002, 2003 and 2004, which were enthusiastically received by the various audiences. Eventually the content of these presentations formed the basis of an article submitted to an academic journal entitled 'Professionalism and politics in language testing'. That article contained four case studies examining the motivations of different actors in various settings, and raising questions about the professionalism of actions within the cases presented. The article concluded with an appeal for a debate about the issues raised.

The reaction of the three anonymous reviewers was very interesting. The first reviewer said:

> This is an interesting and challenging paper, drawing on Author's wide experience of language testing and his/her obvious concern for improving professional standards in the field,

but recommended outright rejection.

The second reviewer commented:

> This is an important paper, and admirable for its courage. It makes fascinating reading and is argued with passion. The points it makes about the abuse of language tests are very powerful, and topical: the power of language tests and the ethical responsibility of language testers is a cutting edge issue in the field, and this paper makes a notable contribution to the debate. The authority, reputation and experience of the person I presume is the author make the paper even more significant. There is nothing in the paper that needs substantial revision.

The third reviewer commented:

> This is a fascinating and provocative article that deserves to be published somewhere in order to prompt the 'open debate' it calls for in relation to ethical conduct and misconduct in language assessment,

but then recommended revision and resubmission.

Encouraged by the journal editors to revise the article and resubmit it, I did so, but the revision was rejected by the same journal. The grounds given were that

> the problem is clearly the research status of the mechanics of the paper, and the Forum (a special section within the journal dedicated to the discussion of important matters) is the place which is most likely to accommodate the genre that you are using here.

I therefore shortened the revised paper, taking account of all editorial comments, and the revised article, in two parts, was accepted for publication by the editor of the Forum. Shortly before publication was due, however, I received a letter from the editor of the Forum, informing me that the publisher of the journal had decided not to publish my two-part article because, in the opinion of their legal adviser it contained possibly defamatory statements which meant that its publication could be a legal risk.

Several supposed problems were mentioned in the letter, including that any claim about unprofessional practice is potentially defamatory; that the body referred to in the second case study, although anonymous, can be identified by those in the know; that cartels are illegal and therefore accusing an organisation of being a cartel is defamatory; that some information may have been gathered in a confidential capacity; and that anonymising those involved is not insufficient protection for such people.

It was argued that the case studies were somewhere between making a justified case against unprofessionalism, and aiming to begin a debate about the issues. The editor agreed that I was raising important issues, but denied that my articles were being censored. The refusal to publish was apparently for my own good! That same editor has subsequently refused me permission to quote from his letter for the sake of this chapter.

However, it seems to me that the reasons given for not publishing my two-part article are unconvincing. I had pointed out in the revised article that the paper I referred to in the first case study was published by the very organisation which was the object of the case study, in the proceedings of the conference where it had been presented, and no changes were requested (including use of the word 'cartel'). An earlier version of the original paper, containing the second case study, was sent for their comments to the organisation discussed in that case study, and I corrected factual errors in response to their reply, to their satisfaction. A much shorter version of the third case study was presented at a conference at which members of the organisation concerned were present and was later published locally. Nobody questioned the interpretation of events and motives contained in that publication. Some of the detail in the fourth case study was contained in Alderson *et al.* (2000) and still remains unchallenged.

To Publish or Not to Publish?

The apparent fear of legal action in the publisher's letter raises the important issue not only of anonymity (which I had made every effort to ensure in my article), but more generally of whether to report at all. How does one publish reports questioning the motives of what might appear to be dubious actions? How does one gather the data, verify it, and then publish it? Should one? Reviewers of an earlier version of the rejected article worried about the potential threat of legal action because 'the presentation may be unfair'. One reviewer, who otherwise felt that this paper should be published without 'substantial revision' thought that perhaps 'X organisation could be given a right of reply, and the author the chance to issue a rejoinder'. Anonymity was attempted as a solution to the threat of legal action, but then the studies arguably lose their force and any insight they may offer. It is, after all, likely that the particular circumstances of each context, and the characteristics and motives of the individuals concerned, are crucial factors in understanding what happened and why. Other than for legal protection, anonymity serves no useful purpose, and is certainly not normal practice in the literature of politics and investigative journalism reporting the actions and motives of those engaged in political action. As Buchanan and Badham (1999: 74) point out: 'Attempts to disguise organisations and actors can separate accounts from their history and context, making adequate interpretations problematic.' It is not clear to me that language education should be any different.

There is a second related issue to be resolved, and that is the issue of research method and of fairness to institutions and individuals, as one reviewer noted. I chose those four case studies for the original article because I had been involved in some way in each, and could therefore claim some degree of insight not available from mere document analysis. Indeed, it is in the very nature of the topic that documentation will not be easily, if at all, available. In the first case study I was an interested bystander, but in touch with developments as they occurred, as well as co-author of a related study. In the second case study, I was a participant observer, as a member of the Advisory Board involved and I attended meetings at which some of the issues reported were discussed. In the third and fourth case studies I was an adviser to examination reform in the country concerned, and thus closely involved in the events and the politics. I thus chose the cases from my own experience. This was not to suggest that these cases were in any way unusual. I argued that accounts like those probably necessarily derive from personal experience, as normal forms of evidence would not be easy to come by. Moreover, much of the content of the article and the cases was verified by discussions and correspondence with individuals involved in some aspect of all the cases.

However, not all parties, and particularly those parties with whom I had little contact, had their views solicited. This was partly for purely linguistic reasons and partly because I suspected that I would not believe the accounts they might give, since the overwhelming evidence I had obtained, and had had corroborated, supported the cases as presented.

A crucial question is: can or should the normal standards of research methodology apply in situations like those reported in the rejected article? How reasonable is it to expect researchers to invite views on matters that are clearly delicate, rarely researched, let alone published, and more usually the subject of gossip in bars at conferences than the object of papers at those same conferences? Indeed, can bar gossip (emphatically not the source of the data in those cases), however widespread and firmly believed, count as evidence, and how can it be verified, when there is every reason to suspect that both individuals and institutions will wish to avoid exposure of their motives and actions? Can 'investigative journalism', as one examination board member dismissively characterised the work reported in Alderson and Buck (1993) and Alderson et al. (1995), count as research, and should it be published in academic journals or volumes like this?

I believe that these questions need to be addressed and discussed, because they vitally affect whether the field of language education will ever be able to come to terms with, describe and understand, let alone guard against, what many consider to be unprofessional behaviour. These are weighty issues, important questions that may never be resolved. But failing to raise them, and failing to describe and discuss unprofessional practices, is surely itself unprofessional, if not unethical.

How to Research These Issues?

Given the frequently hidden nature of power, traditional research techniques are often simply unproductive, and the advocacy of document analysis as a research method is misguided, since such political behaviour is highly unlikely to be documented.

Buchanan and Badham point out that:

> It is notoriously difficult to generate rich and detailed empirical evidence in the field of organisational politics, due to the sensitivities surrounding disclosure. What information we have tends to be in the form of superficial organisational surveys, on the one hand, or ethnographies of management in general ... First-hand accounts from change drivers themselves are rare. (Buchanan & Badham, 1999: 232)

They further point out that 'It is clearly in the best interests of those who possess power if the unequal distribution of power is accepted, taken for granted, not challenged, accepted, invisible' (Buchanan & Badham, 1999: 55).

Buchanan and Badham argue that concepts like aggressiveness or even political behaviour are social constructs which are difficult to define 'outside a knowledge of the meaning attached to the behaviour by those involved'. Thus the interpretations by 'neutral' observers have little force:

> On whose definitions or understandings of the outcomes, means and situational characteristics of particular behaviours are we to rely? The definitions which count are the socially constructed definitions used by the players in the game in a particular context. The observer seeking to understand and explain political behaviour has to adopt the standpoint of the players. If the players label some behaviours as 'political' and other behaviours as 'nonpolitical', then those are the labels which will colour their judgements of, and shape their responses to those behaviours, irrespective of any external definition and judgements. We have to abandon our observers' standpoint and use the labels and definitions that apply in the setting under consideration. (Buchanan & Badham, 1999: 69–70)

'Facts' are always biased by the perspective of the narrator and are always and necessarily incomplete. 'There is a clear distinction between the issues that are discussable backstage, and the language that can be used, and what can be aired and admitted in public' (Buchanan & Badham, 1999: 201). This also applies to research data. The sensitivities of political behaviour in organisations are such that it is frankly absurd to expect that triangulation, observation and semi-objective research instruments can be deployed in order to gather 'objectively verifiable' data that will lead to agreed interpretations. Not only is the behaviour itself often controversial, condemned by many, hidden and even not fully understood by the actors themselves, but the interpretations of such behaviour, even if these could be obtained, would be inconclusive with respect to the 'truth'. That is why accounts from participant observation and even anecdotes, have to be valued, if not implicitly trusted, and why gossip around the edges of conferences and meetings has to be taken as seriously as political behaviour itself.

Nevertheless, research into micropolitics has attempted to develop research methods that might address these problems. The methods reported in Blase (1991), typically ethnographic, took place over considerable periods of time (e.g. one year in one classroom, four years in one school, 92 hours in a seven-week period in another study, 550 hours over three years in yet another) using case study approaches, with or without open-ended questionnaires, formal and informal interviews, private, semi-structured interviews, observation of key meetings, committees and events, interactions in staff rooms and the dining-room. Many verbatim quotations are given from such interviews or comments (it is not always clear whether this is from field notes or from tape recordings – the latter seem likely to be less frank than off-the-cuff comments given informally).

Marshall (1991) points out that given the subtle and often hidden nature of micropolitics 'educators may not even be able to articulate their micropolitical behaviour' (Marshall, 1991: 144), which clearly makes interview-type research difficult. Indeed, it is possible that the reason Marshall, contrary to expectations, found that newly appointed administrators did not distance themselves from the values and goals of teachers was because her interviews were only 40 minutes in duration, and may not have enabled her to probe beneath the surface of politically correct views. There is, thus, an issue of believability of the data in such research. 'Researchers and practitioners alike can see that surface meanings (e.g. staged interviews) may not provide an accurate picture of real values and real conflicts' (Marshall, 1991: 154–156).

Ackroyd and Thompson (1999) make frequent reference to ethnographic and anthropological methods for researching misbehaviour in organisations. Direct participant observation over long periods of time, and reports based on field notes are methods favoured by many authors, although inevitably the very nature of misbehaviour makes it difficult to explore them in depth. Analoui comments on his research in a night club:

> It would have been naïve if not idiotic to approach a member of staff, just after he and two of his mates had 'neutralized' (as the saboteurs put it) a large freezer and enquire, 'Excuse me, I am conducting my doctoral research and I wish to ask you why you and your colleagues destroyed that freezer?'! (Analoui, 1992)

Trompenaars (1993) bases his theories and conclusions on a survey of 30 companies in 50 countries, with 100 respondents in each country. To see which corporate culture one's organisation belongs to, he offers sample questions:

Question 9 Criticism

- In your organisation, criticism
- is aimed at the task, not the person;
- is only given when asked for;
- is mostly negative and usually takes the form of blame;
- is avoided because people are afraid of hurting each other.

Question 11 Conflict

In your organisation, conflict:

- is controlled by the intervention of higher authority and often fostered by it to maintain power;
- is suppressed by reference to rules, procedures and definitions of responsibility;
- is resolved through full discussion of the merits of the work issues involved;
- is resolved by open and deep discussion of personal needs and the values involved.
(Trompenaars, 1993: 183)

I am, however, somewhat sceptical that responses to such leading questions will truly reflect the opinions of the respondents.

Another method used by Trompenaars consists of stories, scenes, situations and questions which put two moral and/or managerial principles in conflict. The researcher forces the respondents to prefer one over the other. For example:

> You are riding in a car driven by a close friend. He hits a pedestrian. You know he was going at least 35 miles per hour in an area of the city where the maximum allowed speed is 20 miles per hour. There are no witnesses. His lawyer says that if you testify under oath that he was only driving 20 miles per hour it may save him from serious consequences.
> What right has you friend to expect you to protect him?
>
> 1a My friend has a definite right to expect me to testify to the lower figure.

1b He has some right as a friend to expect me to testify to the lower figure.
1c He has no right as a friend to expect me to testify to the lower figure. What do you think you would do in view of the obligations of a sworn witness and the obligation to your friend?
1d Testify that he was going 20 miles an hour.
1e Not testify that he was going 20 miles an hour
(Trompenaars, 1993: 164)

Such methods may be useful for arriving at a general picture of culturally conditioned response (presumably by aggregation across a large number of responses) but one has to question whether the sorts of micropolitical behaviours we might be interested would indeed be amenable to such research techniques.

Argyris and Schön (1974, 1978) show, through research in a variety of professional contexts, that people's expressed beliefs (their 'espoused theories') and their behaviour (their 'theories-in-action) do not agree. Thus studying a person's behaviour will reveal more about his or her beliefs and values than listening to them express their opinions. Nevertheless, researchers continue to use questionnaires in an attempt to understand political behaviour. With what success, I leave it up to the reader to judge, from the following questionnaire aimed at identifying 'The Machiavellian Personality', presented in Buchanan and Badham (1999: Appendix II, 234–236). This personality inventory, known as the 'Mach IV scale', was devised by Christie and Geiss (1970). Scores are claimed to be a good predictor of how we behave with other people – whether we become emotionally involved, or whether we simply use others to suit our own ends. I present extracts from the questionnaire to illustrate both the method and the content in Table 11.1.

Respondents are advised to calculate their score by adding the numbers they ticked, and they are told that a score of 45 or below represents a 'Low Mach' and a score of 75 or above suggests that one is highly Machiavellian. Respondents are invited to reflect on whether this is an accurate reflection of their personality, and why?

The question is how believable responses to such instruments are, when it is fairly clear that certain responses are stereotypically valued and others are not, which is likely to lead to respondents being less than honest about their feelings or behaviour. Questionnaires are unlikely to be as effective as participatory observation, but observation of behaviours and attitudes which are often highly negative is itself problematic and reporting the results in a way that meets conventional standards of validity and reliability

Table 11.1 The Machiavellian Personality

		Strongly agree	Agree	Neutral	Disagree	Strongly disagree
(1)	The best way to handle people is to tell them what they want to hear	5	4	3	2	1
(4)	It is hard to get ahead without cutting corners here and there	5	4	3	2	1
(5)	Honesty is the best policy in all cases	5	4	3	2	1
(6)	It is safest to assume that all people have a vicious streak and it will come out when they are given a chance	5	4	3	2	1
(9)	It is wise to flatter important people	5	4	3	2	1
(13)	It is possible to be good in all respects	5	4	3	2	1
(15)	There is no excuse for lying to someone else	5	4	3	2	1
(16)	Most people forget more easily the death of their father than the loss of their property	5	4	3	2	1
(18)	Generally speaking, people won't work hard unless they are forced to do so	5	4	3	2	1
(19)	The biggest difference between most criminals and other people is that criminals are stupid enough to get caught	5	4	3	2	1

is well nigh impossible. The problem is how to gather valid information not only because the method of data collection is likely to influence the data but also because the behaviours and attitudes being investigated may be subversive, controversial, never openly acknowledged, especially to a researcher. And if it is difficult to gather believable data, it is clearly difficult to present convincing accounts of the micropolitics of individuals and institutions that meet the rigorous standards of much academic research. Publication then becomes difficult in its turn.

Conclusion

In this chapter, I have argued that it is impossible to understand language education, and particularly its processes and products, if one only looks at the claimed successes, the theories advocated, the sanitised accounts of behaviour. Much that happens within language education goes unreported, is unacknowledged in the literature, and at best is considered peripheral to academic study, if not downright irrelevant. Yet elsewhere in the social and management sciences, it is increasingly recognised that political behaviour, especially of the micropolitical sort, misbehaviour, hidden agendas, unsavoury actions and irresponsible motivations, need to be studied if we are to understand behaviour in organisations, and the role of individuals and institutions in such behaviour.

Language education should be no exception, but the only literature that even begins to address related issues is that of so-called critical pedagogy, critical applied linguistics and critical language testing. These developing disciplines are, however, concerned with policy matters, with ideologies and with the macropolitics of globalisation, governmental manifestos and actions. It is the contention of this volume that we need better to understand why individuals do what they do, and this can only be achieved by experience, study, research and reporting. The field of the micropolitics of language education has barely developed a research methodology, and has certainly not yet developed an accepted way of reporting its findings. Therefore, there is much reliance on anecdote, personal observation and partial accounts. Once these are published, they can of course be challenged. But if they are never published, then not only do the accounts go unchallenged, so does the behaviour that it is argued underlies the accounts. It is the responsibility of authors and publishers to ensure that reasonable checks be made on the plausibility, at least, of these accounts, but it cannot be healthy for a developing discipline like language education if all attempts to publish are frustrated by the fear of legal action, untested in the courts.

Investigative journalism has become an honourable profession, through the work of reporters like Robert Fisk (see, e.g. Fisk, 2006) and TV programmes like the BBC's *Panorama*. In language education, too, we need similar investigative endeavours, we need to discuss how to gather the evidence, and we need to convince publishers to be brave enough to help us understand this hitherto unexplored area. The publisher of this volume is to be congratulated on leading the way in publishing this volume.

References

Ackroyd, S. and Thompson, P. (1999) *Organizational Misbehaviour*. London: Sage Publications.
Alderson, J.C. and Buck, G. (1993) Standards in testing: A study of the practice of UK examination boards in EFL/ESL testing. *Language Testing* 10 (1), 1–26.
Alderson, J.C., Clapham, C. and Wall, D.M. (1995) *Language Test Construction and Evaluation*. Cambridge: Cambridge University Press.
Alderson, J.C., Nagy, E. and Öveges, E. (eds) (2000) *English Language Education in Hungary, Part II: Examining Hungarian Learners' Achievements in English*. Budapest: The British Council.
Analoui, F. (1992) Unconventional practices at work. *Journal of Managerial Psychology* 7 (5), 3–31.
Argyris, C. and Schön, D.A. (1974) *Theory in Practice*. San Francisco: Jossey-Bass.
Argyris, C. and Schön, D.A. (1978) *Organizational Learning: A Theory of Action Perspective*. Reading, MA: Addison-Wesley.
Blase, J. (ed.) (1991) *The Politics of Life in Schools: Power, Conflict and Cooperation*. Newbury Park: Sage Publications.
Buchanan, D. and Badham, R. (1999) *Power, Politics and Organisational Change: Winning the Turf Game*. London: Sage Publications.
Christie, R. and Geiss, F.L. (1970) *Studies in Machiavellianism*. New York: Academic Press.
Fisk, R. (2006) *The Great War for Civilisation: The Conquest of the Middle East*. London: HarperCollins.
Marshall, C. (1991) The chasm between administrator and teacher cultures: A micropolitical puzzle. In J. Blase (ed.) *The Politics of Life in Schools* (pp. 139–160). London: Sage.
Pennycook, A. (1994) *The Cultural Politics of English as an International Language*. London: Longman.
Phillipson, R. (1992) *Linguistic Imperialism*. Oxford: Oxford University Press.
Shohamy, E. (2001) *The Power of Tests*. London: Longman.
Tollefson, J.W. (ed.) (1995) *Power and Inequality in Language Education*. Cambridge: Cambridge University Press.
Trompenaars, F. (1993) *Riding the Waves of Culture. Understanding Cultural Diversity in Business*. London: Nicholas Brealey Publishing.